Bodega Language.

Behavioural psychologists say individuals give themselves away by their unconsidered gestures.

But an unswerving dedication to *one well considered gesture* is what marks out The Macallan Malt Whisky.

Every drop of The Macallan has been—and always will be — matured exclusively in oaken casks that have previously contained Dry Oloroso and other rare sherries. *Some gesture!*

This is the ancient and now *absurdly costly* way of mellowing pure malt spirit. You can buy perfectly good whisky made without employing this traditional method. But ... one sip of The Macallan ... and *your tongue will tell you the difference.*

To join our small (but devoted) band of merry malt sippers, please call 1-800-428-9810.

THE MACALLAN.
THE SINGLE MALT SCOTCH.

Sole U.S.A. Distributor, Remy Amerique, Inc., NY, NY Scotch Whisky 86 Proof, 43% Alc./Vol © 1995

The Paris Review is published quarterly by The Paris Review, Inc. Vol. 37, No. 136, Fall 1995.
Business Office: 45–39 171 Place, Flushing, New York 11358 (ISSN #0031-2037). Paris Office:
Harry Matthews, 67 rue de Grenelle, Paris 75007 France. London Office: Shusha Guppy, 8 Shawfield
St., London, SW3. US distributors: Random House, Inc. 1(800)733-3000. Typeset and printed in
USA by Capital City Press, Montpelier, VT.   Price for single issue in USA: $10.00. $14.00 in Canada.
Post-paid subscription for four issues $34.00, lifetime subscription $1000. Postal surcharge of $8.00
per four issues outside USA (excluding life subscriptions). Subscription card is bound within magazine. Please give six weeks notice of change of address using subscription card.   *While The Paris
Review welcomes the submission of unsolicited manuscripts, it cannot accept responsibility for
their loss or delay, or engage in related correspondence. Manuscripts will not be returned or
responded to unless accompanied by self-addressed, stamped envelope.   Fiction manuscripts
should be submitted to George Plimpton, poetry to Richard Howard, The Paris Review, 541 East
72nd Street, New York, N.Y. 10021.*   Charter member of the Council of Literary Magazines and
Presses. This publication is made possible, in part, with public funds from the New York State Council
on the Arts and the National Endowment for the Arts.   Second Class postage paid at Flushing,
New York, and at additional mailing offices.   **Postmaster:** Please send address changes to 45-39
171st Place, Flushing, N.Y. 11358.

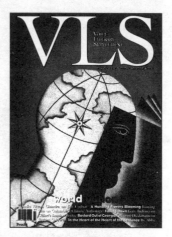

92ND STREET Y
Unterberg Poetry Center

Where Literature Speaks
1995-96 Season of Literary Readings, Lectures & Workshops

—

In order of appearance—
Saul Bellow, Kazuo Ishiguro, Edna O'Brien, Adrienne Rich,
Carlos Fuentes, Umberto Eco, Stanley Kunitz, Annie Dillard,
Rita Dove, Oscar Hijuelos, Jamaica Kincaid, Paul Durcan,
Eiléan Ní Chuilleanáin, Eamon Grennan, John Ashbery,
Ron Padgett, Horton Foote, Romulus Linney, Thomas Lux,
Jean Valentine, Julia Alvarez, Homero Aridjis, Peter Carey,
Nicholas Christopher, John Irving, Louise Glück, Robert Pinsky,
Ann Beattie, Michael Ondaatje, Terry McMillan and
William Kennedy

Special Programs include—
Downtown Readings by T.C. Boyle and William T. Vollmann,
co-sponsored with The Kitchen • Stanley Kunitz: A 90th Birthday
Celebration • A Martin Luther King Day Celebration of Langston
Hughes • Henry James' Short Stories read by William H. Gass,
Richard Howard and Cynthia Ozick • New York Festival of Song
in "Total Eclipse:The Poetry of Rimbaud and Verlaine," songs by
Debussy, Fauré and Hahn • 1995 Winners of the National Book
Critics Circle Awards • James Merrill: A Memorial Reading and
Tribute • Literature and Spirituality with Chana Bloch, Mary
Gordon, Madeleine L'Engle, Alicia Ostriker, Elaine Pagels,
Robert Bly and Coleman Barks

—

Poetry Center Membership, at $135, entitles you to attend all these events,
running from October through May, and much more.
The Unterberg Poetry Center also offers an extensive Writing Program and a
Sunday lecture series, "Biographers and Brunch."

The Unterberg Poetry Center is supported by a major grant from the Lila Wallace-Reader's Digest Fund.

Call **996-1100** for a
brochure or to order tickets.

Unterberg Poetry Center
1395 Lexington Ave NYC 10128
An agency of UJA-Federation

The New American Theater

Conjunctions: 25, guest edited by John Guare

INTRODUCTION BY JOYCE CAROL OATES

In its 25th issue, *Conjunctions* strikes out in a
new direction and brings the stage to the page.
Guest edited by John Guare, one of America's
premier playwrights, The New American Theater is
a celebration of the art of writing for the stage and
will feature over two dozen new plays commissioned
especially for the issue.

Jon Robin Baitz • Christopher Durang • David
Ives • Arthur Kopit • Tony Kushner • Romulus
Linney • David Mamet • Donald Margulies
Ellen McLaughlin • Robert MacNamara • Joyce
Carol Oates • Mark O'Donnell • Han Ong
Eric Overmyer • Keith Reddin • Jonathan Marc
Sherman • Nicky Silver • Paula Vogel • Wendy
Wasserstein • Mac Wellman • and others

Contact your local bookseller or send a check
($12 for this issue, $18 for a one year subscription) to:

Conjunctions, Bard College,
Annandale-on-Hudson, NY 12504

The Paris Review
Put On

100% cotton

Brand new Paris Review tee shirts. White with
black lettering and symbol at only $15.00 apiece.
Sizes: Small, Medium, Large, Extra-Large.

THE PARIS REVIEW • 45-39 171 Place • Flushing, N.Y. 11358

White with black. Quantity: _____

Small ☐ Medium ☐ Large ☐ Ex. Large ☐

NAME. . . . .

ADDRESS. . . . .

CITY. . . . .

STATE. . . . . ZIP. . . . .

PAYMENT MUST ACCOMPANY ORDER
(New York State residents please add tax)

MASTERCARD/VISA CARD # _____ EXP. DATE _____

The Paris Review

Editorial Office:
541 East 72 Street
New York, New York 10021

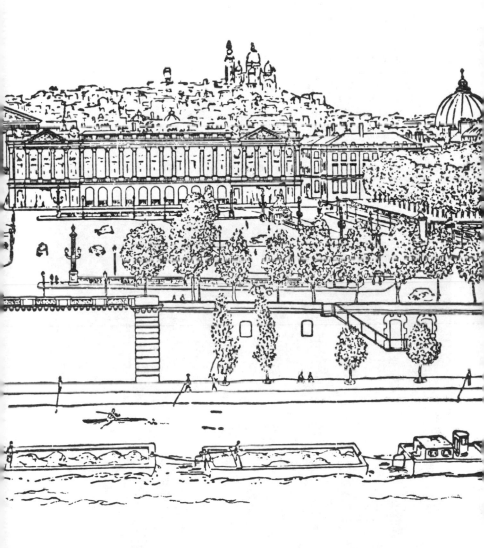

Business & Circulation:
45-39 171 Place
Flushing, New York 11358

Distributed by Random House
201 East 50 Street
New York, N.Y. 10022
(800) 733-3000

Number 136

Table of contents illustration by Raffaele, *Uccelli*.
Frontispiece by William Pène du Bois.

Notice

Longtime readers of *The Paris Review* will be aware that focusing on a single topic—humor—is something we have never done before. Our original statement of purpose was quite simply to steer clear of critical evaluations and concentrate on publishing fiction and poetry. Perhaps because two of the original editors, John Train and the undersigned, as well as the magazine's first publisher, Sadruddin Aga Khan, spent undergraduate years at the *Harvard Lampoon*, the hope had always been to leaven the contents of the average issue with an occasional droll or sly piece, almost as if to keep one's hand in. In 1960 a humor prize was established by Gertrude Vanderbilt who had voiced mild dismay at the lugubriousness in the magazine she had discovered here and there. Its first winner was the novelist Terry Southern (*Candy*, *Flash and Filigree*, *Red Dirt Marijuana*) who won it with sketches about a crazed billionaire, Grand Guy Grand, who used his fortune in bizarre ways to startle the electorate (and indeed Gertrude Vanderbilt!) . . . sketches which became the novel, *The Magic Christian*. Winners since then included Bowden Broadwater, Hughes Rudd, Stanley Elkin, Rosalyn Drexler, Mordecai Richler, and Paul Spike. After a hiatus of fourteen years John Train reinstituted the prize under his name. Winners during his regime included T. Coraghessan Boyle, Stephen Dixon,

D.F. Wallace, Edna O'Brien, Padgett Powell, Robie Macauley and Dan Leone. Then the prize was once again discontinued, largely because of disagreements between the donor of the prize and the editors as to what was funny. Perhaps the contents of this present issue will inspire someone to come forward and start up the prize yet again.

Humor, in fact, has often been a topic raised in the interviews on the craft of writing, which have been running in the magazine since its founding in 1953. It would seem appropriate to offer a number of excerpts. They follow.

Henry Green: If you can make the reader laugh he is apt to get careless and go on reading. So you as the writer get a chance to get something on him.

Bernard Malamud: The funny bone is universal. I doubt humorists think of individual taste when they're enticing the laugh. With me humor comes unexpectedly, usually in defense of a character, sometimes because I need cheering up. When something starts funny, I can feel my imagination eating and running. I love the distancing—the guise of invention—that humor gives fiction. Comedy, I imagine, is harder to do consistently than tragedy, but I like it spiced in the wine of sadness.

S.J. Perelman: It may surprise you to hear me say—and I'll thank you not to confuse me with masters of the paradox like Oscar Wilde and G.K. Chesterton—that I regard my comic writing as serious. For the past thirty-four years I have been approached almost hourly by damp people with foreheads like Rocky Ford melons who urge me to knock off my frivolous career and get started on that novel I'm burning to write. I have no earthly intention of doing any such thing. I don't believe in the importance of scale; to me the muralist is no more valid than the miniature painter. In this very large country, where size is all and where Thomas Wolfe outranks Robert Benchley, I am content to stitch away at my embroidery hoop. I think the form I work can have its own distinction and I would like to surpass what I have done in it.

James Thurber: With humor you have to look out for traps.

You're likely to be very gleeful with what you first put down, and you think it's fine, very funny. One reason you go over it is to make the piece sound less as if you were having a lot of fun with it yourself. You try to play it down. In fact, if there's such a thing as a *New Yorker* style, that would be it — playing it down.

E.B. White: Writing funny pieces is a legitimate form of activity, but the durable humor in literature, I suspect, is not the contrived humor of a funnyman commenting on the news but the sly and almost imperceptible ingredient that sometimes gets into writing. I think of Jane Austen, a deeply humorous woman, I think of Thoreau, a man of some humor along with his bile.

The editors would like to express their appreciation to the considerable cast who contributed to this "theme" issue — the interviewees (Woody Allen, Garrison Keillor, Calvin Trillin), the large number of writers who responded to the questionnaire (*The Man in the Back Row Has a Question*), Harold Bloom, of course, the cartoonists, and lastly the panelists who convened at Drue Heinz's Casa Ecco to discuss "Whither Mirth?" For those readers who find their efforts lacking — not enough laughs, too much pontificating — it should be recalled that Aristophanes warned that his chorus of birds would fly up and defecate on the heads of the judges if his comedy was not appreciated . . .

—G.A.P.

Rapture of the Deep

T. Coraghessan Boyle

"We must go deeper," Cousteau says. He is haggard, worn to bone, his splendid Gallic nose a wedge driven into his face. He uses his utensils to illustrate — his fork has become a crane, his spoon the diving machine, a pool of sauce the ocean. I feel the ship roll under my feet, an undulation as gentle as a breath.

"*Mais oui!*" a chorus of voices sings out. "Deeper!"

I'm working my way round the cramped table, pouring coffee into a desolation of plates, cutlery, crusts of bread and fish bones. "But why?" I hear myself asking. "Haven't we gone deep enough? What crime have we committed that we don't deserve to see a port, a tree, the inside of a good brasserie?"

Twenty pairs of eyes settle on me. I can see that this last bit about the brasserie is having its effect. Cousteau glances up. "I will never rest," he says, "until I see with my own two eyes what lies on the bottom. Who knows what miracles will be revealed, what kaleidoscopic vistas of the unknown and silent world?"

I bite my tongue, though I could say plenty. Cousteau is getting old. We're all getting old. We've plumbed every body

of water on earth, from McMurdo Sound to the Arafura Sea
and the Firth of Clyde, we've found every wreck and frolicked
with every fish, and I just don't see the point of it anymore.
But Cousteau is the perennial Boy Scout, intoxicated with
adventure, if not the *cru bourgeois* the *Calypso* carries in her
three-ton stainless steel wine tank. For him, everything is "kaleidoscopic," "dreamlike," "phantasmagoric," from the life of
the coral reef to the dregs of *vin rouge* left in the bottom of
his glass after dinner. The whole watery world is his to embrace,
but for me it's the galley and the galley only, for me it's a
dwindling supply of veal chops and limp vegetables and nothing but *poisson, poisson, poisson.* Twenty ravenous gastro-
nomes stare up at me from the table each night, and what
do I have to offer them? *Poisson.*

The first to break the silence is Saôut. He has bags under
his eyes, and his chest, once sculpted and firm with his years
of manhandling winches and hawsers, droops like an old woman's. "Bernard has a point," he says. "We've gone over two
months now without liberty."

"Two months without women," Didier growls.

"Or meat," Sancerre puts in.

I try to keep from smirking as I lean over the sun-blasted
nape of this man or that to pour my bitter black brew. But
Cousteau is oblivious. He merely waves the lank flap of his
hand and says, "Deeper."

We are anchored—have been anchored for two months now
and counting—some 160 miles off the coast of West Africa,
hovering over a deep-sea canyon that for all intents and purposes has no bottom. Sense and sonar indicate that it is there,
somewhere between thirteen and fourteen thousand feet, but
because of poor maneuverability, undersea mudslides and se-
nile dementia on the part of captain and crew, we have been
unable to locate it. As if it matters. As if we haven't already
sounded out the sterile bottoms of a hundred canyons just
like it and found absolutely nothing that would change anyone's life one way or the other. The usual complement of

scientists is aboard, of course, eager boyish men with pinched features, oversized eyeglasses, clipboards and calculators. They are geniuses. Learned professors. World-renowned authorities on the sponge or the sea cucumber. *Tant pis*. To me they are simply mouths to feed, mouths that tighten perceptibly at the mention of fish.

I am up, as always, an hour before dawn, preparing breakfast. I still have flour—thank God for that or we'd have a full-scale mutiny on our hands—and am busy fashioning crêpes from thin air. I find myself absently filling them with artificial pastry crème and the obscenely flavorless pulp of defrosted strawberries, but what can I do? Even the batter is bastardized, the eggs produced from a tin in the form of a noxious yellow powder that looks like something you'd use in a chemistry experiment. What I wouldn't give for a dozen fresh eggs. Half a dozen. *Merde*: even a single one. But of course there are no chicken houses on the open sea.

Busy with my whisk, I fail to notice Sancerre creeping into the galley. I hear him before I see him. "Who's there?" I demand, the portholes black with the vestiges of yet another night at sea, the ship undulating beneath my feet in an incipient morning swell.

Sheepish, the sleep still glued to his eyes, Sancerre emerges from the pool of shadow behind the deep freeze. "Me," he says simply.

"What are you doing here?"

I watch as his long mulish face reconstitutes itself in the glare of the galley lights, a face yellowed by the shambling years and the hostility of the sun. He shuffles his big feet, drops his shoulders and spreads his hands wide. "I'm hungry," he says.

"Hungry, eh?"

My first impulse is to toy with him, make him squirm a bit, offer to perhaps fry up a batch of the flying fish that lie stunned on the deck each morning. Fish isn't what he wants. He wants sausage, cheese, croissants pregnant with butter, he wants cold chicken, thick slices of Bayonne ham, beefsteaks and *pâté maison* spread on crusty rounds of peasant bread.

Yes, of course, but he too must suffer through this hell of
fish.

"A little something would do," he says almost apologeti-
cally. "Just a bite to settle the stomach."

And in that moment, even before I reach for the smoked
sausage I keep hidden behind the saucepans, I realize I have
an ally.

As soon as breakfast has been tucked away, down goes the
bathyscaphe, accompanied partway by the *soucoupe plonge-
ante* — our diving saucer — and all hands are hungrily occupied
till lunch. Cousteau himself is piloting the bathyscaphe,
though he's too old to sit for hours in the moist cramped
bubble of steel and glass down there in the ultimate hole of
the earth, too old by far, just as I'm too old to prepare fillets
of *loup de mer* in this straitjacket of a galley or ladle scalding
chaudrée from the pot in an unsettled sea — and I have the
scars to prove it. One of the scientists has gone down with
him, an American with big American teeth and a braying
American laugh that makes me want to kill every time I hear
it. His very name — Dr. Mazzy Gort — sticks in my throat. I wish
no one harm, but sometimes I fantasize. What if Cousteau and
Dr. Mazzy Gort never come up again? What if the lifeline
fails or a mudslide buries them two miles down in ooze a
hundred feet thick and they join the fishes forever? It's an
evil thought. But it's not my first, nor, I suspect, will it be
my last.

For lunch I serve a grouper Falco speared last night. I've
taken some care with it, marinated the fine white flesh in olive
oil and fennel — the last of my fennel — and a soupçon of *pastis*.
I serve it with fresh bread, the remaining potatoes and defrosted green beans in an explosion of aromas, pretending,
for all and sundry, that this is not fish at all, that this is not
the open sea, that we are not prisoners of Cousteau's madness.
And what do I get for it?

Saôut: "Oh, merde, not fish again."

Piccard: "What else?"

Sancerre: "I want my mother."

Didier: "I want a whore. Two whores. One for this—and one for this." (A manual demonstration, very nimble and expressive.)

Afterward, in the interval between morning and afternoon dives, I find my feet directing me to the main deck and the cabin Cousteau used to share with his wife, back in the days when we were young and such things mattered. I am thinking. Talking to myself, actually. Making speeches. In one of the rear compartments of my brain, uninfected by the primordial reek of the sea and the visible evidence of the portholes, is the image of a modest auberge in Cluny or Trévoux, a tasteful little place that specializes in country dishes, viands mostly, heavy on cassoulets, game and sweetbreads, though perhaps, after a year or two on dry land, the chef might consider adding a *pike quenelle* or a *truite aux amandes* to the bill of fare. In the forefront of my consciousness an argument simmers for Cousteau.

Jacques-Yves, mon vieux, be reasonable, I will tell him. *We are out of butter, eggs, cream, vegetables and herbs, we have less than a gallon of olive oil, no meats to speak of, no shallots or onions or potatoes. Release us. Release me. I'm fed up. Thirty years of clinging to the drainboard while the sea jerks my feet out from under me, thirty years of dicing leeks on a counter that won't stand still, thirty years of racking my brain to come up with new ways and yet more new ways to prepare fish, and I've had it. I want to retire. I want to cook for tourists and the petite bourgeoisie. I want to cook meat, I want an herb garden and a chicken house. I want to feel the earth under my feet.*

This is my speech, the one gathering itself on my lips as I seek out Cousteau. Unfortunately, I never get to deliver it. Because by the time I get to Cousteau's cabin and stick my head in the door, he is lost to me, lost to us all, as faraway as if he were on another ship off another coast. The portholes are smothered, the room bathed in shadow: Cousteau is absorbed in the ritual of the voice-over. He sits before the TV monitor, a weird greenish glow on his face, mesmerized by images of the sea. Nothing moves but his lips, his voice murmurous and rapt: "As we go deeper into the somnolent depths, a kaleidoscope of fishes whirling round us like painted stars in a night sky, we cannot help but wonder at the phantasmagoric marvels that await us below . . ."

That evening, as the grouper appears in the guise of a saffronless bouillabaisse that is short on all ingredients except fish, Sancerre takes me aside. We are in the galley, the ship rolling in a moderate-to-heavy swell, the crew loud and raucous in the main cabin. His skin is the color of a baked yam, his eyes sunk deep in his head. "Bernard," he says, lowering his voice to a whispery rasp, "I've been talking to some of the men . . ."

The pans rattle. A knife shoots across the expanse of the cutting board and lodges in the wall. I grab hold of the counter to keep from pitching face forward into the dessert. "Yes?" I prompt.

Sancerre's face is like an old boot. The swell doesn't faze him — he might as well be a fly clinging to the wall. "We want to go home," he says finally.

Relief washes over me. I can feel the tears coming to my eyes as I take the blistered hide of Sancerre's hand in mine and give it an affirmative squeeze. "Me too," I say, "me too," and I can hardly contain my emotion.

Sancerre glances over his shoulder, furtive and sly, then comes back to me with a wink. "We were just thinking," he whispers, and it's a strain to hear him over the habitual roar of the sea and the brouhaha of the crew at their sorry dinner, "about what you said last night over coffee, standing up to Cousteau like that—"

The ship dips to port, then jerks back at the long leash of its anchor, which is mired in the muck on top of a submerged mountain five hundred feet down. "Yes," I say, afraid of moving too fast, afraid of scaring him off, "go on."

But he just shrugs, the big idiot, and jams his hands into his pockets even as the swell rocks the deck under his feet.

"Listen," I say, "Sancerre, old friend, could you find room for another little morsel of sausage? And some cheese I've been saving—some Gruyère?"

Sancerre's eyes leap at me like caged beasts. The ship heaves back again and there's a sharp curse from the main cabin followed by the sound of breaking glass. "Cheese? Did you say cheese?"

I am expansive, generous to a fault. Not only do I break out the cheese and sausage but two neat little glasses of the culinary *pastis* as well, and in the next minute we're seated side by side atop the deep freeze like two old cronies on a country picnic. I wait till he's wolfed down half a dozen wedges of the Gruyère and three plump slices of sausage before I say anything, and when I say it I am already pouring his second glass full to the brim with the clear fragrant liquor. "How many of you are in on it?" I whisper.

"Six of us," he says before he can think.

"And the American?"

A look of disgust creeps across his features, settling finally into the ropy bulge of his lower lip. "The American," he spits, and I know exactly what he means: if push comes to shove, the American will have to be sacrificed, along with anyone else who gets in our way.

"Falco?" I ask.

"He's with the Captain, you should know that. They're like two peas in a pod."

Am I trembling—or is it just the boat rocking under my feet? Are we really sitting here in the galley over a bottomless pit in a rolling swell, contemplating mutiny? The thought thrills me till I feel as if I've been rung like a bell. Strange to say, though, I'm not thinking of Cousteau or fathomless depths or crashing waves or even courts of inquiry, but of forest mushrooms—forest mushrooms growing in sweet pale clumps among the ferns in a deep pool of shade.

It is then that Saôut slips in the door with his old woman's tits and a broken plate held out conspicuously before him, looking secretive, looking like a spy—or a conspirator. His eyes take in the scene and without a word he goes straight

for the sausage. One bite, two: he doesn't bother with the
knife. I watch his jaws work around the bleached-out bristle
of his beard. The ship lurches, but he's glued to the floor.
"Are you with us?" he says finally, and as the sea lashes at
the porthole and the ship comes back up and shakes itself
like an old dog emerging from a bath, I can only nod.

In the morning, though it hurts me to do it, though it goes
against every principle I've held sacrosanct since I successfully
reduced my first béarnaise some forty years ago, I serve a breakfast even an American wouldn't eat. The coffee — strained
through yesterday's grounds — is the color of turpentine, watery and thin and without benefit of cream. There is no bread.
Instead of baking, I make use of the old crusts I've been saving
for croutons, dipping them in a paste made of powdered egg
and water and then frying them hard in twice-used oil and
serving them with an accompaniment of flying fish poached
in sea water and nothing else, not even a dash of pepper or
a pass of the bouquet garni. I feel like an imp, a demon, a
saboteur. I set out the plates in the main cabin, ring the
breakfast bell, and slink away to my berth, heart pounding
in my chest.

It doesn't take long. The rumble of outrage spreads through
the ship like some seismic event, radiating outward from the
epicenter of the main cabin till every last bolt and iron plate
thrums with it. I'm taking a calculated risk, and I know it.
For the moment, at least, the gastronomic outrage is directed
at me, and I'm not surprised when fifteen minutes later a
deputation of the crew seeks me out in my bunk. It is led by
Piccard and one of the scientists — Laffite, the sponge man —
but to my relief, as I look up long-faced from my pillow, I
see that Sancerre and Saôut are hovering protectively in the
background.

"What's the matter with you, Bernard?" Piccard demands.
"Are you sick, is that it? Dizzy spells again?"

The sponge man is more direct: "How could you serve such,

such" — he's so overwrought he can barely get the words out — "such offal? It's nothing short of criminal." I gaze up at them with a composed face, calm as the sacrificial lamb. "Sick, yes," I say. "But not in the body — in my heart." Laffite is a bomb choking on its own fuse. He is a big man, bloated with his cravings, a priest worshipping at the temple of the gustatory pleasures. "What the hell is that supposed to mean?" he cries. "Get out of that bed, you slacker, you assassin!" Fortunately, Saôut is able to wrestle hold of his arms, or the first blood might have been spilled right then and there — and it would have been mine. "Calm yourself, Laffite," he growls, and only I detect the quick slice of his wink. I let my eyes fall shut, and the sea, quiet now, rocks me in my cradle. A minute passes, the four of them squabbling like schoolchildren, and then I listen to the retreat of their footsteps. But my ears deceive me: when I open my eyes I see that Sancerre has stayed behind. He is grinning, and his jaundiced face seems to be lit from within, glowing like a freshly picked lemon. "We are eight," he whispers, and I give him a look. *Who?* I silently mouth. Sancerre glances over his shoulder. "It's all a charade," he says. "Picard has capitulated."

Lunch is a triumph of negativity: the selfsame flying fish, baked to the texture of wood pulp, their veiny winglike fins dried to stumps and served in a crimson jacket of American catsup, with canned niblet corn and sweet gherkins desecrating the rest of the plate under a garnish of seaweed. Again I retreat to my berth, again an incensed mob seeks me out. This time Sancerre shepherds Borchardt, Pépin and Fasquelle into my presence, and by the time they leave, we are eleven.

And then the pièce de résistance, the straw that breaks the camel's back, our ticket to freedom: dinner. During the course of the afternoon, Cousteau and Dr. Mazzy Gort have descended again, ever deeper, seeking their solutions in the eternal muck. The crew has worked doggedly beneath an unsympathetic sun, their wizened biceps and arthritic backs straining, stomachs rumbling, the taste of mutiny burning like some bitter potion in their throats. And I? I have made my slow deliberate way through the reefs and shoals of my saucepans, my cruets, my knives and sieves and whisks. For the first time in as long as I can remember, I am working from a recipe, a curiosity from a thin volume left behind ten or fifteen years ago by a scientist from a place called Missouri: *The Show Me State Cookbook*. I do not have the butter, the crème fraîche, the milk, the champignons or the Parmesan, but the tinned tuna, the yellow wax beans and the packets of egg noodles exist in a sedimentary layer at the very bottom of the larder in a box labeled *Emergency Rations*.

Fair enough. I wouldn't want to spoil the thing with any hint of flavor, after all. The sun slides across the porthole. I whistle while I work.

It is past seven by the time the bathyscaphe is back on deck and Cousteau and Dr. Mazzy Gort have extricated their cramped limbs from its bowels. The crew steps lively, working furiously to secure everything against the night, lurching across the deck on aching feet, their noses turned optimistically to the air in the hope of catching a whiff of what the prandial hour promises to bring them. I overhear snatches of conversation, Cousteau's voice raised in giddy triumph—they've found something, but not the bottom, not yet—and as the sun swells on the horizon the first cigarettes are lit, the first glasses of wine circulated. This is the hour when an air of festivity prevails aboard the *Calypso*, a time when labors are set aside and the mind drifts toward the simple pleasures to come. And so it is tonight, and yet, as bits and pieces of hushed dialogue float in through the open porthole and as this man or that sticks his head in the galley for a premonitory sniff, I can sense the tension underlying it all, the nasty nagging collective memory of that unforgivable breakfast and the obscenity of a lunch that followed it. They tread lightly. They are afraid. Deeply afraid.

This time I stand my ground. With a grand flourish I set

the three big steaming pans down in the center of the table
for each man to serve himself: the moment of truth is at hand.
I note the sly, guilty looks of my co-conspirators as they suck
at their wine glasses like condemned men, resigned to going
hungry, and it props up my resolve. A lull falls over the conversation, hands fiddling with cutlery, with napkins, reaching
out for the saltshaker, the pepper, the quietly oozing pans of
my chef d'oeuvre. And now I have eyes only for the head of
the table, where Cousteau sits absorbed in talk of the deeps
with Dr. Mazzy Gort, Falco and Laffite. They retract unconsciously into the shells of their bent heads and bunched shoulders; their noses sniff the air warily. Steam rises. The first
pan is breached, then the second and third, and all but the
conspirators dig in.

Laffite is the first to react. "Good Christ!" he explodes,
coughing up a mouthful of the stuff.

"I'm poisoned!" gasps Falco; and all round the table men
lurch back from their plates in shock and horror. Even the
captain, whose taste buds must have withered and died long
ago, lifts his head to give me a look of astonishment. Only
Mazzy Gort seems unaffected, feeding the mucilaginous paste
into the slot of his mouth as unconcernedly as if he were
at a hot dog stand in some fantastical place like Peoria or
Oshkosh.

Through the general tumult that ensues, one voice begins
to take command: Laffite's. "Murderer!" he cries, leaping from
his seat in a frenzy. "And what do you call this, this, this
shit?!"

I am a rock, a pillar, the statue of a man in a crisp white
toque, arms folded across my chest. "Tuna noodle casserole,"
I announce, and the place erupts.

Later, after the walls of the main cabin have been scrubbed
down and the belligerents separated and sent wheezing to
their bunks, Sancerre appears in the doorway to the galley to
inform me that the captain would like to have a word with
me. Poor Sancerre. His dried yellow fig of a face is as mournful

as a Greek mask, but his bloodied nose and the flapping rags of his eyes show that he isn't licked yet. "What happened?" I ask, not bothering to look up or offer him a portion of the sausage I'm feeding into my mouth, one compulsive slice after another. "I thought you said we were eleven?"

"Son of a bitch," he mutters. "It was Piccard. Did you see him?"

Only too clearly. Piccard stood with the captain when the fight broke out, and when the food began to fly it wasn't Cousteau who took the brunt of the abuse, but me, as if everything I'd done wasn't for the general good and benefit of all. "What next?" I want to know, my voice a miserable croak. "I've given it everything I have."

Framed in the doorway like some ghost of the larder, Sancerre replies in a voice as miserable as mine. "Give it time," he says. "The men can't hold out much longer. They can't." He steps closer, eyeing my sausage, his hands spread wide in extenuation. "They're sucking on hard candy and drinking wine like it was gravy, they're cracking jars of peanuts, raiding the emergency supplies in the lifeboats. They're in an ugly mood, Bernard. I tell you, if it wasn't for the wine—"

Suddenly we lock eyes. *The wine.* Of course: *the wine.* Deny a Frenchman his bread and he is angry, deny him his foie gras and his truffles and he is savage, but deny him his wine and he is nothing short of homicidal. Sancerre is grinning, and his grin has a country village in it, a kitchen garden, fruit trees, rabbits on a hook. I am grinning too, and my grin contains all that and more. "The wine," I repeat, and though Cousteau awaits and my stomach plunges and everywhere the stink of fish infests my nostrils, I find myself laughing, laughing till the tears begin to stream down my face.

"Bernard," Cousteau intones, and there is nothing left of his face but nose and two huge and liquidly suffering eyes, "I am chagrined. And puzzled too. It almost seems as if you're deliberately trying to provoke the crew."

We are in Cousteau's cabin, a dark void rocking on the

night of the sea and lit only by the subaquatic glow of the
TV monitor. Finned legs kick across the screen, fish appear.
Coral. The deeps. There is a plea on my tongue, a plea for
our thirty years, for understanding and compassion, a *mon
vieux* and a *mon ami*, but I kill it. "That's right," I say. "I
am."

"But what are you thinking?" Here the nose becomes a
slash of shadow, the eyes luminous with the reflection of the
screen — in this moment he looks like nothing so much as a fish.
"Don't you realize that we've almost reached our objective?"

"I don't care."

"Don't care? But what of the kaleidoscopic wonders, what
of the fishes in their undersea grottoes?"

The sea is calm, the ship motionless beneath us, held fast
in a liquid vise. "I'm too old for exploring," I say finally. "My
feet hurt. There are no more wonders for me." I look him
dead in the eye. "I've cooked my last meal aboard this ship."

And now the look of surprise, of consternation, of a befud-
dlement so deep you would have thought I was a talking eel
or a puffer fish reciting *La Nymphe de la Seine*. "But you can't
do that — you've signed the articles. I'd have to, to put you
in chains . . ."

I feel myself giving way — I can't take this anymore, not
another minute. I spit my words out, vomit them up, and I
don't care, I don't. "Spanish rice!" I shout. "Chuck Wagon
Beans, Tuna Surprise, macaroni and cheese!"

And so, the next morning, as dawn breaks over the sea, I
find myself confined to quarters, Laffite, the sponge man,
standing guard over me as if I were some shipwrecked loon or
common provocateur. I can smell from afar the sordid amateur
attempts at breakfast, the blackened and fallen bread, the
ruined coffee. My stomach stirs as I watch Laffite slump over
the farce of his pistol, his heavy face drawn with hunger and
fatigue. "What would you give, Laffite," I say, as the morning
swell drops us into a trough and buffets us back up again,
"for a nice crisply presented *Caneton Tour d'Argent* or a *Filet*

de boeuf en croûte? Eh? How many baskets of your precious sponges? Or would you prefer to eat *them?*"

The big man, with his big head and suffering eyes, looks queasy. "I warn you," he says, and he clutches at the pistol with fat sweating fingers.

"Remember the petites brioches I used to make in the mornings, still hot from the oven? The way the butter would sink into them? Or the *pain de campagne*, a loaf per man?"

"Madman," he snarls. "Fiend. Shut up!"

But I go on and on till he's at the breaking point, till he's either going to have to shoot me or give up the charade and let me climb above decks and guide the misguided. He's giving way, I can see it, but then, right in the middle of my loving recreation of the recipe for Roast Leg of Venison with Poivrade Sauce, there's a shout from above followed almost immediately by the most piteous outpouring of shock and lament I've ever heard. Laffite drops the pistol as if it's suddenly come to life and we leap simultaneously to our feet and fling ourselves out the door and up the companionway. A moment later, out of breath, we emerge on deck to a scene of purgatorial despair. Borchardt is beating his head against the rail, Falco striding up and down the boards shouting "All hands on deck!," Piccard hiding his face and weeping like a schoolgirl. The Captain and Dr. Mazzy Gort, huddled by the bathyscaphe in their deep-sea explorer's costumes, can only blink and stare — they couldn't look any more confused if the ship had hit a reef.

There in the water, all round the ship, is a deep red stain, a stain that might have been the life's blood of a hundred crews, already paling to dissolution in the brine. I look to Sancerre and his reckless smile, to Saôut and his suicidal eyes, and I know that this is not blood, but wine, *cru bourgeois*, five hundred gallons at least. The voyage is over. The bottom will remain inviolate, the fishes undisturbed. Cousteau is defeated.

It is my moment, and I seize it. "Rally round, men!" I cry, my heart contracting like a fist. "Weigh anchor! We're going home!"

No one moves. The wind lifts the hair over our ears, the

wine-dark sea heaves at the hull. All eyes turn to Cousteau. Wearily, sunk into the pouches and wrinkles of his obsession, he takes a step forward and burns us all with his eyes. "Deeper," he says "we must go deeper."

Falco is the first to fracture the tableau. Stooped and sun-blasted, his face unreadable, he breaks ranks with the men to stride across the deck and stand with the Captain. Dr. Mazzy Gort is next. He looks from Falco to Cousteau and then to the rest of us and can't suppress a whinny of apprehension: he may be an American, but he can see what's coming. "It's all over!" I shout. "Give it up!"

Cousteau ignores me. He just pulls on his hood and thermal jacket and climbs into the bathyscaphe, that fat sputnik of the deeps suspended from the crane at the stern of the ship. I can see him there, in hawkish profile, fiddling with the controls through the rictus of the open door. He gestures impatiently to Mazzy Gort, but the American hesitates, and in the moment of his hesitation Falco moves to the Captain's side, disappearing aloft in the shadow of the diving capsule. The steel doors crank shut.

It's up to me now. Up to me to order the bathyscaphe set in motion and dropped over the side into the yawning mouth of the waves, up to me to cut the throats of thirty individual years, one by one, as cleanly and surely as I cut the lifeline with a torch and insure, once and for all, that Cousteau finds what he's seeking. For a moment the responsibility paralyzes me. The men—Sancerre, Saôut, Piccard, even Laffite and Dr. Mazzy Gort—watch me in silence, hardly daring to swallow. And then the breeze shifts direction, carrying all the way out from some distant shore, a breeze smelling impossibly of pork roast, of beef, of goose and quail and duck à l'orange, and I know I can do anything, anything at all.

The Canon of Western Humor: A Conversation with Harold Bloom

It seemed obvious in planning a number devoted to humor that The Paris Review *should approach Harold Bloom, the distinguished Yale academic and critic, author of the recently published* The Western Canon, *to see if he would supply a canon of Western humor—nothing too lengthy, of course, but that anything he wrote about the subject would be most welcome. He wrote back that, alas, he didn't feel he could afford to spend the time writing such a canon, but that he was prepared to* talk *about humor if someone came up to Yale to see him, and would that be all right? Of course it was, and Mr. Bloom was paid a visit in mid-July. Humor was obviously a compelling topic. For almost three hours, seated in an arm-chair in his living room, he held forth with hardly a pause, often when describing a favorite comic scene dissolving into such helpless laughter as to be hardly able to continue . . .*

INTERVIEWER

If you had to put together a syllabus for a course on humor, what would you assign?

HAROLD BLOOM
There would be rather too much. Let's see if we can cut it
down. I would certainly begin with Aristophanes, whom one
could regard as the true founder of Western humor.

INTERVIEWER
Why would you pick Aristophanes?

BLOOM
Well, what is there before him, my dear? There is the humor
of the Hebrew Bible, principally of the Yahwist or J-writer,
but that is a very complex form of literary irony, so far as I
can tell, and isn't normally what we would think of as humor.
The first thing that occurred when I sat down this morning
and started to think hard about the whole subject is that I
suddenly remembered that amidst the many who reviewed
merely the list at the end of my book on the Western canon,
several people rather hurt my feelings by insinuating that I
seem not to care for James Thurber and S J Perelman, to
whom anyone who knows me will testify I have absolute devo-
tion. Quite clearly what one might want to call the canon of
humor is not necessarily the same thing as the literary canon.
There is obviously an equivalent in humor of that sad phenomenon that we speak of when we speak of "period pieces,"
whether in literature or the other arts . . . namely that the
irony of one age is very rarely the irony of another, and what
is humorous in one time and place may not be at all humorous
in another.

INTERVIEWER
That's certainly one of the problems with gauging humor,
isn't it?

BLOOM
One of the great problems of humor is to know who is and
who is not funny. I, for instance, find Philip Roth much the
most hilarious among contemporary American authors, but

it is a humor very much on the border of pain. I don't know if you've looked at the new novel, *Sabbath's Theater?* Of all of Philip's novels it's the first one in which I began to find that even though it was howlingly funny the sheer human pain of it was so great that one began to wonder if such painful laughter could still be laughter, and if it was not, in fact, something else. That doesn't apply to writers as delightful in their way as Thurber and S.J. Perelman, but one rather wonders whether what we find to be profoundly comic can possibly survive into another time. I rather suspect that it can't.

INTERVIEWER

I rather suspect that Perelman won't because there are so many puns, plays on words, topical references, whereas Thurber really is much more in the tradition of Mark Twain.

BLOOM

He is, though, rather less in the Twain tradition than, say, Faulkner's humorous writing, which is probably undervalued, and which can be very funny indeed. Or in the wild and frightening way that Nathanael West is in Twain's tradition — Twain carried to such an extreme point where it's bound to become something insane. I'm not so sure whether Thurber will not seem in the future rather obscure.

Perhaps we should start with something else — that extraordinary phenomenon which I'd like us to pin down together at the beginning. When I'm teaching Shakespearean comedy in the classroom, I always begin with what utterly fascinates me about Kafka. We know when Kafka read aloud to his little circle of Prague Jewish literary friends (we know because this is recorded by several who were there, including Max Brod, his first biographer) that when he read the opening pages of what became *The Trial*, or the opening pages of the story of *The Metamorphosis*, he and the whole group dissolved in absolute hilarity, in hysterical transports, almost *frenzies* of laughter, and that Kafka himself laughed so hard that he was on the point of tears, and had to stop. When you or I or any of us now read the opening of *The Trial*, "Someone must have been telling lies about Joseph K., for without having done anything wrong he was arrested one fine morning," we don't think that's very funny. And poor Gregor Samsa becoming whatever it is, a water beetle, or some horrible bug, we don't find that very funny either. But there was a kind of an extraordinary in-group joke going on there which we can't recover. No circle of New York intellectuals, Jewish or Gentile, in 1995, is going to have read aloud to them those chunks of Kafka and find them absolutely hilarious. So clearly it is a very odd phenomenon that works with laughter.

INTERVIEWER
Should we try to come up with a definition of humor?

BLOOM
Well, I think that all theories of humor have failed. Humor is not only frightfully difficult to define, but I suspect it's indefinable. Definitions of humor have never worked. People who try to think philosophically about humor have always failed: in fact they become funny, but in the wrong sort of a way. It might be more to the point to speak of a *theology* of humor. In a sense, nothing is funnier than theology. I must tell you about my great epiphany, which I shared with my wife, Jeanne. Many years ago, in the early years of our marriage, I had to return a book to the Yale Divinity School Library. We arrived just at high noon. These very apple-cheeked, young future Congregationalist ministers and their wives were coming out of class. They looked like a Norman Rockwell *Saturday Evening Post* cover. Just as the then-young Bloom was getting out of his car and, since I can never remember where anything is, my wife was saying, "Go that way, Harold, that's where the library is," the bells started to ring in the tower. We were both swept up in tremendous laughter, Jeanne and myself, because as we stared at all these kids with their books coming out of class, I realized that they'd been discussing the Holy Spirit, what you might call the theology or the hydraulics or

the physics of a gaseous vapor! I'm not irreligious, I'm rather gnostic, but the difference between those apple-cheeked youngsters and the ineffability of their subject, just as one might suppose the ineffability of any theory of humor, broke me up. I went into terrible hysterical laughter.

INTERVIEWER

Well then, perhaps we should get back to Aristophanes.

BLOOM

Yes, let's begin with him because he is the very first author who, in the extraordinary translations of the, alas, late and much lamented William Arrowsmith, simply takes us away. They are frighteningly funny. They are outrageous. They justify Philip Roth's favorite quotation from Heinrich Heine, which goes, "There is a God, and his name is Aristophanes."

INTERVIEWER

Why did Heine say that?

BLOOM

He was very skeptical: he had converted to Christianity, but was very dubious about it, and he had slipped back not so much to Judaism but to a sort of general Jewish skepticism; I think it was his way of saying that if indeed there is a God at all, he must do everything in the spirit of Aristophanes, that is to say in the spirit of nightmare farce. Aristophanes does seem to be a pretty clear fountainhead—far more than the other origins of Western comedy, which are in fact Alexandrian, Hellenistic: Menander's *The Samian Woman*, Lucian's satires, or their Roman imitators, in Plautus or in Terence, or in the Roman satirical poets, who are behind a lot of our stage and musical comedy tradition. Think of *A Funny Thing Happened on the Way to the Forum*. But Aristophanes works. It is not likely that any of us, students or otherwise, reading him in a really lively translation like Arrowsmith's or Parker's, will not find it very funny indeed. Moreover, it does not turn into a period piece, which may even suggest that really succesful farce always does survive.

I've always remembered Aristophanes' description in the *Symposium* of the original human beings as being round with two heads, four arms, four legs . . . rolling around the earth and being so insolent to the gods that they were split in half and became just as we are today . . .

He proposes that outrageous theory, which is actually in no way in any text of Aristophanes that we have. It is Plato using Aristophanes as a character. If we are going to talk about humorous writers, there we have the subtlest ironist of them all, though it's a question whether one should read Plato straight as he almost invariably is read, or whether he should be read as a skeptical ironist and therefore in a very complex sense. Socrates is certainly a humorist, whether or not Plato is.

What comes after Aristophanes?

In spite of the importance of the Alexandrian or Hellenistic tradition, I suppose next I would jump over the medieval period, looking at Chaucer en route, all the way to the Renaissance—to Boccaccio, Ariosto, maybe Machiavelli's *Mandragola*, or Goldoni's comedies, or to the *Celestina* of De Rojas among the Spaniards. The next great figure after Aristophanes would have to be Rabelais—a kind of apocalyptic mode of humor which starts as satire and quickly becomes something very different. You're really in the great tradition of stage comedy because the next figure to deal with would be Molière. Molière has much more in common with the great tradition of Restoration comedy with its deep emphasis upon societal sophistication, shared with Congreve in some sense, or Sheridan, though these two are very minor figures compared to Molière, who as a comic genius would be second surely only to Shakespeare, or to Cervantes. Cervantes is also at the fountainhead of the novel. The Don and Sancho are the greatest comic creations in literature besides Falstaff. These are all on the road to Shakespeare.

INTERVIEWER

I would suppose that one's use of humor, especially satire, would depend largely on the attitudes of one's patron. I was thinking of Molière.

BLOOM

Molière had more trouble, I think, with the court and the church than he did with the king. If it were not for the great Sun King, Louis XIV, Molière could not have functioned at all. The king protected him at every possible point. Shakespeare, of course, had given up comedy before he really accepted royal patronage. Shakespeare under James—Jacobean Shakespeare after the death of Elizabeth—doesn't write comedy anymore, though he does the occasional tragicomedy.

INTERVIEWER

Does one know why?

BLOOM

As with everything else that really matters in Shakespeare, we can only surmise. We don't actually know why, but the great Shakespearean tragedies are basically under James. *King Lear* is written in a sense for James. *Macbeth* was most certainly written for James.

INTERVIEWER

They're still laced with moments of humor, aren't they?

BLOOM

Laced with very weird humor indeed, but one would not
call even the Fool in *Lear*, or that frightening interlude of the
drunken porter knocking on the gate in *Macbeth*, or that great
scene when the fellow comes in with the basket of figs covering
the asp and has that marvelous dialogue with Cleopatra just
before her death scene, unmixed comedy, though it is astonishing comedy. It is Shakespeare who creates Falstaff, the Eliza-
bethan Shakespeare as it were, who is a pure comic writer,
certainly, I think, the greatest comic writer we've ever had.
There are two basic kinds of comic achievement in Shakespeare. One is most necessarily Falstaff, who is of course a
complete universe in himself. What Hazlitt said about him
is still absolutely true — that he is the finest comic character
in all of literature. He teaches himself how to laugh at himself
and teaches you how to laugh at yourself. Also he's so absolutely comprehensive that even the most casual things that
he says, even if they're not immediately funny, if you brood
on them for hours and hours afterwards, you suddenly see
how gorgeously funny they really are. He says he's not only
witty in himself, but the cause of wit in other men. He most
certainly is that. It's the triumphal quality of the portrait which
is so astonishing — comedy triumphing over everything, over
history, over time, over the state, over the possibility of tragedy
. . . just an endless triumph, particularly in the first part of
Henry IV. The other mode is the mode of high romantic
comedy, of which the great masterpieces are most certainly
As You Like It and *Twelfth Night*, where everything depends
upon astonishing speed on Shakespeare's part. Rosalind, who
must be the most intelligent woman ever represented in literature by anyone, is also howlingly funny . . . the way she cuts
up Touchstone with almost a minimum of words. Also when
her lover Orlando is protesting that he will die if she does
not yield to him — all this is in mockery because they're each
practicing a part — she comes forth with the finest comic formu-
lation in the language when she says, "Men have died from
time to time, and worms have eaten them, but not for love,"
which is quite perfect, and really typifies that whole mode in

Shakespeare. It's a kind of wit or comic perspective which is based upon something quite unique in literature. You cannot get any irony at Rosalind's expense, which is what makes the humor so perfect. Normally with any kind of work by Shakespeare or anyone else, you as the reader have some perspective in which you know more, in some sense, even than Hamlet does. But Rosalind in some amazing way is so perfect a comic consciousness, so much a master of the comic point of view, you can't get round her in any way. It's as though she has already preempted every perspective. That is a sort of pure Shakespearean gift. The divine Oscar doesn't try for that because he knows he can't do it, but certainly more than Congreve, more than Sheridan, more than any playwright in the language after Shakespeare, *The Importance of Being Earnest* must be the most perfect comedy in the English language. It does everything that W.S. Gilbert does in the mode of outrageous laughter, but if one could speak of decorum or tact, it is perfectly orchestrated. Everything that's said is beautifully self-contained, and it goes on reverberating forever. Lady Bracknell's great line is inexhaustible, saying in so many words, "To have lost one parent, Mr. Worthing, might be considered a misfortune. To have lost both smacks of carelessness." Oscar was the last miracle of that kind. I cannot think of a twentieth-century playwright in English who was that consistently and magnificently comic.

INTERVIEWER

Is it possible to be a great writer without having this Shakespearean sense of the comic? How about the Russians? The Germans?

BLOOM

If you start to look at a list of incontrovertible humor, it's almost impossible to find Russian humor. Much of it is Gogolian, that is to say, nightmarish, and farcical, very peculiar stuff, just as Gogol is a very peculiar writer. Isaak Babel's humor, which I've been looking at again, is very much in

Gogol's mode. Then there is Chekhov's, which is gentler, focused in an almost pure vein of theatrical irony. Of course, there's that part in *The Death of Ivan Ilyich* when he's trying to sit down on the ottoman, and there's this alarming noise every time he sits. I forget which Russian critic remarked about Tolstoy that everything is so lively that even the furniture is more alive than the people in other authors' novels.

As for German humor, I don't know what to say about it. Rilke has no sense of humor whatsoever, though he is undoubtedly a great poet. Reading the elegies and the great sonnets, you have a feeling that the fellow never laughed in his life. I suppose the great instance of German humor would be the outrageous second part of Goethe's *Faust*, where Mephistopheles shows up to claim Faust's soul to which he has every right. Amid a great storm of roses, naked little boy-angels descend, who first pelt poor Mephistopheles and his devils with roses, frightening away all the wretched devils except Mephistopheles, who gallantly tries to make a stand; then with an outrage so sublime that only the aged Goethe could surely get away with it, the little boy-angels turn around and wave their rosy round buttocks at Mephistopheles who is so overcome by overwhelming sexual lust for these little cherubim that while he lusts, a couple of them make off with Faust's soul and bear it up to heaven. Now this is in a sense humorous, but humor that is in the worst possible taste. I suppose in that sense we could say that Goethe establishes the bad taste with which all German humor seems to me to be afflicted right down to Günter Grass's very splendid book, *The Flounder*—that splendid trial of the flounder, a terrible wastrel and womanizer, who begins his defense by addressing the all-female court and crying out, "Esteemed and charming ladies!" It's much funnier, in a way, than Goethe, gentler, but in its outrageousness it has Goethean traces in it. Thomas Mann is widely regarded, though he was almost a professional ironist, as not terribly funny, but then there's the Felix Krull book he wrote at the end of his life as a short comic novel. It's very, very funny: the description of Felix Krull working as a bellhop in a fashionable hotel and being seduced by a literary lady, or in a South American country letting himself be seduced by both a mother and a daughter, two Latin beauties — heroically funny stuff. But I don't really know what to make of Russian humor or German humor. From our point of view, at their most successful both are instances of outrageous bad taste. Doubtless you would feel differently if you were German or Russian. Something has got to redeem even the most outrageous humor from sheer bad taste. There's got to be some grace, some saving element, which somehow stylizes the taste and keeps it from being bad. It is evident to me that the humorist traditions are clearly the British, the French, the Italian, not so much the Spanish except for the overwhelming figure of Cervantes. And then of course, the American, which is rather considerable, more perhaps because of Mark Twain than any other single figure.

INTERVIEWER
Is it possible to be a great writer without a sense of humor?

BLOOM
There is the mad example of the greatest of English poets except for Shakespeare and Chaucer, John Milton, who is occasionally unintentionally comic in *Paradise Lost*, but it is always a disaster. When Adam and Eve have just had the Archangel Raphael to dinner, of course before the Fall, they are feeding him on delicious fruits and such and as Adam and Raphael are talking to each other, "No fear lest dinner cool." Or the ghastly, ghastly passage on angelic digestion. He was a very great writer, one of the greatest poets the world has ever known, but he had no sense of humor whatsoever, as I'm sure his three wives would have testified. Perhaps that's unfair actually. Miltonists would come forward and insist that there is savage satire and irony, not only in *Paradise Lost*, but in the prose writings like "The Ready and Easy Way to Establish a Free Commonwealth."

INTERVIEWER
Eighteenth-century England was a particularly rich time.

BLOOM

You have the extraordinary complexity of eighteenth-century English literature being so profoundly a humorous and satirical literature. *The Dunciad* is a screamingly funny poem, as *The Rape of the Lock* is in another way. Swift is a shocking ironist but also powerfully funny. *A Tale of a Tub* remains extraordinarily funny in its account of the projectors as sort of mad visionaries and pseudoscientists. Then you have, of course, that raucous tradition that goes from Thomas Love Peacock's satirical novels, *Nightmare Abbey* and *Headlong Hall*, culminating with his son-in-law George Meredith's *The Egoist*. Then, of course, you have the great novelistic tradition: you have Fielding, Smollett and Sterne, three very different modes of humor all leading on to Jane Austen as a major figure, a hilarious writer, probably the subtlest humorist and ironist since Shakespeare. You have Dickens, an outrageous humorist, from *The Pickwick Papers* on, where it gets all mixed up with every other mode of literature. Then you have Byron, who is the most extraordinary instance of a humorist poet after Pope, perhaps even more than Pope.

INTERVIEWER

Why did Pope say he never laughed?

BLOOM

He did not mean that seriously at all — being both defensive and enhancing himself as a great passionate, sentimental person; in fact, he suffered a great deal: he was a dwarf, crippled, ill in all sorts of ways. He laughed a great deal, he and Swift, before Swift, of course, went quite mad. John Gay was a very cheerful fellow, as befitted his name, the author of the grand *Beggar's Opera* and those very funny pastorals. They all seem to have had a very high old time together. Doctor Johnson, though not himself a humorist, so treasured laughter and so desperately in his melancholia wanted to be amused that though he, morally speaking, seriously disapproved of Sir John Falstaff, he yields completely to him, to the continuous gaiety

of the character; he says again and again that now you can
take Falstaff's stance in literature and in life more, perhaps,
than any other quality. It completely captivated Johnson, and
I think helps establish his greatness as a critic. This rich English
tradition continued until this century when I think it eventually goes to hell. You had, of course, the nonsense writers,
Lewis Carroll and Lear, and W.S. Gilbert of Gilbert and Sulli-
van. You had the masterpiece of that mode in Wilde, particularly in *The Importance of Being Earnest*. George Bernard
Shaw offers a very sly and very successful mode of humor.
Then, the great fantasists of the Edwardian period, Ronald
Firbank and Saki—H.H. Munro—who are not period-piece
writers at all; Munro survives innumerable rereadings. Then
you have the profound comic genius of Joyce . . . certain scenes
from both *Ulysses* and *Finnegans Wake* are really extraordinarily funny. Samuel Beckett's *Murphy*, the first novel that
he wrote, is still a gem of absolute hilarity. I can never get
out of my head his great phrase, "Miss Counihan's hot buttered
buttocks," which is one of the great humorous phrases in the
language. And then of course, Evelyn Waugh, who is anything
but a writer of period pieces. Absolutely permanent humor,
which seems to work in all languages, though his novels are
politically very incorrect, especially these days: *Vile Bodies* and
Scoop are the two grandest along those lines. *Black Mischief*
is a marvelous book, though very politically incorrect just as
the great *Prancing Nigger* of Ronald Firbank is the height of
political incorrectness. *Put Out More Flags* is marvelous, and
best of all is *A Handful of Dust*, a work of comic genius. Then
in a lower register, but still marvelous are the *Enderby* books
of the late Anthony Burgess, whom I greatly lament, and if
I ever reach the same place in the afterlife where he is, where-
sover, he owes me a bottle of Domecq's Fundador Reserva,
which he had told me was his favorite drink. I met him a
couple of times. He was teaching graduate school at the City
University. I bumped into him one day. I had just come out
of the liquor store with a bottle of Fundador Reserva in a
paper bag. Mr. Burgess was sort of blinking. He'd obviously
been writing all night; he was unshaven; he had on what

looked like bedroom slippers. He said, "Bloom? is that you?" I said, "Yes, yes, Mr. Burgess, it's me." He said, "What have you got in that bag?" I said, "Well, as a matter of fact, I'm very much afraid to tell you it is a bottle of Fundador." "Thank God," he said. "There is such a thing as God and providence in this world. Hand it over immediately." I handed it to him, and he handed me back the bag. He unscrewed the bottle and took three tremendous drinks from it, and then tried to hand me back the bottle. "No, no" I said. "My dear fellow, keep it; you can owe me a bottle of Fundador." He said, "It's a sacred obligation. Bloom, it shall be given unto you." He carefully sent me many books through the years, but not the Fundador, and now, alas, he is gone after writing a rather good novel on Kit Marlowe, his very last book as far as I can tell. Not funny, but a very good, very somber book. But the Enderby books are hilarious.

I think we've sort of derailed from our main line. The great Jonathan Swift, the master humorist, teaches us that digressiveness is a form of madness if you take it too far. But that great section in *A Tale of a Tub* called "A Digression In Praise of Digressions" establishes how absolutely essential it is.

INTERVIEWER

Mark Twain is perhaps the best of the digressionists, isn't he?

BLOOM

Roughing It is really one long digression. So is *The Innocents Abroad*. The British hate Twain, you know, because in *The Innocents Abroad* he quite seriously proposes that the British royal family be replaced by a family of pussycats . . . on the grounds that they would be far more interesting, cost far less, and do a much better job. The English nation has never forgiven him, and perhaps they never will.

INTERVIEWER

What about British humor these days? Any entries for a canon of humor?

BLOOM

The decadence of British humor after Evelyn Waugh is so
great that it doesn't really exist, does it? Perhaps it's gone over
into films, or into other modes. I'm not a great admirer of
Kingsley Amis's *Lucky Jim*. I think it is a period piece. I'm
afraid I find Martin Amis heavy going. I think he's an author
of period pieces of a different period, as his father was and
still is. After the Second World War, with the humorous vein
of Evelyn Waugh worked out, except for Mr. Burgess at his
funniest, and Lawrence Durrell in a rather odd way, I'm not
quite sure what to come up with . . .

INTERVIEWER

How about some of the women writers? A.S. Byatt?

BLOOM

Antonia Byatt. Yes, *The Matisse Stories*. *The Matisse Stories*
are so good that I will list them as a very likely canonical
candidate.

INTERVIEWER

The French? Should we talk about the French?

BLOOM

Proust comes instantly to mind. The comic aspect of sexual
jealousy, in a sense very much Molière's subject and the basis
of all the fashionable French farces right down to the present
moment, reaches sublime apotheosis, almost its apocalypse,
you might say, in the *In Search of Lost Time*. An extraordinary
scene, you'll remember, is when Swann is standing just below
the window where he believes Odette is betraying him in a
passionate conversation with a lover; he experiences absolute
hell, plunged into its pits, until he realizes that he's standing
beneath the wrong window.

The entire comedy of sexual jealousy is more powerfully
handled by Shakespeare in *Othello* and *A Winter's Tale* and
in a sense, though it's very Shakespearean, the way Chill-

ingworth's jealousy is handled in *The Scarlet Letter*, but not with much humor. Molière handles sexual jealousy magnificently with humor. But Proust does something brand-new with it. It's the extraordinary way in which he structures it in that vast book: you begin with the insane and magnificent jealousy of Swann in relation to Odette, then to the much briefer interlude of Saint-Loup's jealousy of his beloved Rachel, then on to the immense comedy/tragicomedy of Albertine and André and the other lesbian ladies, and Marcel's, the narrator's, own immense but hilarious infamous jealousy. The greatest comic invention of the century is Proust's insight that compares sexual jealousy to art history . . . that the jealous lover becomes so obsessed (and Proust is always talking about male jealousy, never that of a female) that he becomes an "art historian" of jealousy . . . with the same obsession with the details that the art historian has for, not only the life of the artist, but the provenance of the painting itself. In the way in which it becomes a disease, first Swann and then Marcel need to know every detail about the time and the place, the very decor of the room or the setting if it is outdoors, in which the act of so-called betrayal takes place. The very question of what was worn, not worn, what was said, not said, becomes extravagant, becomes baroque in its sensibility . . . humor that in a writer less remarkable than Marcel Proust might well cross the border into sheer rancidity. He keeps it perfectly balanced; he keeps it heroically comic in the deepest sense of comedy. At one point, he actually does compare it to the kind of comedy of sexual mis-identity that you find in Shakespeare, say in *As You Like It* or in *Twelfth Night*.

INTERVIEWER

Was Proust as a person admired for his humor?

BLOOM

Oh, he was very witty indeed. He kept himself going. The man was desperately ill; he had ghastly asthma. Besides his art, he had the immense aesthetic capacity of high, good hu-

mor about the self. The distance between himself and the
narrator, who only once or twice in the whole novel is called
Marcel, is beautifully maintained until the very closing pages
of *The Past Recaptured*, when the two really significantly begin
to blend into one another, rather in the way in which Dante
the pilgrim and Dante the poet finally begin to blend together
in the closing cantos of the *Paradiso*. Dante, of course, is an
instance of a very great writer whose humor is so savage that
it is very difficult to think of it as being comic at all, though
ironically the great poem is called the comedy.

I think the danger, with French humor, even with the whole
tradition of farce, once you get past its greatest master in
Molière, is that it can too easily stumble into real rancidity.
Ionesco in one sense only is like Proust, not on quite so grand
a scale, but he does not go over the line into rancidity. I don't
know if Jean Cocteau was supposed to have any sense of humor.
He's a very fascinating figure, but his attempts at humor are
very rancid. It's not in good taste. Proust maintains decorum,
no matter how outrageous the humor becomes. Ionesco, in-
sanely enough, maintains decorum. I'm not quite sure that
any other French humorist writer of the twentieth century can
be said to maintain decorum in its deepest literary sense.

INTERVIEWER
How would you define *rancidity* — this thing to be avoided?

BLOOM
Rancidity is when you have a breakdown in decorum, when
you feel that the writer is attempting to amuse neither herself
nor himself nor you nor anyone else, but is essentially sadistic
and is just glorying in the borderline aspect of the whole thing.

INTERVIEWER
The connection with rancid is appropriate. It has an odor.

BLOOM
Yes, it tastes bad. It tastes bad, my dear. May I offer an
example. My first year teaching at Yale back in 1954 or 1955

I had an undergraduate class which consisted entirely of Yale legacies. Back in those days they were not the most intelligent students in the world. They were all male too. At the start of the last class, so as to characterize their relationship to me, I said that they should be deeply moved by a moment in a book I recommended to them, Nathanael West's *A Cool Million*, whose subtitle is "The Dismantling of Lemuel Pitkin." In the climactic scene in Madison Square Garden where the American Fascists are staging a rally, being addressed by Shagpoke Whipple, who is a kind of heroic precursor of President Ronald Reagan, and who is talking about Lemuel Pitkin. Lemuel has been taken to bits part by part, a sort of Horst Wessel of the Davy Crockett boys who are Whipple's S.S. or Hitler youth. Whipple cries out, "Of what is it that Lemuel Pitkin speaks? He speaks of the inalienable right of every American boy to make everything he can of himself without being sneered at or conspired against by sophisticated aliens." I then said to the class that if that read: ". . . the inalienable right of every American boy to make everything he can of himself without being sneered at or conspired against by sophisticated Jews," it would not be funny, but by saying "sophisticated aliens" the taste or decorum of it is very much restored.

INTERVIEWER

What about the Americans? Are there writers—as we were talking about Milton—who are absolutely humorless?

BLOOM

Hemingway is a very interesting case. The closest thing to humor in Hemingway at his best would be the very frightening, but great short story, "God Rest You Merry, Gentlemen."

INTERVIEWER

"Mr. and Mrs. Elliot"?

BLOOM

"Mr. and Mrs. Elliot" is, of course, an attempt to pierce T.S. Eliot, about whom Hemingway remarked at one point

that if he could get the ghost of Joseph Conrad to come out
of the grave by scattering the bones and cinders of T.S. Eliot
over it, he would leave for London the next day with a meat
grinder. A very mean remark indeed. I think that's because
The Sun Also Rises clearly owes something to *The Waste Land*.
And that probably bothered Hemingway. The imagery of the
Fisher King, and Tiresias helps establish the sexual wound
motif of poor Jake Barnes; a central situation of sterility really
reflects the mood and mode of *The Waste Land*. As Wallace
Stevens sublimely remarked, "Hemingway is essentially a
poet."

Hemingway and Stevens knew each other in Key West. If
we're going to speak about humor connected with Hemingway, in a rancid way this is the funniest thing I know.
Down in Key West, when I think Hemingway was thirty-five
and Stevens was fifty-five, they'd had a bit too much to drink
together and they got into a fist fight, Hemingway knocked
Stevens down and perhaps even out, certainly down, and
writes about it with great relish in one of his letters where he
points out how much heavier and bigger a man Stevens was; he
doesn't bother to point out that he was a gentleman knocking
down a gentleman twenty years older. But in spite of the fact
that they had not personally gotten along then and perhaps
on other occasions in Key West, they both had considerable
respect for one another's writing.

But Hemingway is not humorous in that indeliberately
funny book, *The Old Man and the Sea*. The old man and
the boy are talking about whether the great DiMaggio and
the Yankees were going to win the pennant: "But I fear the
Tigers of Detroit." An absolute disaster, and if Hemingway
had had any ear for comedy at all, he could not have committed
that terrible blunder. Fitzgerald is not really a very funny
writer. I always find it difficult to think of a moment in *The
Great Gatsby* or *Tender is the Night* or the short stories which
would strike me as humorous. He's an elegiac writer.

INTERVIEWER

And Twain?

BLOOM

Twain, of course, is hilarious. *The Mysterious Stranger*, which is a shockingly funny book, at least to me, has perfect pitch. He knows exactly what he can or cannot do. Where the humor fails in Twain is occasionally in the *Connecticut Yankee* work. It just turns a little too cute; it turns slightly precious; he gets a little too relaxed; he doesn't maintain his high form. *Huckleberry Finn*, always in the news these days because it has become contentious, is a superb instance of humorous writing — beginning, middle and end.

INTERVIEWER

The last chapters — when Jim is locked up and Tom and Huck cook up crazy schemes to rescue him — are often criticized . . . by Hemingway among others.

BLOOM

The whole Tom Sawyer anticness, which most high literary critics have tended to condemn, I think it works very well. It's beautifully self-contained humor.

INTERVIEWER

Were you enormously upset by the extract Twain discarded, found in some attic, and which was recently printed in *The New Yorker*?

BLOOM

Yes, yes. I saw that. Extremely unfortunate. Twain himself would obviously have objected violently against that. But look what we do all the time. People who keep up with *Entertainment Weekly* called me and said "Demi Moore is now playing Hester Prynne. She's on location with them at this very moment." I said, "Well, you know, she'll certainly be a good-looking Hester Prynne." They said, "Yes, but you know what they're doing with it, Professor Bloom?" I asked, "What are they doing with it?" "Well," they said, "It doesn't begin with her already wearing the scarlet letter in the public scene." I said "What? The whole point is to begin with that marvelous intensity of the scarlet letter right there," and they said, "No, no, it's all different now. It ends happily." The Reverend Dimmesdale is played by Gary Oldman of all people, and he doesn't die. How ghastly, how absolutely ghastly! I would think that Mr. Updike, the novel's greatest admirer, would probably be most offended by all this. That's one of my very rare compliments to Mr. Updike. *There's* a very interesting question: is he a comic writer? I suppose that the reason I liked *The Witches of Eastwick* better than anything else, including the Rabbit novels, is because it does seem to be, in its hallucinatory way, a successful piece of comedy.

I've just thought of a fine humorous moment in Norman Mailer. It's in that crazy book *An American Dream* — when a sort of Sammy Davis, Jr. character comes in and talks jive . . . an astonishing soliliquy of amazing jive talk which is really very funny and which stays in the head but, alas, it's almost a unique moment in Mailer.

INTERVIEWER
You mentioned Faulkner earlier.

BLOOM
Surely one of the many measures of Faulkner's extraordinary eminence is how frighteningly funny he can be. "Spotted Horses" in *The Hamlet* is terrifically funny, as is everything going on in *The Reivers* or in *Go Down, Moses*. Of course, the greatest thing that Faulkner ever wrote, the height of twentieth-century American prose fiction, is the short novel *As I Lay Dying*, which is phantasmagoria; it goes beyond the borders of the naturalistic. There are astonishing moments: this weird collection of her children bringing their mother's body back for burial, taking it on this mad trek, and you enter the conciousness of the quite possibly schizophrenic visionary, Vardaman Bundren, the most remarkable of them . . . that famous section in which he says "My mother is a fish." In a very scary way, in context, that is very funny. In *Sanctuary*,

Popeye's funeral is almost Jacobean humor, the sort of humor that you would expect to find in certain diabolical moments in *The White Devil* or *The Duchess of Malfi*. It's almost a kind of Shakespearean humor in Faulkner, though it obviously owes much to Mark Twain as well.

Do you know Mark Twain's great short story or sketch called "Journalism in Tennessee?" Oh it's absolutely magnificent, my dear. Twain in Tennessee walks into the offices of the highly contentious editor of a magnificent daily newspaper, which rejoices in the name the *Morning Glory and Johnson County War-Whoop*. He starts having a conversation with the editor. Rival editors whom the editor has savaged in his editorials keep dropping by the office with pistols and shooting at the editor. Poor Twain is sort of caught in the crossfire. At one point, the editor of the *Morning Glory and Johnson County War-Whoop* calmly takes aim and shoots off the ear of a rival editor and then makes some remarkable comment to Twain about the whole condition of journalism in Tennessee. It's a marvelous piece. It's deadpan humor in which the narrator, Twain, pretends not to see the humor in anything that's going on. In this perfectly straight-out way he gives you this incredibly outrageous account, which makes Nathanael West seem rather ordinary, of these incredible antics going on between these feuding editors — that old American frontier violence, which in Cormac McCarthy's *Blood Meridian* is such a nightmare, such a holocaust. It's a very difficult piece to describe but I would urge everybody to read it immediately.

Incidentally, one of the great comic writers of this century would be Nabokov, necessarily, because *Pale Fire* may be the most hilarious book by a modern American writer. Russian as he was, one thinks of him as an American writer because he writes in the American language. The notes in *Pale Fire*, and this sort of pseudo-Frostian poem itself, must be the most high-pitched successful humor, deliberately deadpan comic. It's quite astonishing how well Nabokov could do that.

INTERVIEWER

What about the earlier Americans?

BLOOM

You could make an argument that the greatest American —
I won't say novelist — but epic writer, is Herman Melville. Very
difficult to think of *Moby-Dick* as having a comic register at
all; there are whimsical moments in it, but we would not think
of it as comic. Look at Hawthorne: we don't ordinarily think
of Hawthorne as a comic writer when we consider *The Scarlet
Letter*, *The House of the Seven Gables* and *The Marble Faun*.
But one of the last major tales is the howlingly funny story
about a scarecrow whom a witch makes into a live human
being. It's called "Feathertop," and it's very funny in a more
than Borgesian way. Emerson can be hilarious. These days,
when I am outrageously editing what I hope will replace Cliff's
Notes with a series called Bloom's Notes, I am perpetually
cheered up by two great remarks of Emerson. One is, "A
man is seldom so innocent as when he is occupied in making
money," and the other, which always breaks my heart, is,
"Money, in some of its effects, is as beautiful as roses." I might
also add his marvelously humorous remark, which is from the
notebooks: "It is the praise of most critics that they have never
failed because they have attempted nothing."

INTERVIEWER

Is Henry James a candidate?

BLOOM

It's a very curious kind of humor isn't it? Would one think
of it as an aging humorist's work?

INTERVIEWER

Not a comedy of manners, but an inspection of social mores.

BLOOM

Do you ever laugh when you read James, I mean laugh out
loud?

INTERVIEWER

That's the qualification then, that the reader should laugh aloud?

BLOOM

Richard Poirier, my closest friend, wrote as his very first book *The Comic Sense of Henry James*. If Dick Poirier were here he could no doubt tell us a great deal about this, and denounce me for failing to see the splendor of James in this particular department. I don't quite see it at all. Where would one look? *The Portrait of a Lady*, no. *The Bostonians*, no. Certainly not *The Wings of the Dove*. I suppose tragicomedy might be his mode, but it's really a mode of irony rather than of humor.

INTERVIEWER

Perhaps he's one of the humorless major writers we were trying to list?

BLOOM

Well, if one believes the various biographies of him or when one reads his letters or his travel writings, he certainly is an instance of high seriousness, of urbanity in the extreme. He has the elegiac touch. I'm not so sure that the elegiac and the humorous can ever consort.

INTERVIEWER

A contradiction in a way?

BLOOM

Mourning and humor do not often go together. We haven't talked about Walt Whitman, where there is certainly a very curious mode of laughter at the self. But if one takes Shakespeare, Molière, Cervantes, Rabelais and Aristophanes as being the writers who define humor, it's very difficult to admit Mr. Henry James to a place in that pantheon.

INTERVIEWER

To digress a moment and go back to definitions . . . what do you make of Freud's *Jokes and the Unconscious* — that jokes are a manifestation of unconscious wishes?

BLOOM

Freud's basic theory is essentially a comic vision though he may not have realized this. When I think about Freud's outrageous account of the relations between the superego and the ego, I always think of the Italian "Punch and Judy Show" . . . the superego always beating up on the poor Pulchinella or Punch figure, saying, "Stop being so aggressive." The poor beaten-up ego keeps surrendering all its aggressivity; what it gets for doing this is that the superego gets still angrier and hits it even harder. Freud's theory of the joke or of humor is really based upon the essential notion that the superego lets up its severity upon the poor ego, allows it a little space, a little relief, so that — I never thought of it in just this trope or metaphor before — it's rather like a warden or a jailer or even a torturer who occasionally lets his victim laugh and relax a little by withdrawing his censoriousness to a limited degree. Freud's notion of humor is a cat-and-mouse game. It's really a very cruel theory of humor. But as I was saying before, theories of humor are very strange anyway. I mean, the great theory of humor before Freud was that of Henri Bergson — its most peculiar insight that we laugh when the human is reduced to the level of the mechanical. It's very hard to contravene if you think of the history of film comedy. Chaplin quite frequently bases his humor upon what is in effect a Bergsonian theory — that a human being has mechanical movements, and seems to be more like a puppet than a person. Always, of course, it's a question of perspectivism. Think of the grand old Mack Sennett comedies, all that pie throwing involved in those Keystone Cops films. If you photographed somebody throwing a custard pie into somebody else's face, and you see it from a spectator's point of view, you get that marvelous trajectory, the beautiful arc or curve that the pie follows and then *splat*, the pie lands in somebody's face . . . that's very funny indeed. But, if it were photographed, or filmed from the perspective of someone who's standing right behind you, so that you had the pie coming at you, about to land in your face . . .

INTERVIEWER

I have been told your favorite comedian is W.C. Fields—hardly a Bergsonian concept.

BLOOM

Nothing could be more sublimely outrageous than *The Fatal Glass of Beer*. Throughout much of it Fields is strumming a zither and singing a song about the demise of his unfortunate son. It makes an interesting comparison with the next best short of W.C. Fields, *The Dentist*, with the sexual humor of Fields working upon these various ladies and getting between their long legs as he reaches in to pull out a tooth. It really goes beyond the limits of taste. But in *The Fatal Glass of Beer* he walks the line and he doesn't go over it.

INTERVIEWER

Could we discuss Jewish literary humor?

BLOOM

The tradition of Jewish literary humor certainly begins with Sholom Aleichem. It's wonderfully good-natured, but always underneath the good nature there's the terrible sadness. The very barbed irony of it goes into the work of a great Yiddish poet Moyshe-Leyb Halpern—extraordinary poet who wrote New York City poems of a kind of Baudelairean comedy and intensity which are fiercely funny. There are some terrific translations by John Hollander in the late Irving Howe's various collections of Yiddish verse. Jewish literary humor is a fascinating subject because it produces such strange permutations. That marvelous book by Walter Abish called *Alphabetical Africa* is a great Jewish joke done in this mad French style.

INTERVIEWER
Is there something that actually distinguished Yiddish—
Jewish—humor from other types?

BLOOM
The tradition of Yiddish humor is one in which somehow
you've lost already, but survival depends upon the ability to
laugh at yourself and at your predicament. I don't think that's
a very American mode of humor in literature at all, though,
of course it's gotten into film, into radio and televison, into
Broadway. Have you met Mr. Tony Kushner? I have never met
Mr. Kushner. I may never meet Mr. Kushner. The magazine
American Theatre got in touch with me before his two-part
play *Angels in America* opened in New York City to say that,
since I was acknowledged in the prefaces, he—the editor—
thought how interesting it would be if I read the two plays
and attended them, and we did a sort of joint interview/
conversation which they could publish. Then Mr. Kushner
backed out of it. He explained in *The New York Times* that
years ago he was undergoing Freudian analysis. He was reading
my book *The Anxiety of Influence*, and he began to have so
strong a reaction to it, inducing such anxiety in him, that his
psychiatrist forbade him to read any more. He said, "Recently,
I had an opportunity to meet Professor Bloom, but I fled the
encounter the way one of Freud's Aboriginal tribesmen in
Totem and Taboo flees an encounter with the primal father,
the one with the big knife." He thought I was going to cut
off his *cojones* or something. But when I saw *Perestroika* with
Jeanne, it didn't have the scene (at least they didn't play it
that night) which is in the printed version and which I really
thought was a scene of extraordinary distinction. Roy Cohn
is in the afterlife. You're not told whether it's purgatory or
hell or limbo or whatever . . . and God is speaking to him.
You don't hear God's voice. You just hear a lot of thunder.
Roy Cohn hears it and understands it. The various angels are
suing God for desertion, for fleeing his post. Roy Cohn says,
"What's that? You want me to defend you? All right," he
says, "It's a done deal." He talks about how he's going to send

HOLIDAY GIFT DISCOUNT

SAVE $12 off the cover price and $6 off the regular subscription rates with this coupon.

THE PARIS REVIEW

Enclosed is my check for:

☐ $28 for 1 year (new subscriptions and gifts)
☐ $34 for 1 year (4 issues)
☐ $1,000 for a lifetime subscription

(All payment must be in U.S. funds. Postal surcharge of $8 per 4 issues outside USA)

☐ Send me information on becoming a *Paris Review* Associate.

Bill this to my Visa/MasterCard:

_____
Card number   Exp. date

☐ New subscription   ☐ Renewal subscription
☐ New address

Name _____

Address _____

City _____ State _____ Zip code _____

Please send gift subscription to:

Name _____

Address _____

City _____ State _____ Zip code _____

Gift announcement signature _____

Please send me the following:

☐ The Paris Review T-Shirt   ($15.00)
Color _____ Size _____ Quantity _____
☐ The following back issues: Nos. _____

See listing at back of book for availability.

☐ The Paris Review Print Series catalogue ($1.00)

Name _____

Address _____

City _____ State _____ Zip code _____

☐ Enclosed is my check for $ _____
☐ Bill this to my Visa/MasterCard:

_____
Card number   Exp. date

Impress someone, and save.

Give *The Paris Review* for only $28 a year when you renew your subscription at the regular rate. You save $12 off the newsstand price!

BUSINESS REPLY MAIL

FIRST CLASS   PERMIT NO. 3119   FLUSHING, N.Y.

POSTAGE WILL BE PAID BY ADDRESSEE

THE PARIS REVIEW
45-39 171 Place
FLUSHING NY   11358-9892

BUSINESS REPLY MAIL

FIRST CLASS   PERMIT NO. 3119   FLUSHING, N.Y.

POSTAGE WILL BE PAID BY ADDRESSEE

THE PARIS REVIEW
45-39 171 Place
FLUSHING NY   11358-9892

jewelry to the judge, and that he will bamboozle the jury. Then he says to God, "I gotta start by telling you you ain't got a case here, you're as guilty as hell, no question, you have nothing to plead but not to worry, darling, I will make something up." That's a very Yiddish form of humor. Kushner can catch that very well. Very curious, bitter humor.

INTERVIEWER
You are a great admirer of Philip Roth.

BLOOM
Once when I was visiting Philip up in Cornwall, I went for a walk with him out in the woods, and about three or four city blocks down from his house someone had scratched into a tree "Bring back Portnoy." I looked at him and said, "Did you do this?" "Are you kidding?" he said, "I couldn't bring back Portnoy!" This new book, *Sabbath's Theater* raises the issue of whether you can really have humor if it's too much crossed by death. There is the traditional statement about the difference between sexuality and eroticism, which is that as soon as the shadow of mortality falls upon human sexuality, you have the erotic. It is the flavor of death which changes it. In the same way if you put the flavor of death into comedy, then something very curious happens, for which I don't think we have a name. Back in 1947 or 1948 when I was seventeen or eighteen, when they showed documentaries of the Nazi death camps, of Auschwitz in the movie theaters, I could never get myself to watch it. Occasionally, when there is even a little footage of it on a television channel, I dash to the set to turn it off. I am told by some people who forced themselves to go to the camps that after a while, in order to avoid being terribly ill or going mad, they had to start laughing. It's a psychologically defensive reaction akin to the fact that when I was a kid at a really bad horror movie, I would save myself by beginning to laugh, not a forced laughter, but a terribly defensive laughter. I had a bit of that sensation in reading *Sabbath's Theater*. It is about the obsessive love of Sabbath for a lady named

Drenka, a Yugoslav lady who was his mistress for many years, a woman of extraordinary vitality and exuberance and sexual intensity. She dies and he's just inconsolable. In the very last scene of the book, trying to get police officers to at least arrest him if not actually kill him, he's masturbating on her grave out of some terrible frustration. It is written by Roth as high comedy, but it has crossed the line, not into rancidity, not into bad taste, but into whatever the dark equivalent would be when too much humor gets involved with death.

A great literary version of this would be the marvelous scene at the beginning of the fifth act of *Hamlet*, when Hamlet and Horatio are standing in the graveyard and the dialogue takes place between Hamlet and the grave-digger. Hamlet is presented with the skull of Yorick, the king's jester who had played with him when he was a little kid because mama and papa hung on each other and didn't pay him much regard. That entire scene is in a way fiercely funny: the little poems and rhymes that Hamlet makes up: "Imperious Caesar, dead and turn'd to clay, / Might stop a hole to keep the wind away." They're very funny rhymes, and the sort of stuff that he says to Horatio, who plays the straight man more than ever before, is at times howlingly funny. But the whole thing is so gory, so gore-haunted that the effect of it is not humor, but something for which I have not got a term, humor so crossed by death that it just is not funny anymore, but is something else. That seems to be the mode that Roth has gone into, maybe the inevitable mode for him. Roth, I think, is the greatest sit-down and stand-up comic I've heard in my entire life. He is outrageously funny, almost painfully funny, compulsively funny. It just goes on and on and on. I occasionally have the feeling, when I'm having dinner with him and he just won't stop, I sort of lean back and I feel this kind of obsessive, driving, hard-edged comedy that it is like a great flamenco singer who goes up so high and has such pitch that you feel she can't go higher, and then suddenly it gets beyond that. Philip can do the same thing, but finally it begins to reverberate with a kind of painful intensity.

INTERVIEWER

No one else you would put in his class?

BLOOM

With the, alas, precipitous decline of Thomas Pynchon, unless he recovers, I would think there is just no rival to Roth right now, though he seems to alienate a great many readers. I think the comedy is just so harsh. I don't know if we have an important comic writer at the moment except for him. There is Vidal, but unfortunately *Live From Golgotha* did not make it. It does not work at all. It reminded me of *Duluth*, a rather squalid work unworthy of the great man. But *Myra Breckinridge*, I think, is an immortal masterpiece, greatly underappreciated. I suppose Vidal would deny this, but he undoubtedly owes a debt to Evelyn Waugh's wonderful Hollywood novel called *The Loved One*.

INTERVIEWER

We have not talked about women writers.

BLOOM

There is Jane Austen, who is the very best. And Jane Austen is perhaps the greatest ironist in the history of the novel. Much more so than even Henry Fielding, who delighted her so much. But except for a handful of American women poets, if one thinks of French, German, or Italian writers, I cannot think of any major women comic writers at all. If one thinks in general of the great tradition of British women novelists, George Eliot or the two Brontës, or Edith Wharton or Willa Cather in America, all remarkable writers, they are absolutley lacking in humor . . . there isn't a touch of it. I do like *The Matisse Stories* of A.S. Byatt, as we've said, but what else is there? Miss Emily Dickinson of Amherst was a great comic poet when she chose to be. And Miss Marianne Moore and Miss Elizabeth Bishop in their deadpan way, and Miss May Swenson. Some poems of the late Amy Clampitt, who — at her best — is worthy of the four before her.

INTERVIEWER
Does this lack surprise you?

BLOOM
Well, there must be some reason for it, why they elevate themselves to such high seriousness. Perhaps being in contention with the whole world of male writers. Charlotte Brontë—I think this is not often enough remarked—is the most aggressive novelist I have ever read. She basically seems to presuppose throughout *Jane Eyre* that her reader is a male reader; she beats up on him a lot of the time. She keeps saying, reader this and reader that, and she shows just as much aggressivity toward the reader as she does toward poor old Rochester, whom she just about does in. Very fierce personage indeed. Miss Welty is sort of funny . . . *Delta Wedding* has some nice humorous moments in it. But one wouldn't think of Miss Welty as primarily a comic writer.

INTERVIEWER
I have a small, perhaps humorous anecdote about Miss Welty. I visited her down in Jackson, Mississippi a few months ago. A friend of mine wanted me to ask her about Elvis Presley. So at one point I did. She told me she had never met Mr. Presley, but many years after his death she was going up an escalator at Lord and Taylor's in New York. Suddenly the woman in front of her cried out, "Elvis is dead! Elvis is dead!" and burst into tears. Miss Welty told me she had reached out and touched the woman on the shoulder. "There, there," she said. But I digress.

BLOOM
An important reflection, my dear.

INTERVIEWER
We were talking about Jane Austen.

BLOOM

It would be very interesting if one could understand why
it was that Miss Austen was able to be so piercingly funny.
The single most hilarious character ever done by a woman
writer is Mr. Collins in *Pride and Prejudice*. Absolutely superb!
That great first marriage proposal scene between Darcy and
Elizabeth must be the all-time classic for a humorous disaster
in the realm of the proposed erotic. Darcy is proposing marriage to her, saying in so many words, "I don't really want to
do this, but you must understand that you and particularly
your ghastly family are highly inadequate for a man of my
splendid social position. Nevertheless I really am forced to tell
you, you know, that I'm so taken with you . . ." and he's
taking it absolutely for granted that she's going to say, "Oh,
how magnificent!" It's very funny in that scene—the way she
rips Darcy up and then he just collapses—just an astonishing
scene, a deflationary technique, of course; she must be the
greatest master of deflation in comic history. She is so sly, and
the mode of irony in her really is a rugged kind of defense.
I don't know if in Austen you can tell the difference between
irony and high comedy. I think she has found a way of accomo-
dating it. And her influence goes on and on. I mean, my
favorite novel by George Meredith is *The Egoist*—that terrific
scene towards the close when Sir Willoughby has to dash from
room to room, keeping three different women thinking different things—marvelously breathless kind of a pace that George
Meredith keeps up. But if I had to personally vote for one
comic writer, it would be have to be Oscar . . . the divine
Oscar.

INTERVIEWER

Have we left out Trollope? He once declared that, "a novel
should give a picture of common life enlivened by humor and
sweetened by pathos."

BLOOM

Surely one of the greatest comic scenes in the English novel,
except for Austen, is the scene in *Barchester Towers* when an

English lady, an English lady who I think has an Italian title
and who pretends to a fashionable quasi-cripple though in fact
she's perfectly capable of walking, is adorning a big reception
given by the Proudies. She's stretched on this couch, which
someone gives an inadvertent push; it goes across the floor and
cuts into Mrs. Proudie's bustle. Mrs. Proudie almost wordlessly
gives the command; her daughters form up in convoy behind
her and she leads them sweeping across the room so the muti-
lated bustle cannnot be seen. Trollope is very grand at that
kind of thing.

You know who we have left out? That strangely farcical
figure, Kierkegaard, who in that magnificent section of *Ei-
ther-Or* called "The Rotation Method," uses as an epigraph one
of the great choruses in Aristophanes. The chorus is chanting,
"You get too much at last of everything, of sunsets, of cabbages, of love," which is "The Rotation Method" of Kierkegaard in a nutshell. The way in which the whole Rotation
Method works out that strain of Aristophanes is sublimely
humorous. But then one wonders, can one truly think of Kierkegaard as a humorous writer. *Sickness Unto Death* or *The
Concept of Dread* are not works of the highest good humor.
I do feel we've left out a few others, but I suppose one would
have to consult one's own canonical list, which I don't want
to do. To actually do such a thing would seem to be cheating.

INTERVIEWER

I cannot resist asking. Do you treasure jokes?

BLOOM

Oh yes, my dear. Oh, yes, yes, yes. I like religious jokes
in general. There is a very great joke I was told by a Catholic
prelate. The current pope, John Paul II, receives a request for
an audience from Mr. Frank Perdue, the chicken magnate.
Mr. Perdue is ushered into the presence of his Holiness and
his Holiness says, "What can I do for you my son?" Mr. Perdue
says, "Your Holiness, though I am an American Southern
Baptist, I wish to make an unconditional, unrestricted gift of

ten million dollars to the Vatican." Pope John Paul II gravely acknowledges this and says, "That is very good of you, my son. Is there perhaps some very small thing we can do for you in return?" Frank Perdue says, "I'm very glad you asked that, your Holiness. There is one small thing: I want you to change the wording of the Lord's Prayer so it no longer says, 'Give us this day our daily bread,' but instead says, 'Give us this day our daily chicken.'" The pope is outraged. He says, "Mr. Perdue, I will pretend I didn't hear you say that. You can have no idea what you're saying." Frank Perdue says, "Twenty million dollars, your Holiness." The pope is obviously restraining himself. He says, "Mr. Perdue, I really want you to stop going on about this." Mr. Perdue says, "Forty million dollars, your Holiness." The pope says, "Mr. Perdue, I don't think you understand at all. You are talking about the words of our Lord Jesus Christ himself, who said, 'Give us this day our daily bread.'" Frank Perdue says, "One hundred million dollars, your Holiness." The pope says, "Mr. Perdue, come into my innermost chamber where we will talk about these matters further." The next day the pope summons to a secret conclave all of the cardinals resident in or near Rome. After they are all in front of him he says, "My sons, I have some very, very good news for you, and some not so good news. The very, very good news is that Mr. Frank Perdue, the American chicken magnate, is making an unrestricted gift to the Vatican of two hundred million dollars, and in return for this he is asking the trifling concession that from now on all over the world we Catholics, when we recite The Lord's Prayer, will not say, 'Give us this day our daily bread,' but will say, 'Give us this day our daily chicken.'" The cardinals rise to their feet to give his Holiness a standing ovation. He waves them down impatiently and says, "Not so fast. Now for the not so good news: this will ruin our relationship with Wonderbread." Ah jokes. A strange category.

INTERVIEWER

Very nice. Lastly, if you had to supply an epigraph for a canon of Western humor, what might one be?

BLOOM

Actually, *The Western Canon* is the only book I've ever written without an epigraph. I had the perfect epigraph for it, but everybody vetoed it. It is from the divine Oscar's *Importance of Being Earnest*—a perfect instance of why Oscar Wilde is not a writer of a period piece and why Noël Coward, say, is. I wanted to use as the epigraph what that magnificent figure Lady Bracknell says: "Come Gwendolyn, we have missed four or is it five trains already. To miss any more might expose us to comment upon the platform." That strikes me as the highest possible mode of comedy. As soon as you start explaining it, of course, it dissolves. It's really a test for a good reader, because obviously Lady Bracknell is so sublimely crazy and self-centered that it doesn't even occur to her, or even to us because she has such a sway over us, that it isn't *possible* that anybody on the platform would know how many trains Lady Bracknell and Gwendolyn had missed already. So I thought that should be the epigraph. I don't see why it doesn't work in this case. What do you think?

—George Plimpton

John Updike

Epithalamium

MISS TERRIBERRY TO WED IN SUBURBS
— *headline in* The Times, *long, long ago.*

Be ever after merry,
My dear Miss Terriberry:
Enjoy a very very
  Congregational wedding to
  Throckmorton Percy Gardner, who
Esteems it necessary
To rob you of your airy
Maiden name.   How dare he!

The brute, proprietary
And male and tall and hairy,
On lips as sweet as sherry
  Plants kisses ere he leads the way,
  With you in blue and he in gray,
To some suburban cyric
Where years shall pass, contrary
To your nuptial mood, and nary
A hour falls upon unwary

Brides but that, as on some prairie
Time's thrum turns ordinary
The house, the garden.   Scary!

David Lehman

The World Trade Center

I never liked the World Trade Center.
When it went up I talked it down
as did many other New Yorkers.
The twin towers were ugly monoliths
that lacked the details the ornament the character
of the Empire State Building and especially
the Chrysler Building, everyone's favorite,
with its scalloped top, so noble.
The World Trade Center was an example of what was wrong
with American architecture,
and it stayed that way for twenty-five years
until that Friday afternoon in February
when the bomb went off and the buildings became
a great symbol of America, like the Statue
of Liberty at the end of Hitchcock's *Saboteur*.
My whole attitude toward the World Trade Center
changed overnight. I began to like the way
it comes into view as you reach Sixth Avenue
from any side street, the way the tops
of the towers dissolve into white skies
in the east when you cross the Hudson
into the city across the George Washington Bridge.

Three Poems by Brooks Haxton

The Last Confession of Roger Tory Peterson

To see the yellow-bellied sapsucker suck sap,
to watch the oystercatcher at his catch,
and bluebird, woodcock, dickcissel, blue goose,
in bush to find them worth more than in hand . . .
to my mind just to list their names does much
as the tufted titmouse cock's cry does the hen:
Peter peter peter! *Here here here*!
If ever a purple gallinule highstepped
and clucked across a trembling lily pad,
if ever an *anser* answered from the fog,
let buteos be buteos, let whimbrels have
their whim, may limpkins be my lambkins now,
and my works work to call the killdeer dear.

Wisdom

Dim sow is an anagram. They tell me,
"Pigs are the most intelligent of the domestic animals,"
domestic animals a way of phrasing it to leave out
primates and cetaceans (*do swim* is another anagram).

"Cats," they say, "are less intelligent."
But next to pigs, cats look like geniuses
for comfort, diet, incidence of systematic slaughter,
and, despite the rash of neuterings,
loud caterwauling sex. Nevertheless I nod,
"You don't say. Pigs!"

Intelligent, they say. They don't say smart.
This week, in conference with my son's new teacher,
I said, "He's a bright kid."

"More than that," she told me,
"your son is a gifted child."

Let's hope we keep him bright, I thought,
but I said, "Yes. That's what we're told."

I'm also told sows suffocate
their young by accident,
or, being well fed, swallow them alive
on whim. I've seen them
puke their breakfast in the dirt
and eat it warm for lunch,
their faces smeared with shit,
though advocates of pig
intelligence will seldom emphasize
this angle in their adumbrations.

Lately, there's a theory in the news
that people African in their descent
are less intelligent than Europeans.
This we know statistically,
because we have a certain test.
The people saying this themselves are quite
intelligent, according to the test which,
I'm just guessing, is the one they use on pigs.

It Comes to Me: Concision!

One two three: up: and between
the metal ramp and the wooden bed of the truck,
as we shifted grips, my filing cabinet

separated just enough from the dolly, in air,
for me to slip my right thumb into the gap.

When it hit, I felt: *grandes oeuvres*, play, lay,
epic, sequences epistolary, meditative, meta-narrative,
and essayistic, essay, film script, everything,
crank correspondence, refutations of rejections,
every word, I felt land full force on my thumb.

My thumbnail has retained for months the shape
of crimped and beaten-open pipe. Francois Villon
said in his shortest and to me most memorable
poem that from a fathom of rope his neck
would learn the weight of his ass.

Campbell McGrath

Seashells, Manasota Key

Abras, augers, arks and angel wings,

bubbles, bittium,
baby's ears,
bleeding teeth,

crenulate nut clams and pointed cingulas,
dogwinkles, diplodons, donax, dosinia,

emarginate emarginula,

fig shells, frog shells, file shells,
flamingo tongue,

geoducks, gem clams, the bittersweet family *Glycymerididae*,

helmets and half-slippers,
hoof shells and horse mussels,

Ischnochitonidae,
Isognomonidae,
Ilynassa obsoleta,

jewel boxes, jingle shells,
kitten's paws,
loras, limas, lucines, lysonias,
murexes, mactras, moon shells, melampuses,

neptune, nerite, glorious neodrillia,

the San Pedro dwarf olive,
Cande's beaded phos,

quarterdecks and quahogs,
razor clams and ribbed miters,

scotch bonnets, shark eyes, slit worms, solarielle,

tritons, turbans, turrets,
tulips, trumpets,
thracias, trivias, tusks and tuns,

unicorns,
venuses and volutes,
wentletraps, wing oysters, lightning whelks,
xenophoridae,
yoldia,

Zebina browniana and *Zirfaea crispata.*

Victoria Else

Sabbath

The congregation dances perfect golden reels
redolent of sex amid the Sunday chimes;
how sweet, how . . . symmetrical it all is—everything else.
They smile and pray. Today's cassock is Easter grape
and I think Rector Swenson, who calls the dance,
sucks his fringes yellow between services.
I sit in the pew, blighted, thirty-sexless, widowed—
I suppose God knows what She's doing. They pray,

I slyly incant nightmares, then go witching off,
escaping as usual before coffee, achieving unholy
grandiose satori by walking a centerless circle.
Life's a bitch and I the lucky bastard, even though
I'm missing something, like . . . the point. High-ho:
better be god-ridden, than never ridden at all.

Tom Disch

Donna Reed in the Scary Old House

At first she is only mildly annoyed: the car
won't start, it's happened before. She'll phone
her husband—what *is* his name?—at his office,
and he'll come pick her up. Another cup of coffee,
meanwhile, in that funeral chapel of a living room
with old Mrs. Marbleheart, who haunts this old house.

Through the fence's iron trellises, the house
seems strangely familiar. It is her own, and the car
is parked in her own driveway. In the living room
picture window a candle gutters, and a phone
rings, alarm-clock-like, within. What a case of coffee
nerves she's got. It must be Alex, calling from the office.

Only that and nothing more; Alex is at his office,
she's in her spotless kitchen, the house
was built yesterday, on the stovetop the glass coffee
pot burbles its ads, and a mechanic can fix the car.
His name *is* Alex, and it must be him on the phone.
Goodness—imagine falling asleep on the living room

sofa in mid-afternoon. But this *isn't* her living room,
after all. Alex died years ago, and where his office
stood there's now a mall. Her rotary phone
is landfill, and as for the house. . . . The house
is the source of this nightmare, with its tireless car
entombed in the old garage. And worse, this coffee

stain on the bodice of her bridal gown, the coffee
grounds ground into the wall-to-wall living room
carpet, the mice squealing in the walls, and a car-

ving knife with a bone-white handle from the Office
of Lost Wives — who could *live* in such a house?
It dawns on her she's dead. She lifts the phone

from its cradle, and the silence of the telephone
confirms her fear. Ten thousand cups of coffee
ago she *was* Donna Stone, a fictional house-
wife and mother of two, alive in a living room,
full of wise saws and instances, one of life's best office
   managers, licensed to marry and drive a car.

Now she has nowhere to drive any car, no one to phone
but the office of "Please wait." The old brands of coffee
appear on TV, but in another living room, in someone else's house.

Lloyd Schwartz

Proverbs from Purgatory

It was déjà vu all over again.

I know this town like the back of my head.

People who live in glass houses are worth two in
    the bush.

One hand scratches the other.

A friend in need is worth two in the bush.

A bird in the hand makes waste.

Life isn't all it's crapped up to be.

It's like finding a needle in the eye of the beholder.

It's like killing one bird with two stones.

My motto in life has always been: *Get It Over With.*

Two heads are better than none.

A rolling stone deserves another.

All things wait for those who come.

A friend in need deserves another.

I'd trust him as long as I could throw him.

He smokes like a fish.

He's just a chip off the old tooth.

I'll have him eating out of my lap.

A friend in need opens a can of worms.

Too many cooks spoil the child.

An ill wind keeps the doctor away.

The wolf at the door keeps the doctor away.

People who live in glass houses keep the doctor away.

A friend in need shouldn't throw stones.

A friend in need washes the other.

A friend in need keeps the doctor away.

A stitch in time is only skin deep.

A verbal agreement isn't worth the paper it's written on.

A cat may look like a king.

Know which side of the bed your butter is on.

Nothing is cut and dried in stone.

You can eat more flies with honey than with vinegar.

Don't let the cat out of the barn.

Let's burn that bridge when we get to it.

When you come to a fork in the road, take it.

Don't cross your chickens before they hatch.

DO NOT READ THIS SIGN.

Throw discretion to the wolves.

After the twig is bent, the barn door is locked.

After the barn door is locked, you can come in out of the rain.

A friend in need locks the barn door.

There's no fool like a friend in need.

We've passed a lot of water since then.

At least we got home in two pieces.

All's well that ends.

It ain't over till it's over.

There's always one step further down you can go.

It's a milestone hanging around my neck.

Include me out.

It was déjà vu all over again.

The Man in the Back Row
Has a Question

The following questionnaire was sent out to a list of formidable literary figures, many of whom dismissed the fact that junior editors at Harper's Bazaar *are invariably asked to conduct such things, and sent in lively replies. The question about Turkish humor was tossed in to give a slightly more quirky feel to the questionnaire and, oddly, a surprising number of the literary worthies, perhaps because of the mundane quality of the other questions, leapt upon it with relish — eliciting far more response than one would have expected.*

What is the state of humor today?

Without a doubt, Arkansas. (Rim shot)

— Dave Barry

Robust. We live in unfortunately funny times.

— Christopher Buckley

An issue of *The Paris Review* devoted to humor suggests that humor is in need of saving; indeed the allowable range of

humor has suffered from the political correctness of our time —
the good-taste police are patrolling in legions. And there has
always been the suspicion among humorless book reviewers
that a novel that's funny can't be as serious as one that's . . .
uh, well, *serious*. (Concomitant to that notion is the presump-
tion that it's *harder* to be serious than to be funny, which
anyone who's ever *tried* to be funny knows is a lie.)

—John Irving

My love is pre-ironic humor: wit that was earnest in its intentions. P.G. Wodehouse and S.J. Perelman were no strangers
to the snide turn of phrase, but they were sincere in their
efforts to get a rise out of their readers. They didn't take our
modern-day humor shortcuts: the pop-culture reference that
substitutes for a punch line; the deliberately hokey joke we're
suppose to laugh at because it's deliberately hokey. I often
wonder how much experimentation and rejiggering and cross-
ing out it took for Wodehouse to achieve the pared down
magnificence of my favorite paragraph in all of comic literature—a single sentence of Bertie Wooster's describing his
awful Aunt Dahlia's reaction to his latest girlfriend: "The rela-
tive uttered a yowl."

—David Kamp

Terrible. There is much to laugh at in our holier-than-thou
politicians, but they are such obvious hypocrites and scoun-
drels that there is nothing concealed, nothing to puncture.
We live in desperate times; there are no heroes to take down.

— Alfred Kazin

Any discussion of humor is doomed, because (a) it won't be
funny, and (b) it supposes humor to be a distinct genre, when
in fact it's inextricable from any writer's voice. Is fiction shelved
in libraries by "anger" or "coldness"? One of my creative-writ-
ing students showed up for her first class with a five-hun-
dred-page manuscript. "Here's my novel," she announced

"It's all finished! All I have to do is add some humor!" She might as well have said, "All I have to do is add a *point of view!*"

Humor—or the more macho-sounding *comedy*—uses an outsider's perspective to point out absurdities the naked eye may have missed. People often cite hostility as a source of comedy, but they miss the crucial point that humor, unlike mere violence, also requires at least some high spirits. It's the inevitable combination of outrage and glee (as distinct from the more complacent happiness); it can be scalding or tolerant, but it exists to some extent in everything worthwhile, from *Hamlet* to *Waiting for Godot*, and even, in a way, on "Home Improvement." Its fun is reconciliatory: humor acknowledges that Life Is Hell, but adds, Oh, what the hell.

—Mark O'Donnell

Humor seems to be in particularly fine shape right now, in fact it's the only aspect of pop culture I feel completely at home with—maybe because it spends so much time beating up on the other aspects.

—Wilfrid Sheed

Terrible with notable exceptions (Dave Barry, Jerry Seinfeld, top political cartoonists, *Calvin & Hobbes*). At all levels lacks appropriate dosage of irony. Humor involves an ironic disconnection from, or distortion/inversion of normal (universal?) contexts. Context requires reference other than to self. Today's world is probably too mean-spirited, self-regarding and, well, brain-deadened. Compare Laurel and Hardy to *Dumb and Dumber*.

—Michael Thomas

It is hard to separate history from one's personal history. In my adolescence I thought "humor" was a sublime and prevalent genre; I greedily and happily consumed books by James Thurber, E.B. White, Robert Benchley, S.J. Perelman, Frank Sulli-

van, Peter DeVries, P.G. Wodehouse, Thorne Smith. I drew
the line at Max Shulman — he struck me as vulgar. I read the
poems of Ogden Nash, Phyllis McGinley, Morris Bishop, Arthur Guiterman, Don Marquis. In my hunger to be amused I
searched out older writers like Stephen Leacock, Ring Lardner,
Clarence Day, and Mark Twain. Laugh! I loved these volumes,
available in abundant supply in the bookstore and the local
library, and could imagine nothing finer than to join, some-
day, the jolly company of humorists.

This was all in the forties, drawing heavily on books from
the thirties. By the time, in the fifties, I grew to be a man,
there were still humorists practicing, but somehow the entity
called "humor" was fading away, drying up, even as I scribbled
and sold some late examples of it. What was happening? Could
the Cold War be chilling a genre that had thrived through
horrors of the Depression and World War II? Could the human
animal be shedding its ancient release mechanism of laughter?
One answer would be: of course not, humor still thrives,
though in slightly different milieus than the Algonquin Circle
and *The New Yorker*. A book of parodies called *Politically
Correct Bedtime Stories* has been on *The New York Times*
best-seller list for over fifty weeks, and chaps like Roy Blount
and P.J. O'Rourke seem to do all right; Art Buchwald and
Russell Baker continue to troll for chuckles in the daily papers.

But this answer, though defensible, doesn't sing. Things
have changed; *Zeitgeistig* energy has ebbed away from "humor" — look at the very way I feel obliged to put the word
in quotation marks. For one, the culture is less literate, less
print-oriented, and there are fewer to appreciate, even if suitable targets were around, the kind of literary parody that Roger
Angell and Veronica Geng, say, should be producing more
of, or the sort of hyper-literate prose that Sid Perelman and
George Jean Nathan used to spin. Light verse required a deli-
cacy of ear and a shared treasure of allusions that are gone;
its metrical ingenuity thrived in the shade of a body of serious,
stanzaic, rhymed verse that was common knowledge, and there
is no such body now. Secondly, the humor of Benchley and

Thurber assumed a kind of generic American experience —
white, Protestant, male, bourgeois, basically genteel, timid,
and well-intentioned — that can no longer be assumed. Much
of what used to be considered funny would now seem classist,
sexist and racist, in ascending order of unfunniness. Humor
draws on stereotypes, and where *stereotype* is a dirty word,
the humorist will find himself washing his hands too often.
Thirdly, humor, to be a valuable release, needs something to
be released, and what, in let-it-all-hang-out America, is that
something? The cartoons of Thurber and Arno flirted with
our privately held sexual knowledge; what sexual knowledge
is now privately held? Humor used to let us peek from our
excessively ordered and repressed lives into possibilities of
cheerful confusion, dishevelment and de-inhibition; now culture serves up those possibilities in rap and heavy-metal music,
in boisterously shameless talk shows, in blatantly sexual movies
and television serials. How strenuously, for example, television
comedies like "Roseanne" and "Married with Children" must
cavort to be more outrageous than what is happening in the
American living rooms where such programs are turned on.

Humor, to use a dichotomy dear to Camille Paglia, is a
subversive voice of Dionysius whispered in a society con-
strained by Apollonian ideals. The less the constraint, the
louder the voice has to be to be heard; and the louder the
voice, the less exquisite, the less artistic, the humor will be.
In my career as a would-be humorist, I discovered that simply
describing, as reverently and calmly as possible, my fellow
Americans in action was fun enough, and funny enough,
for me.

—John Updike

I have no idea. I think of humor, if at all, not as an absolute
but as incidental. There is so much of the absurd around me
I don't need humor or humorists. Yet I gather that things I
say or write amuse people who listen or read.

—Paul West

How important is humor in a literary work?

The party line, of course, is that there should always be at least a modicum of humor, even in the darkest of tragedies. I don't know, maybe I missed the boat on this one, but I never thought *Heart of Darkness* was all that funny, and I stopped laughing at Solzhenitsyn years ago. Saying that every drama should contain a little comedy is not unlike saying that every bowl of rice should contain a little pasta. If you subscribe to such a view, then I suppose you believe its obverse, too — that in every comedy there must be tragedy. So Thurber should have made Walter Mitty a delusional alcoholic, abused by his parents since birth; so Wodehouse should have had Jeeves hang himself, unrequited in his affection for Bertie.

— Henry Alford

It is crucial. Try to imagine *The Brothers Karamazov* without the pie-fight scene.

— Dave Barry

Depends. It might be a little out of place in, say, Marguerite Yourcenar, but it mostly works in the rest of it.

— Christopher Buckley

Holden Caulfield put it this way: "What I like best is a book that's at least funny once in a while." And I'll go as far as to say this: without humor at least lurking about somewhere, literature cannot exist. Hugh Kenner said that Irish humor came out of trying to deal with the two things that are impossible to deal with: sex and death. Since every novelist must deal, on some level, with those two subjects, he or she would be wise to learn from the Irish example. Humor doesn't mean jokes; it's an attitude toward life. With humor, humanity gets to one-up existence. Humor is our refusal to take what we've been given lying down.

— Jeffrey Eugenides

My three favorite living authors are Robertson Davies, Günter
Grass, and Gabriel García Márquez. And what do they have
in common? Well, they are all Dickensian, in the sense that
they mesh a fantastical plot, an interwoven narrative (or many
narratives) and larger-than-life characters with the most socially and/or historically realistic detail imaginable; they all
believe in the obligation of the novelist to prove a plot, a
better-than-what-you-can-read-in-a-newspaper story; they all
believe in developed characters and the emotional power of
the passage of time (in a story); and—no surprise—they are
all comic novelists.

—John Irving

There is no vitality in literature without humor. Even the Bible
is full of ridiculous incidents as well as the improbable ones.
But in a lot of writing and "art," humor has always been
replaced by *travesty*. And the trouble with that is that while
a little goes a long way, some people see nothing but absurdity
and senselessness.

—Alfred Kazin

Important, I think, but beware: it must be part of the generic
whole. It must illuminate the heart.

—Willie Morris

Vital! I once tried to make a list of major writers who were not,
in some essential way, humorists. It was very short: Theodore
Dreiser. That was it. Dostoyevsky, Balzac, Faulkner—all had
the crazy twist of humor.

—Daniel Stern

It's not essential but it's not a barrier either (viz Jane Smiley,
Elmore Leonard). I'm talking humor now—not wit—not P.J.
O'Rourke, which is intellectually the equivalent of farting in
church.

—Michael Thomas

Are there concepts that are universally funny?

Absolutely . . . and our wild-card search ferrets them out in the convenient multilingual dictionary of inoffensive terms.

—Walter Abish

The federal government. Also, weasels.

—Dave Barry

Farting, alas.

—Christopher Buckley

H.L. Mencken, 1920 Democratic Convention, in gracious San Francisco: "If one rings for a bellboy he comes. If one falls over or smashes a dressing table a new one is put in at once. If one complains that a delegate next door is drunk and noisy an anaesthetist or a mental healer is sent for to silence him." Universally funny concepts: a bellboy; any form of room service; falling over (cf. falling down); smashing something; large Mencken-type male in proximity to fragile feminine furniture; smashing a dressing table; complaining; a drunk if hypothetical or offstage. Then "an anaesthetist or mental healer is sent for to silence him." This is a non-universal concept nobody would come up with except Mencken. It's an intuitively compressed thought, which is—what? That there's a fine line between proper hotel management and eugenics? It don't mean a thing if it ain't got that???

—Veronica Geng

Stanley Elkin once said that all jokes are about powerlessness, and, as the bloom fades a little on my youth, I come to see how his assessment is right: humor hinges on a lancing of pretension (or affectation or fantasy), on a sudden and painful recognition of the folly of human dignity, thus of the folly of power. This recognition amounts to a coming to terms with a fact even more base—as Elkin also noted—that *everybody dies.* We're all powerless, all struggling, all faint of heart, and once we get the drift of this joke, shit, *everything's funny.*

— Rick Moody

In autobiographical writing, I've discovered, readers respond to your poking fun at yourself, or putting yourself in embarrassing or belittling situations and seeing how you get out of them, if indeed you do. (Mailer's *Armies of the Night* is a good example.) In *New York Days*, the section on arriving at an intimate political meeting for George McGovern at Arthur Schlesinger, Jr.'s apartment with dog shit on my shoes, and the surreptitious sniffing of the other guests, got more response than almost any other thing in that book.

— Willie Morris

Death and desire.

— Paul West

Is it easy? Why is the answer so often in the negative?

It would be easier if the paper would laugh occasionally.

— Henry Alford

It is extremely easy. Consider Calvin Trillin, who has been a top humor writer for years and still finds time for a very successful career as a professional swimsuit model.

— Dave Barry

It's bloody hard. For one thing the word-processing program you use in your computer always goes down just when you get to the funny stuff. I have lost my most inspired material by pressing DELETE when I should have hit SAVE AS. The reason the ozone is thinning so rapidly is that all the funny stuff escapes from the screen and rises because humor is lighter than air.

— Art Buchwald

Humor is founded on surprise, the unexpected, a sudden show of alternative reality. Much humor basically tries to take down one or another of the authorities (in fact and in memory) that rule our lives. But alas, too many Americans in our day have joined the enemy. Or have become so "ethnic" or civically virtuous that they dare not laugh at one another. Years ago, lecturing on *Huckleberry Finn* before a European audience, I was astounded to see a famous American black historian take a front seat. "What the devil are you doing here?" I asked him. "Because I wanted to make sure, you damned liberal, that you would say *Nigger* Jim," he replied.

As for Jews! You can make fun of Sharon, Begin and other such beasts in Israel, but not in America.

—Alfred Kazin

Are humorists necessarily funny in real life?

They are except when they have to stand in line for an hour to get an airline ticket, a sidewalk machine eats their banking card, *The New York Post* rejects a piece they wrote on the anniversary of Jack the Ripper, and when anyone—ANY-ONE—tells them something they produced is not funny.

—Art Buchwald

Are housekeepers happy in their work? Are custodians still shoveling coal into public school furnaces? Do undertakers make jokes after work, when they've had a drink or three, or do they cry more than laugh?

—Stephen Dixon

No. I recently had the pleasure of meeting Calvin Trillin. It was at a benefit, and I went up to him and said what amounted to, "Hey, you're Calvin Trillin!" He agreed. He was also the night's master of ceremonies. He began to speak to me, extremely slowly, more slowly, really, than anybody has ever spoken to me in my life. I kept waiting for the punch line. It didn't come. Then the ceremony began and Mr. Trillin took the podium. And while I watched, he repeated, more or less, what he'd just said to me a few minutes earlier. Only this time he was funny. Hilarious! He'd been using me as a warm-up audience, trying out his material, which he'd managed to perfect in the time it took to walk across the room.

—Jeffrey Eugenides

No; humorists are not necessarily funny in real life, although some are. Grass isn't especially funny. Rob Davies certainly can be extremely funny, but he isn't always. Kurt Vonnegut and Joe Heller—very funny in real life, but very serious, too. I once attended one of those black-tie fund-raisers where I was seated for dinner beside a wealthy matron who "interviewed" me relentlessly, through a relentless number of courses. Finally, I could discern that I'd displeased her. Possibly, I'd been vulgar, I thought—she was a woman of my mother's generation. But when I asked if I'd unwittingly offended her, for she had turned her back on me and was holding her dessert in her lap, she said: "Not at all. I just expected you to be more interesting."

She didn't even say "funnier"—it was the "interesting" test that I'd failed!

—John Irving

From what I hear of Woody Allen (neighbors, co-workers) he's a kvetch. But don't get me wrong. There's nothing to laugh at in these gossipers either.

—Alfred Kazin

In short, no. Two of the funniest writers I ever read were Evelyn Waugh and S.J. Perelman. *Scoop*, Waugh's book on journalism in Africa, was first published in 1938 and has grown more hilarious over the years. I never met Waugh, but I gather that he was not funny in real life.

Perelman's short pieces in *The New Yorker* I found genuinely humorous when I was growing up and reading most everything interesting I could get my hands on. Perelman became a sort of literary hero. Many years later, I encountered him face to face at a small airport in northern Burma, where he had just lost his luggage and was taking it very badly. I thought, My God, here is the man who wrote *Westward, Ha!*, or *Around the World in 80 Cliches* and he is being done in by some lost baggage.

His face was pinched and pallid. He looked terribly unhealthy. He was berating the Burmese airport manager in a way I thought would guarantee he would never see his luggage again. To make matters even worse, he was dressed in tweeds with a British hat and must have seemed incredibly colonial to the Burmese official he was humiliating. The whole scene was so depressing, I fled. But I still enjoy reading the short pieces he did for *The New Yorker*, even for the second and third time. Like *Scoop*.

— Sean Kelly

Are there pitfalls one should look out for when writing humor?

My old teacher, John Hawkes, used to tell me that my college stories suffered from too much surface comedy. Overall, it's best not to have anybody slip on a crack vial, or to bring a bird right in over somebody's cocktail. Leave that stuff to Chevy Chase. With the danger of sounding like a tired workshop instructor, I'd probably echo that old rule that true humor comes out of character. Alexander Portnoy's character we know. Now let's see what happens when his mother sends him to the store to buy liver. Humor is always generated by the leap from a premise to a logical but unseen conclusion. It works according to the Hegelian thesis-antithesis-thesis dialectic. For example, take the vaudeville joke (reprised by Buddy Glass): First comedian: "I just spent two weeks in bed with an acute hepatitis." Second comedian: "You lucky stiff! Which one? They're both cute, those Hepatitis girls." Here the thesis is hepatitis, a disease. The antithesis is the Hepatitis girls, two people. The final thesis — the humor — comes with the recogni-

tion of the unseen connection between these two dissimilar
items (in this case, the tendency of some names, usually Greek,
to sound like a disease).

—Jeffrey Eugenides

Unless you're a professional humorist like Calvin Trillin or
Garrison Keillor, don't *try*. If you're writing a story or a novel,
just find the sound and let it sing.

—Daniel Stern

Is there one ethnic group that is especially funny and why?

For a special risible ethnic flavor we suggest coupling seasoned
Aztec drolleries with Outdoor Roasting jocundity.

—Walter Abish

Absolutely not. (Mormons.)

—Dave Barry

The best Jewish jokes used to be made by Jews. Sholom
Aleichem's Tevye the milkman: "With God's help we starved
to death." Don't try that now. In his old age, S.J. Perelman
told me that *The New Yorker* no longer took his stuff. "Too
old-fashioned."

Ralph Ellison had a joke about a Black maid in a Jewish
household who answered the telephone when the family was
out. "Who is this? Who is this?" "This is the *schwartze*."
A lot of history there. But don't aim your peashooter at Al
Sharpton.

—Alfred Kazin

American Southerners, if you can call them ethnics, which I
do with impunity. They are bigger scapegoaters than Poles or
Texas aggies, which is why they are so funny.

—Willie Morris

The minimalists in all arts. Given an electron microscope they produce tiddleywink. Given English, they produce immigrantese.

Paul West

Which writers, past or present, do you think have succeeded admirably at humor . . . who have written classics of the genre?

Our favorite is *Rumpelstiltskin* by The Brothers Grimm. A close runner-up is *A Question of Lay Analysis.*

—Walter Abish

We must not overlook James Beard. His New Fish Cookery contains the sentence, "Here are grunions at their best." This is my very lodestar.

—Henry Alford

My hat is off to whomever writes copy for the Internal Revenue Service.

—Dave Barry

Present: Henry Beard, P.J. O'Rourke, Roy Blount, Jr., Woody Allen, Dave Barry, Tom Wolfe, Fran Lebowitz.
    Past: Twain, Amis (*père et fils*), Benchley, Thurber, Waugh.

—Chistopher Buckley

For me the list begins with Aristophanes (who happens to be a distant uncle). Then we come to Catullus, who is sad and lovelorn but also funny. Plautus was not very funny when I read him in college, but I'll include him to impress Harold Bloom. The Middle Ages were not funny for me, either, and so we jump, over the gaping chasm in my learning, all the way to Cervantes and to the marvelous Swift with a stopover at Laurence Sterne. Closer to our time we have Joyce, of course, and Nabokov. Pynchon, Donald Barthelme, Gilbert Sorrentino, and lots of others I don't have room to name. One of the funniest writers I've read recently is a woman from Brooklyn named Elinor Spielberg. Martin Amis is pretty funny. And Mark Leyner. But, of course, the whole thing leads up, for me, to *Portnoy's Complaint*.

—Jeffrey Eugenides

I once wrote a piece for *The New Republic* called "Kurt Vonnegut and His Critics"; I was angry at how many critics wrote dismissively of Vonnegut—he's much funnier, and more original, than Mark Twain. But Twain is dead and taught in schools—the latter takes the fun out of everything, and being dead is one way to be revered. This was in the summer of 1979; I was enjoying the considerable paperback success of *The World According To Garp*. I had not yet been subjected to the kind of critical condescension that is commonly meted out to best-selling authors by book reviewers who are unable to read a probable best-seller without foaming at the mouth in anticipation of the sales. And I have never been treated, even since that time, to the degree of patronizing slander that greets Mr. Vonnegut's publications.

I suspect the reason that I escape much of the fatuous malice with which Mr. Vonnegut is treated is that I am not half as original a writer as Vonnegut; I'm also not half as entertaining. Originality is almost as offensive to critics as success; I suspect that comedy is *more* offensive to critics than originality and success combined.

Whenever I'm in Europe for a publication, a translation of this or that, the European journalists unfailingly ask me why Kurt Vonnegut and his colleague in originality and humor, Joseph Heller, are treated so badly by the American book reviewers. What is there to say? Kurt Vonnegut and Joseph Heller are the most original American novelists alive; they are also the funniest. Everyone in Europe seems to know this—but not here. ("So it goes," as Mr. Vonnegut has written. "Go figure," as Mr. Heller has said.)

Vonnegut is simply more one-of-a-kind than any writer I've read. And I've said before that Joe Heller is my cleverest

friend; he's also the *smartest* writer I know. But then there
are critics: they don't want you to be successful, they detest
originality—or they fail to recognize it—they can't stand it if
you're funny, and they don't like *smart* either. (Go figure. So
it goes.)

—John Irving

I won't name all the usual suspects. I will say that Wodehouse
continues to be underrated as a *writer* by too many people. he
never put a word wrong. Other favorites: George and Weedon
Grossmith's *Diary of a Nobody*, Jerome K. Jerome's *Three
Men in a Boat*; most of Peter DeVries; the first two paragraphs
of *Fear & Loathing in Las Vegas*; the Amii at their best; Paul
Rudnick's *nonpareil* one-liners; George S. Kaufman's "If Men
Played Cards as Women Do;" Bill Franzen's story "Hearing
From Wayne," which remains one of the funniest things I've
read in the last fifteen years; and about a zillion others.

—George Kalogerakis

The roster is lengthy. For the sake of irony, I'll cite two of
the most tragic twentieth-century American novels: Ellison's
Invisible Man and Styron's *Sophie's Choice*—the first long
pages of *Invisible Man* are among the most uproariously funny
in our literature, as is the Leslie Lapidus "seduction scene"
in *Sophie's Choice*. Faulkner, for all his desolate and dusty
matters, could be wildly funny. Try "Spotted Horses." Saul
Bellow's *Herzog* made me laugh out loud. You can go on and
on. By the way, the first half of Mark Twain's *Roughing It*,
which people don't read much anyway, is outrageously funny.
The second half doesn't work because the humor doesn't relate
to much of anything. Once at a dinner party down here in
Mississippi I read the hilarious early section of Walker Percy's
The Moviegoer about William Holden strolling through the
French Quarter to Gene Hackman and other Hollywood peo-
ple. "Percy knows what he's talking about," Hackman said.

—Willie Morris

Max Beerbohm's stories: "Enoch Soames", for one. Thurber's "The Figure in the Carpet" is a classic send-up of Henry James. Also, any short story by Bernard Malamud.

—Daniel Stern

Intentionally: Wodehouse, Dickens (the American scenes in Chuzzlewit), Benchley, Dave Barry, Peter DeVries, John Wells and Richard Ingrams (the "Dear Bill" letters in *Private Eye*), E. Waugh, Molière, Juvenal, Anthony Powell (its wit is *A Dance to the Music of Time*'s best achievement), Joe Heller, Ogden Nash, S.J. Perelman.

Unintentionally: to start with and possibly topping the list, that mistress of the self-parody of self-absorption, Cynthia Ozick, Robert Bartley of *The Wall Street Journal*, Hilton Kramer, most supply-side economists.

—Michael Thomas

The place to start is with *Don Quixote*, if you regard the displacement of elegance and lofty dreams by cudgels and quotation cruelties as comic. And that may simply depend on your humor when you wake up. I wake on the side of finding comic some novels others find "classics" of untinged high seriousness. I include, then, among these classics of humor: Flann O'Brien's *The Third Policeman*; Celine's *Journey to the End of the Night*; Gertrude Stein's *The Making of Americans*.

Molly Bloom's soliloquy apart, Joyce's *Ulysses* joins this canon as a comedy of postures, language being the thing worked into unusual and funny shapes: syntax and structure as comedy.

And it is the riot of language that shapes Nabokov's *Lolita* into a hilarious, unsentimental modern handbook of heartbreaking, impossible love. The intellectual clown and the teenager guru, both sharing a sitcom stage the size of America, which for Humbert's delusions and for its indifferent vulgarities could well be the landscape of Don Quixote's Spain.

Thomas Mann's *The Magic Mountain* — too often shrouded in misty intellectual overcast — is, I promise, a time-release novel, slowly and quietly leaking out its comic irony through its pages and into your heart. Finally, I add Melville's *The Confidence Man*, the greatest — with Twain's *Huck Finn* standing close by — nineteenth-century comic novel in America. An April Fool's Day bouquet, fit for a minor devil who has not had such a good laugh at humans and their trials since Satan cast Job in his one-man show.

—Frederic Tuten

Beckett for symphonic ridiculousness. I suspect humor is not the word for him but liturgical sarcasm.

Clive, of India: Having seized Sind, he wired London the one word *peccavi*, thus, I'd have thought, keeping the secret from those with little Latin and less Greek, but positively attracting the attention of all the officials who, to enter Oxford or Cambridge, had had to pass a matriculation exam in Latin.

—Paul West

I'm a great, and envious, fan of certain English Edwardian comic masters: Jerome K. Jerome, Saki, Wodehouse (that eternal Edwardian).

But, *incomparably*, Max Beerbohm inhabits a realm beyond mere fandom, beyond envy (the latter is perhaps not actually possible). He is . . . what, a kind of pearly god? His book of eight stories, *Seven Men and Two Others* (the ninth man is himself, of course) contains some of the most delicately wrought, uproarious set-ups in the history of . . . well, in history. The secret to his humorous wizardry, for me, is his diabolical mix of contrasts: an impeccably voiced, exquisitely tailored well-manneredness, refined and courteous and utterly, urbanely self-effacing and mild-toned, in the service of slapstick howlers, of cunningly delicious punitive whimsies, of lapidary, devastating humiliations and monstrous psychological needlings and pinpricks. Max Beerbohm is really not so much a pearl, come to think of it, as an exquisite Fabergé egg, which, when you open it with reverential, proprietary care, squirts you in the eye.

And lately I find myself wondering: aren't certain qualities that make the incomparable Max such a great humorist—the acute eye for foibles and pomposities, for unworthy ambitions and *amour propres*; the hyper-acute touch for exactly where and how to deliver the most egregiously painful, intimately humiliating nick, all this done with an absolutely mild, self-deprecating mien—isn't all this a bit akin to the capacities of . . . a sadist?

Yes, I think so. For what it's worth, a little bit, I think so.

—Barry Yourgrau

Can anyone speak on behalf of Turkish humor?

I can. We are fine. Although we could use some clean underwear.

—Dave Barry

You should never ask a Greek to speak on behalf of Turkish anything.

—Jeffrey Eugenides

As everyone knows, in Istanbul clubs, people don't laugh at the jokes of the stand-up comics; they just yell "Ataturk! Ataturk!".

—Donald Hall

What do you mean, *Turkish* humor? I was once food-poisoned in Istanbul. I spent the whole night vomiting in a bathtub (because the toilet was stopped up), and in the morning I returned to the restaurant and took a copy of the menu with me to the doctor. I wanted to be able to show him what I had ordered, and eaten, because I couldn't pronounce it—and of course I hadn't the faintest idea what it was; I only knew the word for it was printed on the menu. I pointed to the item, the cheapest meat dish on the menu, and the doctor laughed and laughed and laughed. Then he took me out to the street, and we walked to a butcher shop. There in the window, hanging alongside the more familiar hunks of flesh, were several cats. They were skinned, except for their heads and tails. I had ordered and eaten a *cat*. The doctor laughed all the way back to his office; the degree of his mirth was so distracting to him, he forgot to write me out a prescription — I had to remind him. Ah, Turkish humor — is there anything that can compare to it?

—John Irving

Not I — my late grandparents are spinning just at the thought. But I will allow that in proper context, *ottoman* can be a very funny word indeed.

—George Kalogerakis

One morning in spring we sat at the cafe on the dock in Bodrum, Turkey — not Bodrum today which is fashionable, but Bodrum yesterday when everybody knew each other. Sara Maitland, the English novelist, a young poet from Oxford, and I were drinking tea in little glasses which is what everybody did at that hour in that place at that time. The chief of police came up and joined us, looking very worried.

"I must warn you. A cobalt bomb has exploded in Antalya. She has killed many people." Turkish has no gender pronouns. So she is very popular when speaking English.

"My God," the young poet said, "I must cable my family to tell them I'm all right." Antalya is at least five hundred miles or so to the east.

"Ha" in Turkish, "What you call the April Fool. She is celebrated here," the chief of police said.

Sara said, "We will send your family the cable, 'We are sending your son back on Monday.'"

"And Tuesday," the chief of police added.

"And Wednesday," Sara finished.

The Turks have jokes and puns and bawdy songs. The children sing, "Gelyor yavash yavash yavash, patlican arkadash." He comes slowly slowly slowly, my friend the eggplant — Turk-

ish eggplants are the shape of cucumbers. The Turks speak
with straight tongues and poker faces.

— Mary Lee Settle

Turkish humor is like eating halvah. After a Turkish joke
you're thirsty for days.

— Daniel Stern

Q: What is Greek?
A: Turk impersonating an Italian. (It's even funnier told in
German.)

— Michael Thomas

Why the need, if any, for humor?

It's better not to intellectualize this. Humor's mandate should
be ineffable. I am reminded of Mrs. John Gotti who, when
asked by one reporter about her husband's livelihood, said,
"All I know is, he provides." Humor is the same way. All you
need to know is, it provides.

— Henry Alford

It is what separates human beings from Ross Perot.

— Dave Barry

There is a theory (God knows whose) about tickling. The theory holds that a tickle is halfway between a blow and a caress.
Mousey-mousey up and down the ribs thus produces oxymo-
ronic reflex reactions. The victim doesn't know whether to give
you a kiss on the mouth or a punch in the kisser. So he laughs.
I think this explains most laughter. Humor is an automatic
response to sudden contradictions and absurdities, but to surprises of the kind not quite painful enough for tears but too
ugly to hug. Is humor necessary? Anything involuntary may
be called a necessity, more or less. Humor fulfills a need
whether we want it to or not and even if we don't know what
that need is. Anyway, as a means of expressing upset and

confusion, laughter is more attractive than the alternative. Compare: "vomiting out loud," "vomiting up your sleeve," "getting the last vomit," "vomit and the world vomits with you," etc.

— P.J. O'Rourke

I don't think novelists have to do anything in particular about humor except bear it in mind. People laugh *a lot*; in fact, to judge from my own grandchildren, they were practically born laughing, as if just being alive were inherently hilarious. And ever after that they will burst out laughing every chance they get, whether in classrooms, offices, or on the steps of churches and courthouses—and it can't *all* be nervousness. Yet if you asked any one of them, "What did you laugh about today, dear?" he or she probably wouldn't remember having laughed at all about anything.

So whether one really means it or is just being polite, laughter seems to be our badge, our identifying noise, and if a given fictional character can't even be *imagined* producing it, at least as easily as, let's say, Joseph Stalin, Tammy Bakker, or O.J. Simpson can be so imagined, he may still be a fascinating character but he probably isn't a human being, if of course that's what you were aiming at.

— Wilfrid Sheed

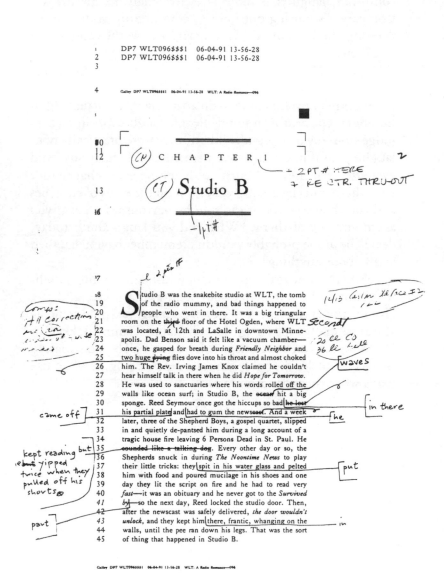

A revised galley from Garrison Keillor's WLT: A Radio Romance.

Garrison Keillor

The Art of Humor II

Garrison Keillor was born in 1942 in Anoka, Minnesota. He attended Anoka High School and the University of Minnesota. In 1969, he began writing for The New Yorker. *In 1974, while at work on an article about the Grand Ole Opry, he was inspired to create a live variety show for radio. The result was the award-winning* A Prairie Home Companion, *an inspired program in which Keillor—invariably appearing on stage in the World Theater in downtown St. Paul in a tuxedo, red suspenders, and jogging sneakers—brought his listeners the latest news from the fictional town of Lake Wobegon. The show was "sponsored" by, among others, Ralph's Pretty Good*

Grocery ("if you can't find it at Ralph's, you can probably get along without it"). His chronicling of a midwest culture and its gentle homespun ways (in the tradition of Booth Tarkington and certainly Mark Twain) have resulted in a number of books, among them We Are Still Married, Happy to Be Here, Lake Wobegon Days, WLT: A Radio Romance, Leaving Home, *and* The Book of Guys. *He left* The New Yorker *at its last administrative change and at what he perceived to be a shift in its editorial policy; he now contributes regularly to* The New York Times *and* The Atlantic Monthly. *In addition to* A Prairie Home Companion, *Keillor also hosts "The Writer's Almanac," a daily poetry program distributed by Public Radio International.*

This interview was conducted on the stage of the YMHA at Ninety-second Street and Lexington Avenue in New York as part of a continuing series arranged between that institution and The Paris Review. *The auditorium was packed, the balcony as well, many in the audience with his books — well-thumbed copies of* Lake Wobegon Days *in particular — which they would get him to autograph afterwards.*

Keillor is a large man, very tall, built along the lines of professional football's tight ends. He has a heavy crop of dark hair which is distinguished by a forelock clump that reaches almost to his right eyebrow. His is a large and expressive face which with his dark-rimmed glasses gives him a somewhat solemn and owlish appearance: he never appears to laugh, even at his most hilarious. The pace of his replies is slow and measured, giving one the sense that he has applied a good deal of thought to the question, however uninspired.

The introduction on the stage concluded with a listing of some of the more distinguished literary figures who have been interviewed on the craft of fiction for the Review — a pantheon Keillor was now joining.

INTERVIEWER

The *Paris Review* interviews on the craft of writing started back in 1953, the first interviewee being E.M. Forster. The interviews have appeared in the magazine, which is a quarterly, ever since. We are extremely glad to welcome Garrison Keillor to the pantheon and to their good company.

GARRISON KEILLOR
I'm glad that sales of my books have dropped to where serious literary journals now take an interest in me.

INTERVIEWER
Well, fortunately, we had to wait a long time for that to happen. Could we start by asking if the process of writing is pleasurable?

KEILLOR
Sometimes, but it doesn't have to be; you still have to do your work. I write for a radio show that, no matter what, will go on the air Saturday at five o'clock central time. You learn to write toward that deadline, to let the adrenaline pick you up on Friday morning and carry you through, to cook up a monologue about Lake Wobegon and get to the theater on time. That can be pleasurable, but only if the material you write is good. If it's not, you're filled with self-loathing. If the material is good and funny, you still loathe yourself, of course, for writing comedy and lighthearted fluff instead of writing serious and loathsome fiction, but . . . what was your question?

INTERVIEWER
No, you were doing fine. During this time from Friday until Saturday a part of your brain must be working on what you are going to put down. What is the genesis of a particular piece? Can you describe what that is like?

KEILLOR
You mean the Lake Wobegon stories? They aim to be truthful, so that's where they originate, in the search for truth. I

told a story a month ago, for Halloween, about the terrible
pranks that were played in Lake Wobegon just before I came
along that I never got to participate in. Things such as pushing
over an outhouse when some sterling citizen was in it, tipping
it forwards so it fell on the door and the poor man had to
crawl out the hole. I never did this. It existed for me only in
my uncle's stories, but the stories were severely edited. So I
had to reconstruct what happened when an outhouse was
tipped, how it must have felt to the man inside and what a
pleasure it must have been to the tipper.

INTERVIEWER

When does your own imagination take over a story that an
uncle told you?

KEILLOR

Well, my uncle was not willing to tell me the whole story,
only to acknowledge that he had heard of people doing that
sort of thing. He wasn't willing to put a hand on the outhouse
himself. In his version, he was far away, at a Bible reading,
which diminished the story. I don't consider it fiction to complete someone else's story that they for the wrong reasons cut
short or revised. Although I never tipped an outhouse over,
I could tell about it—any writer could. How many ways are
there to tip over an outhouse, after all? And who wouldn't
do it, given the chance to? And you know whose outhouses
would be really worth tipping over. And would you tip it over
onto its back? No. Of course you'd tip it onto the front.

INTERVIEWER

I would think so.

KEILLOR

Leaving your victim only the one exit, and so it's uh . . .
I don't consider it fiction, it's more like working out a theorem.

And if you can imagine how to tip over an outhouse, you're ready to go on and write about homicide.

INTERVIEWER

Well, how about the genesis of something longer? For example, "My North Dakota Railroad Days," your marvelous story about an imaginary railroad train?

KEILLOR

My father worked on the railroad, for the Railway Mail Service, sorting mail in the mail car, and his run was St. Paul to Jamestown, North Dakota and back. Their trains were very romantic to me as a boy in Minnesota. You could hear the whistles from miles away when I was a teenager. I rode the Burlington Zephyr to Chicago, and the North Coast Limited, and years later I set out to write about a train that was even greater than those trains, a train that those trains were trying to be. The Prairie Queen, which crossed North Dakota, a state in which it was possible to lay straight track for hundreds of miles without hitting anything that couldn't easily be removed. The passengers stood on the rear of the platform of the parlor car in the trans-Dakota Canal, and trolled for fish, and they played pocket billiards onboard. After I wrote that for *The New Yorker*, it was republished in North Dakota, in a magazine for railroad old-timers, and it drew some testy letters from old-timers who couldn't recall any sort of train like that. When people take pure fiction as journalism, there is no greater compliment.

INTERVIEWER

I take it you did not write back to the railroad magazine.

KEILLOR

No. I clipped out those irate letters and framed them.

INTERVIEWER

Being considered a humorist, are you constantly aware that it's time to come up with something as clever as you've just described, or to be comic in some way?

KEILLOR

No, I think that past the age of thirty there is no obligation
to be clever at all. Cleverness is a burden after that. You are
supposed to settle down and be a good person, raise your
children, and be good to your friends, which you may not
have been back when you were clever.

INTERVIEWER

So you are not really aware of an audience, as you write,
that you have to entertain in some way?

KEILLOR

There is an audience that listens to "Prairie Home Companion," and I feel obligated to do something for them, just as
you would be obligated to clean your house and make food
if you had friends coming over at seven o'clock. They don't
demand that you be clever or profound, only to be in good
humor, or lacking that, to be brief.

INTERVIEWER

Do they read *The New Yorker*?

KEILLOR

The audience for the radio show?

INTERVIEWER

Yes.

KEILLOR

No, I don't think they do. They never mentioned it if they
do. Most people I know used to feel bad that they didn't
have time to read the magazine and now they don't anymore.
Anyway, I don't write for *The New Yorker* anymore.

INTERVIEWER

You once wrote about *The New Yorker* as being an immense
literary ocean liner off the coast of Minnesota, so it must have
had an enormous impression upon you at one time.

KEILLOR

It's moved off the coast of Minnesota, and now it is firmly
anchored off the coast of Staten Island.

INTERVIEWER

Have you informed them of this?

KEILLOR

Yes. When I heard that Ms. Brown was the new editor,
having read magazines she had edited in the past, I decided
that twenty-some good years was privilege enough, and I
packed up my office into cardboard boxes, loaded them into
an elevator and went away in a cab.

INTERVIEWER

Where will these marvelous pieces of yours now appear?

KEILLOR

I don't have a magazine. I've been de-horsed. So I'm a
pedestrian now.

INTERVIEWER

Now, does that mean you are not going to write, or will
you continue to write stories that would have been in the old
New Yorker?

KEILLOR

No, I am saving them up. And looking for a home, like
the boll weevil.

INTERVIEWER

Has Tina Brown of *The New Yorker* tried to call you on
the telephone?

KEILLOR

No, I don't think so. Has she mentioned anything to you?

INTERVIEWER
I am perfectly willing to be an intermediary if you would like.

KEILLOR
Ms. Brown, God bless her and God help her, is one of those crazy people who do not realize that the Midwest exists. The country is collapsed between two coasts in the minds of these people; the interior terrifies them. They are afraid to go to Cleveland or Chicago, afraid people won't know who they are, afraid their ATM cards won't work.

INTERVIEWER
Well, that's why I would assume that she'd be very anxious to publish your work. The Minnesota correspondent.

KEILLOR
There are no famous people in Minnesota and no good murder trials. Nothing there to interest her.

INTERVIEWER
Well, when you did work at *The New Yorker* what was the atmosphere like then? I mean about editing, in particular?

KEILLOR
It was a wonderful place for a writer. It could be disconcerting, in that editors avoided by word, deed, or nuance ever suggesting what they might like you to write about, for fear of spooking you. I found it weird. But once you got going on something, it was a great place to work. There wasn't a lot of hanging out at *The New Yorker*. When you went into your office and closed the door, people didn't bother you. They had the respect that writers have for each other's time. When you finished, you would run up to the nineteenth floor and stick it on Chip McGrath's desk, the managing editor. And you'd walk back to your office, and he would tell you within an hour if they liked it or not. It would go into proof

right away if it was a casual or "Talk of the Town" piece, which were what I wrote, and you'd get to see it in galleys that same week. And the next week, you would correct it and a couple days after that it was on a newsstand. So it was a shop that took writing very seriously, and had a great reverence for writers, and it also had the feeling of a country, weekly newspaper which was where I started to write. When I was fourteen, I wrote for the *Anoka Herald*. It smelled somewhat like *The New Yorker*, the ink proofs, the piles of old newspapers, and the people were a little run down at the heels. And you got to see what you'd written right away afterward. That was joyful, to work on a weekly schedule for a magazine that cared about writing.

INTERVIEWER

Did Mr. McGrath ever say, "I'm terribly sorry we don't like this very much? This is not quite up to snuff," or however they would put it?

KEILLOR

Well, when *The New Yorker* rejected work, they did it in an elaborately polite way, apologizing for their shortsightedness, that undoubtedly it was their fault, but somehow, this story fell slightly short of your remarkably high standard. They had a way of rejecting my work that made me feel sorry for them, somehow.

INTERVIEWER

How easily did the "Talk of the Town" pieces come to you?

KEILLOR

I just walked around the city. I think a midwesterner does not have to walk around New York very long before something springs to mind. If you can't find something to write about by walking around, then you find it by standing in one place and waiting.

INTERVIEWER

But you have extraordinarily capable equipment to do this: an eye for detail, even a sense of smell.

KEILLOR

I don't have much equipment at all. I have a very poor sense of smell. I don't have a great eye for detail. I leave blanks in all of my stories. I leave out all detail, which leaves the reader to fill in something better.

INTERVIEWER

Come on.

KEILLOR

Like Hemingway. Hemingway burned off the underbrush, and his stuff leaps to life.

INTERVIEWER

Well, I was reading a story of yours the other day, in which you go on at great length about creamers and automatic milking systems. Nothing left to the imagination at all.

KEILLOR

Automatic milking systems? In a story of mine?

INTERVIEWER

Yes indeed.

KEILLOR

I didn't know you read dairy journals.

INTERVIEWER

But you must rely on a lot of catalogues. The Wobegon pieces are marvelously full of detail about what's in a barbershop, what is here, what is there, what are in the store windows. No?

KEILLOR

No. The Lake Wobegon stories are remarkably empty of detail. They are like twenty-minute haiku, they are absolutely formal and without detail. This is what permits people who grew up in Sandusky, Ohio or Honolulu, Hawaii, or people who grew up in Staten Island for God's sake, to imagine that I'm talking about their hometown.

INTERVIEWER

Really? I see very little similarity between here on Ninety-second Street and Wobegon, at least as concerns the milking equipment.

KEILLOR

Well, it depends on whether you're talking about East Ninety-second or West Ninety-second. No. You see I talk very slowly, especially when I do those Lake Wobegon stories, because as I talk I am thinking about what comes next, if anything. I talk so slowly that I couldn't possibly put in details or I would never get to the end. I talk in subjects and verbs, and sort of wind around in concentric circles until I get far enough away from the beginning so that I can call it the end, and it ends. I'm passing on a lot of secrets to you right now.

INTERVIEWER

I can hardly wait to try them out, starting with talking slowly. When you do the Wobegon radio pieces, will you then turn them into stories for, not *The New Yorker* anymore, but for a collection?

KEILLOR

I did that once, for a book called *Leaving Home*. Those stories were very close to what I did on the air. I had to fix up my grammar, of course. Those stories seemed to work so well without any detail that now I use even less, but they were very close to what was on the air. I did want them to have a little more shape than what they'd had on the air, and I tried

to make myself look more literate, goodness knows, than if
you simply did a transcript of those stories. But beyond that,
no, I didn't add that much to them. It seemed to have worked
so well the first time without any detail that I wouldn't want
to add any to it.

INTERVIEWER

Why is humor such a rare commodity? Why are there so
few American humorists?

KEILLOR

Well, I think there are quite a few. How many should there
be? How many do we need?

INTERVIEWER

More than there are, I think.

KEILLOR

You think we need more?

INTERVIEWER

Well, I'm thinking really of editors, who pray for something
they can put in their magazines that is, not wit necessarily,
but humor.

KEILLOR

I don't know. Humor has to surprise us, otherwise it isn't
funny. It's a death knell for a writer to be labeled a humorist
because then it's not a surprise anymore. It's what's demanded
of him. And when you demand humor of people you will
never get it. I have been working on editing an anthology of
humor, a hellish task, and you wind up beating the bushes
for humor, looking for it, demanding it, expecting it, and
suddenly nothing looks funny to you anymore now that you are
a professional humor anthologist. When you were an innocent
reader, and they sprang up at you out of the weeds, they made
you laugh out loud. S.J. Perelman used to make me laugh

out loud on planes. We don't have more humorists because
we don't need them. And nobody wants to live with one.
They're very hard to live with. I've been told that. So the fear
of loneliness discourages people from going into the field.

INTERVIEWER

What about rereading E.B. White, who was one of your
great idols. White, A.J. Liebling and indeed Perelman you
thought were the great titans of the time. Have you dared
reread White and Liebling?

KEILLOR

They are all three of them beautiful writers, and you could
teach a year of English just using the three of them.

INTERVIEWER

What did you learn from them particularly?

KEILLOR

I tried awfully hard to imitate them, and that helps you to
get through a lot of your own dreadful early writing and get
into something else. A.J. Liebling, who for years you could
only find in used bookstores, now has been very handsomely
reissued. My favorites were *The Road Back to Paris* and *The
Earl of Louisiana*. But everything that he wrote was gorgeous.
He was the most elegant American writer ever, very sweet,
and a funny man. E.B. White was a master of the educated,
democratic prose style. As a teacher he is the equal of Mark
Twain. And S.J. Perelman will teach you how to do what E.B.
White teaches you not to.

INTERVIEWER

Any of your contemporaries make you laugh out loud?

KEILLOR

Yes, Ian Frazier and Nora Ephron, Veronica Geng, Roy
Blount, Calvin Trillin. So does Dave Barry. I think a lot of

Dave Barry. Even though all of Dave Barry's books are entitled *Dave Barry*. But Blount is the best. He can be literate, uncouth and soulful all in one sentence.

INTERVIEWER

What is the first mistake that someone trying to write humor almost invariably makes? What goes wrong almost invariably?

KEILLOR

When some people sit down to write humor, they adopt a giddy tone of voice, a whooping or comic warble, so that the reader will know it's funny. It's the writing equivalent of a clown suit. This does not wear well. Humor needs to come in under cover of darkness, in disguise, and surprise people. You don't want to get that *gdoing, gdoing, gdoing* sound in your writing. It makes the reader feel sorry for you.

INTERVIEWER

Isn't it possible that one of the problems with humor is that a lot of it is devoted to the topical, which then disappears so you no longer know quite what you should be laughing at?

KEILLOR

That's true of stand-up comedy; it goes bad in about six months. But the problem for written humor is that nobody reads anymore. This makes humorists feel invisible, which is okay for poets, but humor is the only literary genre labeled by the effect it is supposed to have on people. So humor without an audience is pointless. No humorist has unpublished stuff. There is no great unpublished humor.

INTERVIEWER

I'm not so sure about that.

KEILLOR

No, no, take my word for it.

INTERVIEWER

Once you write it, it is noticed?

KEILLOR

Yes. It's like sugar-beet farmers. You don't hoard your crop. You put seeds in the ground, you get the crops out. But if people don't read books, then we'll have to switch over to soybeans.

INTERVIEWER

What should failed humorists do?

KEILLOR

Well, they should go into the ministry. Or they should write the sort of things that people want to read, which are profound essays about the future of our society that, though they are profound, nonetheless mention the names of celebrities.

INTERVIEWER

Have you tried this yourself?

KEILLOR

No, I haven't.

INTERVIEWER

Have you ever imagined seeing some of your stories filmed?

KEILLOR

I have. I went out to Los Angeles twice and talked to people about making Lake Wobegon into a film and discovered that film executives are much younger than I, and have never been to the Midwest. They've flown over it, but the movie was showing during that part of the trip. Nonetheless, these executives wanted to make a film with me, but . . . a midwesterner of my upbringing is a pessimist, so I began the meeting by saying that my work is full of problems and probably wouldn't

translate to the screen, and even if it did, people wouldn't
get it. This was a ritual of false modesty drilled into me as a
child. I'm helpless to avoid it. I did it so well that I convinced
them not to do it. When you grow up in a religious home,
it makes a mark on you, and it's not easy to get away from.
They teach you, "Don't think you're somebody, 'cause you're
not; you're no different than anybody else." And I believe
that, because it's true.

INTERVIEWER

You spent some time abroad in Copenhagen. Did that
change anything about your outlook or your habits or your
view of things?

KEILLOR

You learn a great deal about yourself living in a foreign
city, that's for sure. When I had been there for a while, I
started to meet some rural people whom you could really learn
Danish from because that was the only language they knew.
But at first, the only people I met were educated Copenhagen-
ers. You go to their homes for dinner, you see volumes of
John Updike and Philip Roth and the Yale Shakespeare, and
of course they speak perfect English, and it was hard to wrestle
them out of English and into Danish so I could practice speaking my childlike, ungrammatical Danish. I'd wrestle them
into Danish and then they'd stay in Danish and when they
talked I couldn't understand a word they said. I strove valiantly
to be as Danish as possible so that when I walked into a bakery
and said, "*Goddag, jeg vil gerne køb tre stykker*" and the
bakery girl looked at me and said, "Oh you want three of
those?" it was a defeat. Danes don't care about these exercises,
they want to get it done, get it over with. I discovered, speaking
Danish, that it was warping me, because the only Danish I
knew was about food and love and beauty, and it was cheerful,
bright, the language of complimenting people on the food,
and "Thank you for last time," and "Thank you for the herring,
it was delicious." It was like living in a YMCA of the mind.

I never found a way in Danish to express my meanness or
make cutting remarks. All of my weapons were taken away
from me.

INTERVIEWER

Why were you doing this in the first place?

KEILLOR

Because I was in their country, and I thought I should do
the right thing and learn their language. But I couldn't. I
could only be a six-foot three, two hundred pound four year
old.

INTERVIEWER

So you came back.

KEILLOR

Yes. There's not much future in being that large a child.
But I had a wonderful time, and I am happy every time I go
back. I talk my head off in Danish for about half an hour,
until it's used up, and then we speak English.

INTERVIEWER

I have forgotten the quintessential *Paris Review* question.
What tools do you use when you write?

KEILLOR

I use a laptop computer. There are dangers in using a computer to write; it's a fluid tool and you lose some of the concentration that a percussive tool like the typewriter gives you.
But I'm tired of retyping the third draft. It's too easy to write
on a computer, the writing flows on and on like hot chocolate.
So you have to print it out every so often and deal with it as
a typescript, mark it up with pencil. As a final check, you
force yourself to read it out loud. That is, I think, the surest
detector of — I'm trying to think of a term other than horseshit, but I can't — the clearest horseshit detector is to read it

out loud. You can always tell when you're putting on airs or lying when you hear yourself say it.

INTERVIEWER

Do you think it's important to make a point in writing humor?

KEILLOR

Yes. Humor has to take up absolutely everything in your life and deal with it. Humor is not about airline luggage or foreign taxicab drivers. It's about our lives in America today, the ends of our lives, and everything that happened before and after. Why make jokes about food blenders or TV or the perils of dating after the age of thirty? It's not an interesting way to spend your life. You'd much rather write pornography, and it would be better for everybody. When I am funny, I hope to be funny about Republicans, not about Pakistani taxi drivers.

INTERVIEWER

Which do you prefer, performing or writing?

KEILLOR

Well, that's a good question. I keep on doing both performing and writing until I figure out the answer. But the only performing I do is of my own writing. So they're almost the same thing.

INTERVIEWER

When did you actually decide to become a writer? And why?

KEILLOR

Well, it was surprising because I didn't know anyone who was a writer. I grew up in a fundamentalist Protestant family that stressed very strongly one's separation from the world, that we were a select people, selected by God to receive the revelation of His truth through the Word and that we should conform not to this world, but renew our minds constantly through the faith. We were to avoid contact with others who did not share our faith. We were isolated, I think, just as much as the Hasidim or other religious minorities. Growing up in this world you got, as a birthright, a reverence for the word and for language. God spoke to us through the word. God did not give us pictures or ideograms, or speak to us through nature. God spoke to us through the word and in our family this was the King James Bible, which was an everyday part of our lives. Such a childhood gave fiction great power because it was proscribed. We were not to touch it. My family was shocked when I came home with a volume of Hemingway when I was boy. There was a price to be paid for being interested in fiction and in writing, you lost your family. I went to the University of Minnesota and fell in with writers, and after that writing was all I thought about. It's a decision that always seems temporary and troubled, you're never quite sure. Someone once asked John Berryman, "How do you know if something you've written is good?" And John Berryman said, "You don't. You never know, and if you need to know then you don't want to be a writer." It's a choice one makes that has constantly to be renewed. I'm only fifty-two, so I made a sort of a tentative choice that has lasted this long, but I could still fall back on radio. Or retail sales.

— George Plimpton

The Birth of a Notion: Cartoonists Have Their Say

To provide an art portfolio for this issue devoted to humor, the editors asked a number of leading cartoonists if they would contribute a work they considered representative along with a description of the thought-process that went into its making—all of this very much in keeping with one of the primary ideas behind the magazine's on-going interviews on the craft of writing, namely to seek out and have explained the genesis of a particular work. Surely one of the questions that bedevils cartoonists—indeed far more than it does writers—is, "How on earth did you come up with the idea for that latest cartoon of yours?" It was a question, incidentally, that George Price, who was one of the *New Yorker*'s most prolific artists (he died at the age of 93) never had to answer since his ideas were supplied by so-called "gag writers" provided by Katharine White. Only one idea of his own ever appeared—a cover of a gaggle of department store Santa Clauses standing in a subway car, staring rather shame-facedly at each other. This nugget of information comes from a delightful volume entitled *The Art of* The New Yorker *1925–1995* (Knopf) edited by Lee Lorenz, the *New Yorker*'s art editor from 1973–1993 and its present cartoon editor, as well as being a distinguished cartoonist in his own right. We went to him for advice in putting together the portfolio which follows; we are grateful for his assistance.

—G.A.P.

Safely behind the plate-glass window of the pet store this cat is making faces at that stupid looking canine bully. There's a lot of me in that cat. That's why it's one of my favorite cartoons.

I was an only child, and if you're going to be a cartoonist that helps. I can remember long before I knew what funny was, my father getting angry . . . "Pay attention to me when I'm speaking to you," he would shout leaning his face close to mine. He was an excitable man, who could without warning burst into laughter or fly into a temper tantrum. Whenever any of this was focused on me he needn't have worried that I wasn't paying attention. I was. He had already gotten his message across. I was studying the way his anger worked on the topography of his face inches from mine. This was not the arena in which I felt I could safely express my feelings. I became a cartoonist.

—Frank Modell

This cartoon appeared in the Winter 1994/1995 issue of
The Journal of Blacks in Higher Education accompanying a
review of *The Bell Curve* by Hernstein and Murray. Naturally,
I hadn't read the review because it was being written even as
I drew. I hadn't read the book but had read much about it
and had heard the authors interviewed many times.

We are in an era when most individuals realize themselves
only as members of large groups. Organizations based on race,
gender, height, weight, reach, sexual proclivity, culture, et cetera
clamor for equality and its incumbent, inherent sense of supe-
riority. Scientific proof of that sense is absolutely necessary.

It is ironic that nature groups humans by occupation only,
and that the one superior group (scientific proof available
when ready) is cartoonists . . . who get to do drawings such
as this one.

— **Arnold Roth**

"Your father and I want to explain why we've decided to live apart."

A long-married couple with children has decided to separate. "We have decided to live apart," one of them tells a friend. That friend, in a moment of delicious gossip, tells it to the fellow with antennae for ears and magnifying glasses for eyes: the cartoonist. He leaps at the verbal crumb — "decided to live apart" — and impales it with his pen.

The problem: how to make this awkward and stiff piece of dialogue — shorthand for a mountain of stress and anguish and family failure — and transform it into something that transcends the cliché used to express it? And how to illustrate the effect on the noncombatants in the family?

The solution: mice. Huge numbers of mice kids, row upon row of them. And mice parents, awkward in their clinical effort to tell a cataclysmic piece of news to their children. This prompts questions about the nature of this particular family, their life together, how and where they live, their "lifestyle." There are also questions of timing: what happened before the frozen moment of the cartoon itself, and what will happen next? Pandemonium? Stunned silence? Cheers? An explanation? Whatever the outcome, it won't be the mice we laugh at.

— Edward Koren

One of the joys of my job as an editorial cartoonist is skewering hypocrites. As you can imagine, I was elated when Phil Gramm provided just such an opportunity.

Phil's ex-brother-in-law revealed that Phil had once invested money in a "T and A" film. This from the guy who in the current political season is the altar boy for the religious right? How to depict this irony? I looked for similarities between soft-porn and religion. I came up with "God" or should I say, "Gawwd." In this case, that's where the humor derives—from taking something or someone and transfering it to another situation that it's alien to. Hopefully, Phil Gramm trying to take "Oh, Gawwd" into the religious sphere is funny.

— **Mike Luckovich**

"Now look what you've done!"

In my experience, the general public seems to consider cartoonists to be socially marginal types of independent means, pursuing a harmless, if self-indulgent, hobby. The truth, of course, is that the field of comic art is just as difficult, painful, and financially precarious as is any other area of creative endeavor.

Why does one do it?

One answer, among many, is the occasional self-revelation produced in the relentless attempt to transmute the awfulness of daily life into a redemptive chuckle.

The accompanying drawing, which summed up eight years of therapy, provided such a moment for me, and, judging from my mail, many readers of *The New Yorker* as well.

—Lee Lorenz

Roz Chast - "Stores of Mystery"
appeared in The New Yorker January 13, 1986

September 29, 1995

I did this cartoon about nine years ago when I was still living on the Upper West Side, which at the time was undergoing its first spasms of the commercial rebirth of the 1980's. What was once a dingy linoleum outlet was suddenly a neon-highlighted tofutti shop. Then, fifteen minutes later, it would be a boutique that imported pottery from only Tuscany, which would close and reopen as a workout clothing emporium.

Anyway, amidst all this hubbub, there were these stores that just sort of sat there. The one that never failed to stop me dead in my tracks was this grim little place with fractured, indifferently-taped windows that sold nothing but "typewriter supplies." Its display case, unchanged for the entire ten years that I lived in that neighborhood, held a grimy, nondescript typewriter, a couple of dusty boxes of ribbon, and a handful of those plastic brush-typewriter eraser combos depressingly laid out around these other items. Nobody ever walked in or came out. I never even saw anyone inside working there. It always seemed to be closed.

This cartoon expanded to include other varieties of Stores of Mystery, but this place was the kernel around which the rest of the cartoon formed.

STORES OF MYSTERY

Fred's Drugs

Surrounded by cut rate drug and cosmetic emporiums that sell, let's say, a bottle of XYZ shampoo for 79¢. Same bottle at Fred's? $2.09 !!! How does he do it?

Beauty-Moi Frocks

Weird clothes, always five seasons out of date. Has been there forever. Store is usually pretty empty except for racks and racks of pants suits and the like. Who shops here?

M + O Typewriter Supplies

This place has been closed whenever one has walked by it. However, it's always there, meaning somebody is continuing to pay rent on it. Why?

Tip-Top Goods

Boxes of saltines next to cartons of hair spray. Wigs. Christmas decorations, halter tops, institutional-sized jars of olives. Did all of this stuff "fall off a truck" or what?

r. Chast

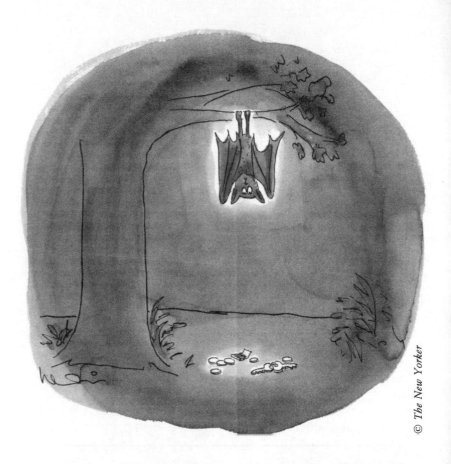

Like most cartoonists I follow the standard routes in search of material—looking in the newspapers, magazines, eavesdropping at cocktail parties and sifting through the numerous suggestions given me at Bar Mitzvahs from those who "know what would make a great idea for a cartoon," and I could use for free, providing their name appears prominently somewhere in, on or near it."

But my natural style of humor comes from physical action—akin to that of the French filmmaker Jacques Tati. I interact with objects, sounds, colors, movements, patterns. The important thing is to actually hear and digest what's being said.

The results are often in the abstract, but form a crazy kind of logic that we're all familiar with. From there I look to create a story that will both embrace the concept and allow for some kind of a dramatic visual presentation.

—Arnold Levin

"Hi. I'm, I'm, I'm... You'll have to forgive me, I'm terrible with names."

MANKOFF

Every week I draw about ten cartoons (the batch) to be submitted to *The New Yorker* for their Tuesday afternoon art meeting. If one of the batch is selected for publication by the powers that be, it's a good week. (A batting average of .100 in the cartoon field will put you in the "Cartoon Hall of Fame".)

One never knows when a good idea will appear. And this time it happend *after* I had drawn my quota and was hurrying through my morning ablutions. I was in the shower when the phrase "I'm terrible with names" just popped into my head along with the notion that if someone says this while introducing himself, rather than someone else, it would be funny. *The New Yorker* bought that idea while rejecting the other ten.

—Bob Mankoff

Reprinted with special permission of King Features Syndicate.

A National Public Radio commentator was yammering on about Bill Clinton's management style as I sat through my third green light at a gridlocked intersection. I was on my way home from my studio at the newspaper and my mind was typically uncorking a stream of images and half-thoughts, like a can of Coke that's been shaken all day and finally opened. A newspaper office, with its phones, beepers, and fax machines always piping up, is a bad place for playful thinking, but my drive home often provides the necessary odd juxtapositions of images and thoughts that lead to cartoon ideas once given a depressurized place to fizz.

I heard the word *free-associate* from the radio, but immediately it felt fertile. On rare occasions, I know I have a cartoon making its way down my forehead even before I know what it is, and so wrote the word on the Post-it note on my dashboard that also included a grocery list. It felt clear to me that I had a cartoon, though I had it only by the toenail.

The next morning I drew Clinton with a faraway stare surrounded by a team of frustrated bureaucrats. It sat like that, with only his voice bubble filled in, for a week while I went on to more lineal matters.

The joy was in describing the loops of musings. The process mimics my own as I daydream my way from cartoon to cartoon, so there was no sweat involved. My personal favorite is in going from Haiti to Tonton Macoutes to Wonton Soup to China.

—Jim Borgman

The parrot is just a spot drawing, but it tickled me. I've forgotten what the parrot is saying. I think it's something I picked up from a Chinese menu. I don't remember too much about the history behind the shooting of the fiscus tree. My wife has a greenhouse and the house is full of them. The cartoon may very well be the result of some defense mechanism kicking in. I write notes immediately if I think of something, otherwise the ideas get away from me. I've always worked through the night, because about six o'clock the world, the commotion stops.

I never thought I'd fit into the sophisticated *New Yorker.* I tried and tried, and finally broke in when I relaxed and started drawing what I thought was funny. Somewhere along the line I got on a kick drawing the orneriest-looking dog I could figure out—a wide-bodied cur because I don't know anything about breeds. Then some woman wrote in and asked,

"Isn't that a English bull terrier?" I went to the library and checked it out. So I decided to improve his breeding and make him an English bull terrier. So that's what he is, though some people call him a spade-faced mutt. The dog's got a name. Some years ago a young man, a teacher, came out here to Stony Brook with a little black curly-haired dog with him on a string. He said her name was Snarfie Sue and that she was about to die. He wanted to know if I'd name my bull terrier Snarfie Sue. I liked the name, so that's what the critter's called. When he's a male in the cartoon, he's Snarfie; when she's a female, she's Sue. And you thought the dog was nondescript!

—**George Booth**

Dear Vince,

Saw your "Potato Eaters" in Paris. Whew! Dullsville! Didn't you absorb _anything_ I said?? My Super Bowl series currently in 45th printing! Big bucks rolling in!!
Best, Leroy N.

Dear V.,

"Starry Night" O.K. Could have used a couple of football players and those big stadium lights for some extra zip, but not bad. Off to Vegas to unload some of my Kentucky Derby series dough!
Awright!
L. N.

This drawing has no real story behind it beyond it being just another affliction of my constant, peripheral quandary as to whether what I, or any of us do, can actually be considered "art."

—Jack Ziegler

I like cartoon ideas that are natural — unforced, spontaneous and direct — the kind the reader gets instantly. Nothing has to be deciphered or figured out. Nobody has to think, "Oh, I see what you're driving at." There is no distance, no gap between the original impulse, that electrical charge of wit or insight, that leap of the synapses called inspiration, and what shows up on paper. It is as if the artist's neurons are firing directly onto the drawing paper, like his ink supply flows directly from his carotid artery. These kinds of ideas come up from the cellars. They come as a result of a highly developed capacity for free association combined with a killer instinct.

Recently, the California Supreme Court ruled against affirmative action. I wanted to comment on it. Here is a rough rehash of the kind of chaotic thinking process that led to this cartoon: I begin by thinking about affirmative action, reverse discrimination . . . The fact that the ruling came from California's university system made me think of racism in California, which leads me to think of the famous video images of the LAPD beating up Rodney King, which prompts sketches of a figure labeled California Supreme Court beating up lady justice . . . Or maybe Mark Fuhrman beating up . . . uh . . . Mark Fuhrman . . . Hold on . . . Start over . . . Let's see now . . . Reverse discrimination in California . . . What is that like? . . . Hmmm . . . Come to think of it, you never heard Ray Charles do a cover of a Beach Boys tune! . . . I try to remember the lyrics of "Help Me, Rhonda", which reminds me of Kato Kaelin and how he kind of looks like one of the Beach Boys . . . Maybe Dennis Wilson on Prozac. But wait— I'm getting off track. I keep drifting to the O.J. trial . . . Let's see . . . What do we have here? . . . Angry White Guys in California . . . First, I think of Bobby Hurley drafted by the Sacramento Kings . . . L.A. Kings, Wayne Gretzky . . . No . . . Angry Middle-Aged, White Guys . . . Hmmm . . . Barry Diller, David Geffen, Katzenberg, Spielberg, Mike Ovitz and ten thousand short, Armani-suited CAA agents in Tai Chi stances . . . Wrong way. Dead end . . . Hmmm . . . Angry white guys, angry white guys, ulcers, Pepto Bismol, high blood pressure, clogged arteries, florid faces, Michael Douglas, Kirk Douglas, Douglas MacArthur, MacArthur Foundation, Genius grants, Foster Grants . . . No, I'm getting away from it again . . . White and Colored water fountains . . . White and Colored entrances . . . White Guys singing "We Shall Overcome" . . . We Shall Overkill . . . We Shall Overcompensate . . . Naaa . . . Discrimination . . . We Reserve The Right To Refuse Service To Anyone . . . White Men Can't Jump . . . White Men Can't Jumpstart Their Careers . . . Wait . . . Let's start over . . . Why do privileged white guys feel victimized? . . . What kind of jobs do whites feel that blacks have taken from them? Good question . . . Power Forward for the Houston Rockets? Vice President for Vertical Affairs . . . Band leader for the Tonight Show? African American studies professor at Berkeley? NFL running back? Blind blues singer? . . . Vice President for Blind Blues Operations . . . Wait. I'm onto something. What kind of jobs do angry whites feel would be okay to give minorities first dibs on? Porters, housekeepers, chauffeurs, bussing tables, shoeshine stands . . . Shoeshine stands! . . . Now that's a classic image. There's got to be something there! . . . An angry white guy getting a shoeshine by a black guy at a shoeshine stand! I bet some whites would even feel cheated out of traditional racially stereotypical jobs . . . Hey! So why not just show that?! Bingo! The caption wrote itself.

—Doug Marlette

This cartoon, referring to the Waco massacre by the government, came as a complete surprise. Usually I labor over my
cartoons, but this one came as swiftly as a rabbit out of a hat.
I did the basic drawing in one try, without any preliminary
sketches. The only revisions were minor: I drew Uncle Sam's
head in a three-quarter position because a full-face view
wouldn't read as well, and redrew the eyes so that the figure
would have eye contact with the viewer; I added the drops of
rabbit blood to dramatize his death. Finally I drew an aureole
around Uncle Sam—to ironically comment on the situation
as for decorative reasons.

—R.O. **Blechman**

Lucille Clifton

Lorena

*Woman cuts off husband's penis,
later throws it from car window.*
—**News Report**

it lay in my palm soft and trembled
as a new bird and i thought about
authority and how it always insisted
on itself, how it was master
of the man, how it measured him, never
was ignored or denied, and how it promised
there would be sweetness if it was obeyed
just like the saints do, like the angels
and i opened the window and held out my
uncupped hand; i swear to god
i thought it could fly

Two Poems by Robert Phillips

Cherry Suite

Gesturing toward the master bedroom suite,
"Solid cherry wood!" Mother said grandly.
Two bureaus, two mirrors, four-poster bed,
night-stand, and her personal vanity.

It was the best furniture we owned.
The rest, mere veneer. Weekly she sprayed
that suite with Lemon Pledge, buffed it
till it shone deep and red as Beaujolais.

I was drawn to its many drawers, sliding
as if on casters. Hers contained paste
jewelry, perfumes, prom programs (Jefferson
High 1933, 1934), photos of her smug-faced

aviator brother, a handbag made of beads,
scarves, cosmetics, a desiccated starfish,
my stellar report cards since first grade,
an autographed photo of Miss Lillian Gish.

Besides shirts and suspenders, his held
underwear, PJs, new wallets, socks,
reeking pipes, a porno comic with Dagwood
doing Blondie, and under his hankies a box

of Trojans—red and white, "Young Rubber Co.,
Youngstown, Ohio, Sold for the Prevention
of Disease Only." They smelled like artgum
erasers at my middle school. For comparison

I unrolled one, tried it on, despaired
I would ever fill such a thing. Ten rubbers
in the twelve-pack. The next time I looked,
only seven: Jeez, he's done it to Mother

three times in two weeks! (It never occurred
to me, They've done it three times together.)
He's crucifying her, I thought, on a cherry-
wood cross, just as I had had to bear

his cod-cold indifference. (At school
beer-breathed boys lied about sex.
I knew "nice" ladies didn't do such things.
At church mother'd deeply genuflect,

afterward have the rector home for tea.)
Yet she seemed none the worse for wear,
warbling "When it's springtime in the Rockies,
and the birds sing all the day," as she'd prepare

pancakes and sausages for her family of six.
Trundled across the globe to make me bourgeois,
the cherry suite's mine today—I'm orphaned.
My performance in bed? At times a faux pas.

I never enter that room with its bric-a-brac
without thinking, Mom, Dad, old fuckers, come back.

"A Pretty Mocking of the Life"

Mother in champagne-colored dress,
    neckline with navy-blue crenelles,
Father in dress-white uniform,
    their heads precisely parallel,

they face the future. "Our wedding
    portrait," Mother proudly averred.
For half a century it dominated the air
    above her cherrywood dresser.

In flattering lighting and pastels,
    they were the picture of connubiality.
Mona Lisa smile and military bearing,
    they could be in *Town & Country*.

Sorting the homeplace after both died,
    I found the individual photographs —
Mother's from a high school prom,
    Father's a college yearbook — halves

of the composite in their bedroom.
    Friends knew they were wed by a Justice
of the Peace over Christmas break, but
    only I now knew it was in such a rush

they didn't pose commemoratively.
    Later Mother paid a studio to retouch
what haste and pregnancy disallowed,
    her wedding at last made illustrious.

Two Poems by Gary Mitchner

Athena, Tour Guide; Aphrodite, Nympho

Morgan saw Athena's face in the crowd
at the Athens International Airport
where the Chaos became a genesis for
a journey toward an archaic revelation.

Athena guided him through the confusion
to Olympic Airways for another flight
to Crete. Like Icarus he dared to
rush and the clerk placed him on standby.

At Heraklion in a beach resort he saw
Aphrodite emerging from the blue-green waves.
Mother asked for a diversion of eyes
but topless bathing did not offend him.

Morgan could not guess the exploits he would
participate in with this goddess of the black curls
nor the instruction from this owl-like goddess
of art history and beer, escapades galore.

Mother warned him not to return if he dallied
among the epicureans and hedonists but
being led astray by these wonderful goddesses
proved more entertaining than their decadence.

At Knossos, Athena took ill, dizzy from
the heights and he lead her down
from the palace steps by the bull relief
until safe on the theater slabs; she vomited.

On Santorini known as Thera, Aphro, as he called
her, met a sailor, staying more than two weeks
instead of the one day she had planned.
Morgan envied her abandon and masturbated.

When Athena, the hygiene queen, went topless
on Hydra at Kalamari Beach, he wouldn't look,
afraid that her breasts might entice him
into a rash act like taking a picture for home.

His real fantasy appeared when the curled one
took a Greek boy to bed and he imagined
the flesh moving together in erotic pose;
Mother would never learn of these notions.

Morgan crawled in the below-temple chambers
at his favorite site in Delphi, searching for
contemporary oracles to give him necessary answers
to the great questions: what would he have learned

here? Did his purification sweep through him
so that this new state of relaxation could
last when he returned home? Would a Penelope
be waiting for him without Mother's notice?

Morgan's Delphic Purification

The pain began in the left groin at high tea
in The Cincinnatian Hotel; Mother refused
to consider the possibilities of hernia
much less mentioning the word *loins*.

After several incidents, he reported
to his doctor who pronounced kidney stone.
An X-ray would be required but first cleansing.
Like Apollo he purified himself with pills

and liquid laxative and suppository.
He felt he would die in Venice or succumb
to Hades on the Delphic slopes. But no.
Mother would say the stone must be removed.

His plans for going to Colonus interrupted?
No, he would persist. Morgan dreaded
the on-coming pain. He needed an oracle
to predict the moment of hospitable

agony but none came until the last
morning: a black lentil containing his sins
dropped into the bowl with minor discomfort.
Mother permitted him to writhe in anxiety.

At the oracle he crawled through sub-
terranean chambers where priestesses
gathered their prophecies. He understood
the seven-day purification, the stadium

and theater. Spirituality opening out
to the majestic mountains in proportion
and submersion of fragments into
an omphalos. Morgan's navel ached.

Gary Fincke

Johnny Weismuller Learns the Tarzan Yell

For public appearances, for the crowds
Who expected perfection, he managed,
Take after take, to mimic the sound
The studio had built for an ape-child.
Practice was like swimming all those laps
In the pool, building his breath again
To fill the audio needs of Tarzan:
Camel's bleat, hyena howl played backwards—
He couldn't admit to plucked violin,
A soprano's high C added, one
After the other, to his own best roar,
His champion's howl so much a common cry
The audience would think "explorer caught
In quicksand," "hunter surrounded by spears,"
Not Tarzan loud in the natural world
Where the hybrid voice develops into
Their great arpeggio of beast and man.

Beth Gylys

Not an Affair a Sestina

You're crazy if you called this an affair.
We slept together, and you made me come.
No big deal. You've got a lot of strange
ideas. You think you know so much about me,
think because you've seen me naked that counts
for something. Just because I put my head

between your legs, because you gave me head,
you tell the world we've had some big affair.
We've been together twice — no one counts
that time behind my desk. I didn't come.
(How could I relax, you simply grabbed me?)
I'm not the one you need. You're really strange.

You try to make this seem important, this strange
relationship we have. I'm no head
to place upon a platter. I'm married. Me,
I'm not the kind of man who has affairs.
I like you — that is all. It doesn't come
to any more than that. Do you know what counts

in things like ours? I'll tell you what counts.
Let me put it simply: it's not that strange
to meet in places in the dark, to come
between your hopes and what you have, and head
for someplace warm and soft. To have affairs —
a real affair — is wrong. It seems to me

you give too much away. You're telling me
as well as all your friends these wild accounts
of us and me and our intense affair,

as if to have a little sex was strange.
I know you think I'm messing with your head,
but you're the one who kept going. You came

to see me. You knew my life was set. I've come
to take things as they are: I know you want me.
It's hard to be alone, to move ahead
with no one there, when nothing seems to count.
Believe me, I've felt like that. You aren't so strange.
Listen, I do care; this wasn't an affair.

I hope you come to see that, take what counts
from what you tell me is a big affair,
and head to love more real than strange.

John Drexel

Chance Encounters

On a street in a city a thousand miles inland
a woman I'd never met grabbed me by the shoulders
and shook me and shook me and shouted
"Look! Look! Don't tell me you can't see
the sea from here! Don't give me that bull!"
Okay. Maybe if I listen long and hard enough
I can just hear *La Mer*
somewhere in the distance.
(But please, if I've a choice,
play the original monaural record by Barbirolli
from Lady Barbirolli's collection.)
Did the fact that I once lived by the sea,
that I looked at it day after day,
heard gulls in my dreams,
smelled sea weed and sea fish and ship wrecks
make any difference? Did some look in my eyes
make her go batty?
In any event I certainly was not there
when the first Romans stepped ashore
bearing oysters for their dopey drowsy emperor.
And what would be the advantage(s),
if any, of eating oysters in the Summer Isles
with a poet who might praise the sea in Scots?

Albert Goldbarth

Two Cents

Academia 1994: these dead white males
I've been hauling about in this brick of a box of a book
called *Western Civilization* — Homer, Plato, Melville,
and the rest of the Anglo-Sultans of Civ. — have
seemingly weighted me down: at least, I'm told so.
I shake the book; I hear the rattle
of its ponderous Goliath beetles of history,
while elsewhere someone holds a copy of something like
New Rainbows: Multi-Voices, and
its ladybugs and mayflies lightly hum and lift
their reader into higher realms of consciousness,
as if the neocortex were merely another layer
of gray, confining atmosphere to rise above.
Good-bye, good-bye, I heavily wave. That's

one example. Another — a friend confides: the woman
she calls her "female mentor" (a lauded lit-crit doyenne
exemplary at both oracular wisdom and daintier,
humbler, daily graces) suddenly hemorrhaged and
two hours after that died: "and on her deathbed
told me, I guess by way of finally cleaning
every interior surface, that she'd once done something,
I won't say what, but something, *so* demeaning
involving this man she knew to be completely meretricious,
and yet . . . Well, what I'm saying is, that's
two deaths. First, the person I *thought* she was, died;
then she died in her wholeness. Now . . . how can I say it?
She left 'us' . . . *incomplete*, and so I carry her everywhere,
invisibly, my osteoporotic hump, my camelback, whispering
    to me."

Examples swarm me: D-Day's 50th anniversary, and
the local paper rehashes the Japanese soldier
found on that island twenty years after the War, still
loyal to Hirohito and armed with a bayonet. The man
who weeps for the fallen Führer. The woman whose self
is predicated on membership in D.A.R. — who
harnesses herself every morning, and all day drags
the Mayflower in her wake. Or this: "I know by now
how tired a cliché it is, but, hey: my father drank,
I drink" — and then the long tale of DNA in a gene pool
spiked like a frat party punch. The truth is: everybody
alive is small against the dead,
in ways sustaining and misshaping simultaneously.
A favorite page in *Western Civilization* tries

describing Rome in 1100: cowherds and rush-weavers
living amid the abandoned grandeur, patching huts together
of mud and thatch inside the walls of public buildings
— temples, garrisons, arenas — so unthinkably vast,
the work of gods or demons, they were seen as plains
and mountainridge escarpments. Huts
against those columns like lesions on bones. And
life, of course, unceasingly buzzing in each of them:
a cooking-stone; a sexual musk; a hide to soften . . .
I also think of a tale I've read of two wanderers
who sheltered overnight in a magical cave the fates
provided: the skull of a whale Time had worn clean,
into a fabulous sanctum. Huddled all night, in its head,
like a thought, like two cents clinking together.

gesture, he said, to demonstrate his contempt for the farm-workers'

acceptance of "a Latin society based on **machismo** and the oppression

of women." He had spent hours working on a treatise ~~XXXX~~ arguing that sexual dif-
ferences among wild animals were cultural rather than biological--
a study he ~~had~~ (was) tentatively ~~entitled~~ (calling) "The Myth of Robin Red Breast."

Bernie had become particularly concerned about ~~XXXX~~ the Melissa,

in a magazine
Mohlers' only child. After he read ~~XXXXXXXX~~ that little girls

because of
unconsciously accepted the limitation of sex roles ~~by~~ associating

fathers
~~XXX~~ with going to the office and mothers with staying home, Bernie

began staying home more and more. Even before he became aware of the

a purist about daily
crippling power of sex roles, he had not been ~~XXXXXXXXX~~

office attendance.
~~XXXXXXXXXXXXX~~ Bernie's ~~XXXX~~ grandfather had done well in

the paper towel business, and Bernie had spent his time at an

investment house managing the portfolio he inherited. His concern

for Melissa caused him to spend less and less time at his desk, until

finally he just gave up the office altogether -- a decision that

had effect one way or the other on the health of his portfolio.

It also had no effect on the way Melissa viewed the world.

"I can't believe this could happen to us," Bernie said ~~one night~~

as soon as Greta got home from the office, "Melissa wants to be a nurse."

A Calvin Trillin manuscript page.

Calvin Trillin

The Art of Humor III

Calvin Trillin was born in Kansas City, Missouri in 1935. He graduated from Southwest High School in 1953, and in the fall of that year, as he mentions in his book, Remembering Denny, *he was one of the "brown-shoe" freshmen to enter Yale University: "the bright student council president from white middle-class high schools who had been selected by Yale to be buffed up a bit and sent out into the world prepared to prove their high-school classmates right in voting them most likely to succeed."*

After graduating in 1957, while waiting to enter the army, Trillin had a temporary job at Time, *working at the magazine's bureaus in London, Paris and Tunisia. When he finished his stint in the army, which had been spent mainly on Governor's Island in New York Harbor, a position at* Time's *Atlanta bureau was available. After a year covering the civil rights struggle in the South, he worked as a writer for* Time *in New York — but not for long. He was soon assigned his first article for* The New Yorker, *a three-part series on the two black students who desegregated the University of Georgia. The articles were published in 1963; he has been a staff writer there ever since.*

In 1967 Trillin began traveling the country for his New Yorker *series, "U.S. Journal." For the next fifteen years, his journal entries chronicled American life in the small towns and cities he visited every three weeks. Along with his travels, he also began writing occasionally about eating; these essays, in which, as he says, "I wrote about eating rather than food, and I wrote as a reporter rather than as an expert," have been published in his* Tummy Trilogy. *While still keeping his journal for* The New Yorker, *he began writing a column for* The Nation *in 1978. These columns, written first for* The Nation *and then for newspaper syndication, have been collected in five books.* Uncivil Liberties *and* With All Disrespect. *In the summer of 1990, prompted by the sound of John Sununu's last name, he wrote the first of a series of short poems, "If You Knew What Sununu," which presently appear in* The Nation.

He is now settled with his wife in a town house in Greenwich Village, where this interview took place in a large sun-lit room. From time to time the phone rang, invariably for his daughter Abigail, who was sunbathing up on the roof and studying for the California bar examination. Finally, Mr. Trillin rose and attempted to turn off the answering machine, but in the time-honored tradition of humorists' confusion with machines, was unable to do so. This interview could be punctuated with long messages for his daughter, but they have been excised for reasons of respecting privacy, and for length.

Mr. Trillin (known by all as "Dad") is very much a family man. Married to his wife, Alice, in 1965, he often refers to her and family members in his columns and in the monologues he gives in public performances — "around our house we often . . ." being a constant refrain. The Trillins celebrated their thirtieth anniversary earlier this year, indeed shortly after the symposium on humor (described elsewhere in this issue) in Menaggio, Italy.

INTERVIEWER

Here's a simple question for you. As opposed to spoken humor, what's the secret to actually writing it? Why can't people sit down and write funny stuff?

CALVIN TRILLIN

What is called "getting it onto the page." That's a really good question, so good it's probably unanswerable. We all know funny people who can't get it down on the page — even funny *writers* who can't get it down on the page. I suppose that there is the necessity of some sort of structure in written humor that you can get away without in spoken humor by the use of timing and gesture. Everybody knows people who are funny just by the way they talk. Remember that comedian Jack Leonard — this big, fat guy who appeared on the Johnny Carson shows? He talked very fast. He would always say something like, "IjustwantyoutoknowJohnnyifyoueverneedafriend-youwon'tbeabletofindone." But if you listened to him carefully, after a while you realized a lot of things he said weren't funny at all. But he had a wonderful delivery. Or take the joke about the telegram that Trotsky sent to Stalin from exile in Mexico: "I was wrong. You were right. I should apologize." Somebody says to Stalin, "Trotsky's given up. He's asking forgiveness." Stalin says, "No, you don't understand: Trotsky's

Jewish. What he's saying is, '*I* was wrong?? *You* were right?? *I* should apologize?!?'" So that's one thing. When you're writing, you are robbed of your delivery. People, particularly comedians, always say it's all in the timing. But in written humor, the reader has to do his own timing—you have to build in the timing for the reader, which is difficult.

Also, I find that written humor and spoken humor are really so different. For instance, I have been on a book tour with this recent collection of newspaper columns and "Shouts and Murmurs" pieces from *The New Yorker*. Occasionally I gave readings in bookstores. It's amazing how few of the pieces wore well when read aloud. A number of them, partly for purely technical reasons—they have too many quotes in them, or too many parenthetical phrases—don't read well. It is hard to read quotes, or parenthetical phrases.

INTERVIEWER

When did you realize that you were funny?

TRILLIN

At Sunday school when I was about eleven. We came to the part in the Bible or the Talmud, whichever it is, with the famous phrase, "If I forget thee, oh Yerushalayem, may my right hand lose its cunning and my tongue cling to the roof of my mouth." I stood up with my right hand gradually becoming noticeably weird and said: "If I forget thee, O Yerushalayem, may my right hand lose its cunning and my tongue cleave to duh woof of my mout." Everybody laughed except the teacher who ejected me from the classroom and accused me of self-hatred. A very weird epiphany. I guess I already knew I wasn't a solemn little boy—shy, but not exactly solemn.

I actually think of being funny as an odd turn of mind, like a mild disability, some weird way of looking at the world that you can't get rid of. It's odd: one of the questions that people ask me constantly is, "Is it hard having to be funny all the time?" The difficult thing for me is being *serious*. It's a genetic thing—being funny—like being able to wiggle your ears. I don't have any trouble being funny, that's my turn of mind. Or at least attempting to be funny. Whether it really is funny is for the audience to judge. But I actually do think that some people are and some people aren't. We all know, say, a lot of lawyers who aren't funny and some who are. A lot of dentists who aren't funny. The dentist who just took a fractured root out of my tooth — we refer to him as the butcher of Fifty-fourth Street — is a pleasant, friendly man, but he's not funny.

INTERVIEWER

I would have thought most people who find themselves very funny early on think of themselves as potential stand-up comics or actors.

TRILLIN

If I had been raised in a different house, I might have done something like that. As it was, I was raised to be a kind of champion, sent out to make something of myself. My father, who was technically an immigrant — he came when he was an infant — wanted me to be an American, preferably an American president. He didn't go to college. Before I was born he wanted me to go specifically to Yale, which he thought would help. It was easy for him to think I could be president: he didn't have to worry about being president himself, being ineligible because he wasn't born in the United States.

INTERVIEWER

Did he worry about your comic streak?

TRILLIN

I think that he enjoyed it, but yes, he did worry about it a little bit. It never seemed to me a bad thing, or something that I was supposed to suppress or anything like that. On the other hand, if I'd had the ambition to become, say, a stand-up comic, I don't think I could have gone to my father very comfortably and said, "This is what your dreams have come to."

I do remember in high school I wanted to be a disc jockey. I remember even going around to talk to a disc jockey. The disc jockey said, "Well maybe you could be in your family business and then just be funny when people come in." By then my father was out of the grocery business, and he had a restaurant. The disc jockey was suggesting I could be one of those great maître d' jokesters. I saw one in Italy last spring. We stopped at one of the best restaurants I've ever been to. I saw the guy who ran it talking to three or four regulars who obviously came in for lunch every day. I had no idea what he was saying, but you could see he was telling a joke. At the punch line he would turn his back as they laughed and take two steps in the other direction, spin around, and come back. It's an old vaudeville move. In that motion you could see that every day he told this wonderful sort of restaurant-proprietor joke. So this disc jockey was telling me to think of it in some way like that, the sort of thing to do on the side, like the very serious lawyer who makes a funny speech at the Bar Association dinner.

INTERVIEWER

Did you do a lot of reading . . . Twain, for instance? Thurber?

TRILLIN

No. I didn't. It's always embarrassing for me to be asked, "Well, I suppose you really grabbed a hold of Thurber and Perelman when you were in high school." I only knew one person who took *The New Yorker*—a cousin of mine who was considered a little bit strange. One person I read in college who I thought was funny was the very déclassé Max Shulman. I thought he was hilarious.

One time I was asked, by the New York Public Library, for a book put out in connection with some Literary Lion function, to submit a passage of prose that I particularly admired. A lot of writers were asked, and I suppose a lot of Proust found its way in there. It gave me the chance to quote Max Shulman.

I found this passage about Dobey's dog where his mother says, "Dobey you're going off to college and I'm no smarter than your old hound dog Edmund lying there in the corner." Dobey says, "Don't talk that way about Edmund, Mom. He's a smart dog." He whistles to him and says, "Play dead, Edmund. Look at how he obeys. All four feet sticking in the air." His mother says, "Dobey, I hadn't wanted to tell you. He's been dead since Friday. You ran over him with the car." It fit perfectly.

INTERVIEWER

Were you employed by *The New Yorker* because you were funny . . . they'd seen funny pieces?

TRILLIN

The first one I wrote was about the integration of the University of Georgia, a fairly serious piece. The first pieces I did were all fairly straight, I think partly because I hadn't really figured out what I sounded like. Then I started writing a series of pieces that were all about the same guy, Barnett Frummer who had a girlfriend named Rosalie Mondle he was trying to impress. Each one was about a different kind of trendiness. At one point she became a radical; he tried to be radical. She got interested in gourmet cooking; he tried to do the same. These were what *The New Yorker* called casuals—short pieces that were signed. At the time, they had a special deal on them, like a cut-rate special in the fiction department: if you sold six of them in one year, something wonderful happened to you. It was sort of like hitting the pinball machine in "The Time of Your Life": flags went off, you got a lot of money, piano lessons for a year, a new pair of shoes, all that stuff. So I wrote these really sporadically at *The New Yorker*.

I didn't really find an outlet for just purely I'm-going-to-try-to-be-funny-now-for-a-certain-number-of-words until I started doing *The Nation* column, which I think was in 1978. I always thought of writing humor as some sort of little, weird thing that I could do in the way some people could play the piano

INTERVIEWER
Is it that easy?

TRILLIN

It's not easy, but it's natural. Once I started having to do it, it turned out it wasn't that hard. I did a *Nation* column every three weeks. We set it at three weeks because at the time I was doing this U.S. journal series for *The New Yorker*— a reporting piece from somewhere in the country every three weeks—and I'd settled into a week of reporting, a week to write it, and what we call the "off week" when I did things like look for another story and pay bills. I started writing *The Nation* column during that off week. Then I started syndicating that column in 1985 or 1986 once a week. Russell Baker said I would find it easier doing one a week rather than one every three weeks. That was, I think, a little prank on his part. It was exactly three times as hard.

INTERVIEWER

I imagine one column a day would be twenty-one times as hard.

TRILLIN

Exactly. But then it turns out if you have to do it, you do it. You start writing and eventually you think of something.

INTERVIEWER

Is that how it works? Especially when you have to get something ready for tomorrow?

TRILLIN

Well, sometimes I tear things out of the newspaper and throw them in this file. When I'm desperate I look through the file, which is often painful. "Oh God, not that thing, why didn't I throw that thing out years ago?" I think one approach to writing this sort of column is to apply the rules of your own house to Washington or Washington to your own

house. That is, the contrast between ordinary life and the life
of government and general big shots. For instance, I once did
a column that started, "Reading in *The New York Times* that
the Pentagon has in its warehouses thirty billion dollars worth
of equipment and supplies that it had no earthly use for makes
me feel a lot better about my basement." So then you start
thinking, "Well, that column is either going to go toward the
basement or toward the Pentagon or both." What you read
in the paper and what happens to you are often the normal
sources of supply.

INTERVIEWER

Do people send you ideas?

TRILLIN

Not for columns, usually. Perhaps for stories. I find that
for writing humor, people's ideas usually don't work very well.
Occasionally they do. Bill Vaughan was a really funny humor
columnist for *The Kansas City Star*. Once, when I was visiting
him in Kansas City, he told me, "I think these car-washing
places are really sexy. All that water sluicing around. You
should write a story about that." Which I did—for *Playboy*
needless to say. Then Bob Bingham, my editor at *The New
Yorker*, told me once he had heard from a friend that people
were using their safety-deposit rooms for midday trysts. Better
than a hotel room: "Would you and your secretary like a room,
sir?" So I wrote a piece about how a couple who did that
regularly lured the guard into the safety-deposit room and
disarmed him. A heist. I mean this was all fiction. So to that
extent people suggest things. There's a guy I know who called
me a year or two ago and said, "Seat belts for dogs. Good-bye.
See you later." So I wrote a piece about a division in the animal
rights community over seat belts for dogs. Do you owe it to
your dog to try to get mandatory seat-belt legislation for pets
or are you invading his space by doing that, et cetera, et cetera.
Sometimes people call, but not usually. I find something has
to sort of marinate in my own weird juices before it comes
out.

INTERVIEWER

To be turned down for a straight piece of reporting is bad
enough, but to be turned down if it's supposed to be funny
and isn't must be especially discouraging.

TRILLIN

I think in some ways it's harder to have a factual piece turned
down. Assuming that they liked the idea to start with, if they
turn down a factual piece, then there's really something wrong
with it. It's flawed. But if the person in the second row doesn't
laugh, then it only means it's not funny to that one person.
When I used to try to write casuals for *The New Yorker* I had
a very low batting average. I never sold the sixth piece that
would have made all these wonderful things happen. I always
assumed I just had a different sense of what was funny than
they did. Roger Angell was the main editor I dealt with. Roger
is such a gentleman that he would sometimes try to explain
to me what the problem was. I said, "Roger, if you don't
think it's funny, it's not funny." The piece of mine that's
anthologized as much as any I've ever written was turned down
at *The New Yorker* and appeared in *The Atlantic*. *The New
Yorker* simply didn't think it was funny.

INTERVIEWER

Which one was that?

TRILLIN

It was a piece called "A Nation of Shopkeepers Loses Three
of Them Through Contact with a Nation of Violence." It was
about different ideas that Americans and English have about
retail trade, about standing in line and being fair and saying
"thank you." That sort of stuff. The American who goes into
a typewriter shop and says, "Do you have typewriter ribbons?"
"No, we don't *do* typewriter ribbons. Odd, people come in
here all the time asking for typewriter ribbons, simply because
we sell typewriters and various pieces of office equipment."
And the American says, "What do you tell those people?" "I

tell them we don't *do* typewriter ribbons." Americans trying
to *out*-thank you English people. "Thanks awfully." "Thanks
very much." It was appreciated by Americans who had lived
in England. Probably not by very many other people. So, I
think of humor as being subjective. Take comedians. There
are some comedians who don't make me laugh even though
I know they are talented and greatly appreciated by some
people whose opinions I respect. It just somehow goes over
me, or around me or something. I once dedicated a novel to
my sister at her request. Originally the dedication said, "To
my sister, Sukey Fox in a first tentative step toward forgiving
her for trying to throw me down the laundry chute in 1937."
But Alice made me take out that part about the laundry chute.
Anyway, Sukey said when she read it, "I thought it was a
comic novel. Was this supposed to be funny?" "Well, yeah,
one or two people thought it was moderately humorous. Fortunately, a couple of them were reviewers."

INTERVIEWER

Do you test the pieces on Alice, on anybody? Daughters?

TRILLIN

On Alice.

INTERVIEWER

What does she usually say?

TRILLIN

A wry smile sometimes. Fortunately she doesn't often say,
"Why would anybody think this is funny?" A couple of times,
maybe. I suppose it's very weird being married to a writer. Alice
could be married to — using an example we've mentioned — a
dentist whose methods of dentistry she might not like, if she
thought much about it. But of course she *wouldn't* think about
it. What if you had a wife who simply didn't think you were
funny, and you were trying to make jokes on paper? I suppose
you wouldn't show her your stuff. Because, you know, it's not

a requirement in marriage. But I do show things to Alice, not just the things that are meant to be funny, but the things that are meant to be serious. Alice has a very good eye. Also, she doesn't have any axe to grind. She doesn't happen to have a constituency. When I first got to *The New Yorker* I didn't know Alice. I used to show things to a friend of mine there, Gerry Jonas. I proposed to him, and he refused to marry me: he said he was already married.

INTERVIEWER

How many drafts do you tend to do?

TRILLIN

It's harder to tell now with the word processor. With reporting pieces, I actually do a kind of pre-draft, which sort of starts out in English but degenerates very quickly. I've always been terrified that someone will find an early draft. When I used to write more at *The New Yorker*, there were two or three Polish cleaning women who came in late at night, and I was always afraid that they would find my early drafts and read them to each other, howling with laughter, slapping their brooms against the desks like hockey players do . . . "Ha! He calls himself a writer!"

I've always written humor slightly differently. I've always paid more attention to the paragraph on hand before I go to the next paragraph.

About twice a year I make myself laugh when I'm writing. Something just sort of gets out without my knowing it. Alice says, "What's going in there?" I've actually giggled a little bit at my own line, but usually something that nobody else finds particularly funny. It means that if I ever had to spend a lot of time locked up in solitary confinement, I wouldn't be totally without resources.

INTERVIEWER

Do you have any explanations as to why there are so few women writers one thinks of as funny?

TRILLIN

Well, funny is obviously not one of the things women in this country have traditionally been expected to be. In the bad old days there was certainly a feeling that being funny was not feminine. I suppose the number of female stand-up comedians these days is an indication that this is changing. But if a girl in my Sunday school class had thought about pretending to take that passage about forgetting Jerusalem literally, I don't think she would have stood up and put on the little performance. The female class cutup has not been a staple of American folklore. I don't know whether or not that has meant that fewer women have felt encouraged about writing humor. There are, of course, some very funny women writers. Molly Ivins, for instance, writes about the characters in Texas politics better than anyone. She once mentioned a Texas gubernatorial candidate — this was a real candidate — who visited San Francisco and was so afraid of getting AIDS that when he took a shower in the hotel he wore shower hats on his feet.

INTERVIEWER

What is it like working at *The New Yorker*? Do writers sit around as they presumably did in the day of the Algonquin and fire off clever quips and sallies at each other?

TRILLIN

Alas, no. Unless that's going on somewhere every Tuesday and Thursday and I haven't been invited. Years ago, when I spent more time in the office, I used to go to the Algonquin for a drink sometimes, but the people I went with seemed to be the most morose people on the staff. Actually, when people used to ask me if there were any truly funny people at *The New Yorker* — not funny on the fourth draft but verbally very funny — I always said, "There's this guy in the makeup room . . ." His name was Johnny Murphy, and he did both quick comebacks and the sort of joke that would have been a bomb at Knights of Columbus meeting if it had been told by someone

without the gift. Johnny never seemed to think it was odd
that the funniest person on the magazine was someone who
didn't write anything. He was very Irish, of course, and someone once told me that in Ireland a writer is a failed talker.

Are there any subjects which the humorist should avoid?
Swift didn't seem to shy away from nibbling on tots, or at
least suggesting it was okay.

TRILLIN

It's not so much that certain subjects are out of bounds
because of rules set down somewhere or because of a policy
that a writer has decided on. It's that writing about certain
subjects wouldn't be funny. I think that if the goal is to be
funny, the subjects sort themselves out naturally. Also, the
passage of time makes some subjects okay. It's common to
hear jokes about Lincoln and Ford's Theater, for instance. I've
never heard anyone object to Zero Mostel's great line about
Rumanian-Jewish cooking. As you may know, the Rumanian
part of Rumanian-Jewish cooking is garlic, and the Jewish part
is schmaltz — chicken fat. My theory is that the garlic is to keep
away vampires, and if they get through the first line of defense
the schmaltz gets them with heartburn. Anyway, Mostel always said that Rumanian-Jewish cooking has killed more Jews
than Hitler.

INTERVIEWER

Is the humorist given more poetic license to stray away from
the truth to make a reader laugh?

TRILLIN

Straying from the truth is one of the ways the humorist
makes the reader laugh. Exaggeration is obviously one of the
tools. I once wrote, for instance, that the Quebec language
laws are so strict that in a school assembly you can't show a
film of English-speaking mimes. The mime has to be someone

like Marcel Marceau who is not speaking French. A couple of paragraphs later, I admitted that I made that up, but presumably the reader would have known that anyway. Or maybe not. I've often said that someone trying to write satirically in this country faces the problem of writing something sufficiently bizarre so that it might not come true while his article is on the presses. The Reagan Administration was difficult that way. Once, at a reception for big-city mayors in Washington, President Reagan was approached by his own Secretary of Housing and Urban Development, and the President said, "Hello, Mr. Mayor, how are things in your city?" Now, what does that leave for me?

INTERVIEWER

Have the targets, the victims of your humor ever coming knocking on the door?

TRILLIN

That has never happened. Where have I gone wrong?

— George Plimpton

Henry V, Part 2

Marcia Guthridge

She was choosing cucumbers at the grocery store and wondering what sorts of genitalia cicadas had when someone
touched her on the shoulder. She prepared her public face
and turned, expecting to see her friend the produce man.
There was no one behind her. The automatic sprinkler over
the vegetables switched on and soaked the sleeve of her new
suede jacket. She wanted someone to be behind her. She
turned all the way round and there, at the far end of her
cart in a wet mist which rose faintly pink from a heap of red
cabbages, stood Henry V of England.

"He's awfully young," she said aloud, or nearly aloud. There
was no one else around. She hastily chose a cucumber and a
red cabbage, though her sons hated red cabbage, wheeled her
cart in a half-circle and went fast away from the boy-king past
the oranges and the garlic, to the checkout counter. He strode
behind her. She did not look back, but she could hear his
sword hitting his boot at every step. He helped her unload
her groceries for the cashier, who asked her if she was in a
hurry. Maureen didn't answer. Henry V followed her out the
door to the parking lot, carrying both bags of groceries. She

told the bag boy she didn't need his help. The king walked
to the rear of her car and waited, grinning, while she fetched
the keys to open the trunk. After setting the bags inside he
tossed his mop of blond hair, which was cut as if with a bowl
and stood out like eaves over his longish ears and away from
his forehead, with a twist of his neck. Then he stood straight
and grinned some more. He made Maureen think of a golden
retriever puppy her parents had bought her as a child, which
had dug under the fence and disappeared after two weeks.

"Where did this guy come from?" she asked herself. The
after-work rush was beginning. Several people passed by her
car without staring. Could they possibly be so anxious to get
their shopping done that they don't notice a boy wearing
studded gloves, a tooled scabbard and a tunic emblazoned
with the Lancaster lions straddling two parking places behind
a Honda Accord? Henry V, for his part, didn't seem to notice
any of the hurrying shoppers or the line of cars building up
behind Maureen's, waiting for her to vacate her parking place.
He only had eyes for Maureen. "I must have made him up,"
she decided. "This is very sick. This is terrible."

She decided to kill him quickly. After all, he'd been dead
already for hundreds of years. Who would arrest her? She
jerked open the car door. It stuck a bit because of the dent
from a couple of weeks ago. She scrambled into the driver's
seat and it hit her that she didn't have the keys. He had opened
the trunk and held onto the keys. How could she run over him
when he had her car keys? Suddenly his large head appeared at
her window. She started. He tapped on the glass, still grinning.
He was so close she could see that his teeth were very bad:
brown nubs, medieval teeth, disgusting. She rolled down the
window to accept the keys he dangled between their faces,
and she smelled wood smoke and manure. When she had
taken the keys and started the car he walked back behind it
again and stood waiting for her to mow him down, grinning
into the rearview mirror. Her fingers tapped the emergency
brake but didn't release it. She had always suspected that her
puppy had been run over by a car and that her parents had

never told her. One of the cars behind her ground its gears irritably and screeched away, and the next car in line honked loudly. She closed her eyes and let her head sink back against the headrest. Henry V bounded along the side of the car and appeared in the seat next to her. "I definitely dreamed him up. But I had no idea he was going to arrive; I am not prepared," she said to herself, and to him: "Fasten your seat belt. I'm a conservative person." He obeyed immediately.

She had a good deal of trouble getting used to him. That first night and several afterward he spent in the garage. When she got into the car to drive to work the next day he was in his seat waiting for her, his seat belt snugly buckled. He stayed in the car while she answered phones at the radio station where she worked. He followed her into the house that afternoon and sat at the kitchen table while she fixed supper. Once or twice he rose to look out the window, but mostly he stared at her. She stared back. She asked herself questions: how long would he stay, could he speak? When one of her sons came thundering up the basement stairs to report that someone had spilt something black and oily on the beige carpet downstairs, she jumped so high she broke a plate. She gazed blankly at her son, cleaned up the broken china and went to the pantry for baking soda. She gave it to him and told him to pour it on the carpet and to leave her alone, she was busy. She realized as he thundered back down that she had given him the wrong stuff; she turned dizzily to call him back and ran into Henry V who had followed her into the pantry. She tripped on his armor-toed boot, and he caught her by the hand to stop her falling. She thought once more of the golden retriever pup, who had been always underfoot, whose nose had been soft and damp like Henry's glove, and who had slept in the garage.

She pulled her hand away from his and raised it to him as a warning, against what she wasn't sure. She felt it was time for her to say something. Her thoughts were disorganized. She had never been good at initiating conversation. She didn't even know if he would understand her sort of English. But she began anyway.

"I'm having some difficulty," she said. "I seem to have a transition to make here, and I'm afraid it's too much. You know I remember when my sons were babies both of them were fussy babies. It's funny, I don't know anymore which one did what cute thing or bad thing, which one's first word was *mine* and which one's *mama*. They run together. My sister-in-law was always giving me scrapbooks with those plastic quilted covers, you know the ones — no, of course you don't — and telling me I'd be sorry if I didn't write things down, my babies would be gone forever. Well anyway, they were both fussy, that I remember, and I'm not too sorry that's gone forever either, it wasn't colic or anything, they were just always fussing. And the pediatrician asked me if they cried when I picked them up or when I put them down or when I changed their diapers or when I started feeding them or when I was finished, and I said, 'Yes, yes, yes, all of those,' and she wrote DIT in her file. That's for 'Difficulty in Transition.' That's what I'm having. Can you talk?" Henry V stared at her, his gloved hand still outstretched where it had held hers. "Please sit down again," she said.

She sat down with him at the kitchen table and looked him over carefully. He had a couple of days' growth of beard (a soft, flimsy teenage beard like the whiskers her sons were beginning to sprout) with a pink Celtic skin underneath, a deep round scar on his lower left cheek — smallpox, an arrow? But his face was essentially unclear to her; even when she gazed at it point-blank it seemed curiously as if she were looking through welling tears. The setting sun blazed in through the window behind his head and cast him still further into shadow.

She sighed. "So maybe the deal is, since I made you up I can do anything I want to do with you, if I want to do anything. If I do anything, the first thing I'll do is send you to the dentist."

She balled her hands into fists and closed her eyes. She willed Henry V's teeth capped, opened her eyes and took a breath. He was gone. She didn't know whether to be relieved or disappointed. There was no trace of him left. His pungent smell had disappeared. The glove he had removed in order to scratch himself was no longer on the table. Then she heard a clatter behind her, by the sink. She turned and saw him rummaging in the dish drainer, then raising a colander toward the window into a shaft of sunlight. The light gently freckled his face through the holes in the colander. She breathed again.

"Grin at me," she said. He did. His teeth were beautiful. They glinted in the sun shaft like a movie star's. She blinked her eyes and yellowed them a bit. She didn't want him to be a movie star. The teeth were now perfect; nevertheless, she could not avoid thinking that she might as well have a lemur hunkering at her sink, so primitive a primate was this man, so attenuated was their connection on the evolutionary time line. He gave her the shivers.

He, on the other hand, appeared to be comfortably settled in her kitchen. Having found a knife in the dish drainer, with one foot propped on the table, he was scraping mud from his boot, his mouth folded inward in concentration. But how could she manage to squeeze herself into his unfathomable life? Did Maureen come before Queen Katharine or after? Was Falstaff dead? Had the boy-king known sorrow? Boredom? Impotence? How could she fit him into her life?

This would be more difficult than the teeth. She dragged a broom over and began sweeping clods of dirt from under the table: he had finished cleaning his boots. He picked something from his wild hair—she worried he might give fleas to her sons' pet white mice—squashed it on his thumbnail, turned his face up to her and obligingly showed his new teeth. She was proud of her dentistry, and hoped it hadn't caused him any pain. So this was how she would proceed: she would ignore Falstaff and Katharine and make him fit her, if she had the power.

She got to work right after supper that night. She dug out both *Henry IV*s and *Henry V*, and the encyclopedia. She looked him up in the indexes of her college Western Civilization textbooks. There was not much to be found out that she didn't know already: two paragraphs in each text and one in the encyclopedia. The *Henry IV*s she ended by skimming: she did not enjoy seeing this boy as a jackanapes. It wasn't constructive. She decided to go to the video store the next day and rent Olivier's *Henry V*, though only in the spirit of scholarly thoroughness. She knew already Olivier would be too elegant for her. So it seemed her ministrations would have to be delicate. In all her imaginings she still couldn't imagine why it was such a man she had come up with. "God knows there have been plenty of things I wanted to change about nearly every man I've known," she confided to Henry as he helped her empty the dishwasher. "And I couldn't fix them either."

Getting ready for bed that night she wondered if it would work to make him the actor from the new *Henry V* movie she had seen recently. She didn't think so, but she decided to give it some consideration. At least the actor, whose name she couldn't remember, could be dressed in a shirt and jeans. Maureen was put off by those studded gloves. So she ran down the stairs with her toothbrush in her mouth, passing her husband on his way up (Kirk didn't seem to see her), swallowing toothpaste. She rummaged through old newspapers until she found an ad for the movie. To her surprise, the actor in the picture bore little resemblance to her Henry V; the blurry newsprint picture was as inscrutable as her Henry's fuzzy face. A fantasy life with an actor wouldn't work anyway, she said to herself as she refolded the paper and stacked it on the recycling pile. Most of them are gay, she had surmised from meeting them when they came to read at the radio station where she worked, also self-centered. And if he weren't gay, who could tell when she might pick up *People* magazine and find pictures of this guy with his gorgeous wife and his cottage in the country and his two unctuous Siamese cats. No, the idea of an actor was too unruly. Though as a medieval warlord he might prove stubborn, Henry, being dead, could at least be pinned down.

Then there was the question of age. His youth was embarrassing to Maureen. But he had died young—it had happened—and here he was now, with her. The enyclopedia didn't say how he had died, and she simply decided she couldn't worry about that for now, nor his studded gloves, nor even his age. She spent a sleepless night and a long day at her office phone, in her car and on her kitchen stool fooling with Henry's clothes, his adolescent grin, his wispy budding beard; and she couldn't do anything about them. Apparently she had to live with him a while before she was sure what she wanted and how much she could do. At least she'd taken care of those teeth. Fuzzy as he looked, he had a hard center and she would have to leave that alone for now. And, need she worry about his age? Why should *she* be embarrasssed? Who would see them and laugh? And after all, princes matured early, didn't they? They had to. This boy had whored with Falstaff, fathered a king, decimated the French army. She spent days trying to figure things out. She kept tripping over Henry in the kitchen and locking him in the garage every night. "Fuck it," one day she said to the whistling kettle, where she was boiling water for tea. She had switched from coffee to tea because it was British. She told Kirk she hadn't been sleeping well and was cutting down on caffeine; when she offered him some tea he made a nauseated face. "Fuck it and 'od's bodkins. It's my fantasy, isn't it? I'll imagine that nothing matters. Maybe I'll change a few things gradually, and then I won't have so much trouble with transitions. Meanwhile this is the king I'm stuck with."

She decided to work on her seduction. She sat on her stool at the kitchen counter with a pot of steamed beets in front of her needing to be peeled and sliced and closed her eyes to begin an outline. She wondered about his underwear. Did he wear any? She thought not, dispatching hastily from behind her closed eyes a picture of him in a chain mail jock strap. She could not think of any appropriate words, so there would be none. They could come later. Leave the wordy wooing to Shakespeare.

First she tried squeezing herself into the nightdress of the newlywed Queen Katharine. Demure and virginal she could muster, but no, in her fantasy she didn't want to be anyone's wife—not even the wife of a boy barbarian. She would have to be Maureen, keeping Kirk, stretch marks, and all.

She got down to details. She tried out a soap-opera type kiss—necks twisting, mouths wide open. It wasn't right for his big canine head, too modern; she felt sodden from it. She tried a continental kiss on the hand. That was wrong too, not Gaelic enough. She kept her eyes closed tightly through an interruption from her son Justin, who reported that indeed his white mice had gotten fleas. She snapped: "Don't be ridiculous, mice don't get fleas. And even if they did, where would they have gotten fleas?" Justin asked why her eyes were closed, she ignored him and after a while he clomped clumsily back down the stairs.

Then she remembered a scene from the movie, and she knew she had her scenario. After the Battle of Agincourt, Henry and his men had carried their dead a long distance across the bloody battlefield, tripping over dead horses, to heap the bodies onto a cart, while singing a requiem. She sketched her scene briefly. She didn't want to prepare too much. She wanted it to happen. She thought at first she would keep her eyes closed, that it would be easier that way. But by the time he had moved across the kitchen and reached for her, she didn't know whether her eyes were open or closed. Her arms flailed and upset the beets. Red steamy juice spilled over the counter and trickled onto the floor. Henry heaved her over his shoulder so that her head and one arm dangled down his back and bounced as he walked. He carried her up the stairs, huffing through his mouth. She couldn't see anything: her hair was in her face. When they entered the bedroom he kicked the door closed and stooped to set her on her feet. She staggered. His cheeks were red, and he breathed heavily into her face. She smelled leeks and vinegar and sank stiffly backward onto the bed.

He towered over her like a hero, his feet planted widely apart. One of the lions on his tunic was almost completely obscured by gray dirt. The others heaved with his breathing. His eyelids fluttered, as if he were about to sink into a trance. Maureen thought for a moment he might faint or disappear, but instead he fumbled under his tunic with his left hand and drew his sword with his right; she was pleased to see he had shed somewhere his studded gauntlets. Maureen clutched a handful of skin on her stomach—loose skin from pregnancies—and wondered if he could kill her.

He brandished the sword three times over his head. She turned her face to the side in fear, saw the orange daisies on the bedspread, heard the swish of the sword in the air. Then he cried, "Once more unto the breech!", threw the sword clanging against the wall and leapt on top of her. She gasped, felt him between her legs. He thrust at her once: "For England!" he yelled painfully into her ear. Twice: "For Harry!" Again: "And for St. George!"

She felt him quiver and go limp. He must be densely built, more muscular than he looked, from jumping onto moving horses. He was absurdly heavy. Her lungs and belly were squashed. Her eyes felt like they would pop soon. She struggled for a breath. He was motionless. She managed to wriggle one of her arms out from under him. She pushed frantically at his shoulder—dead weight. Finally she got hold of the thick shock of hair at his forehead and jerked his head back from her chest. Something cracked in his neck, but she was able to inhale. His face was as limp as the rest of him. His jaw fell open and he drooled a little. "Poor thing. I'm not a horse," she sighed. "We're going back to the drawing board."

So in the weeks that followed Maureen made subtle adjustments. She still wanted to be careful, not do too much; for essentially she was satisfied. Orgasms were simply a matter of mechanics. For all his puppy-dog gracelessness, and despite the deceptive ease she had fixing his teeth, she came to appreciate this man's royal recalcitrance. She had some power. He was hers. But she could not remove the dusty lions from his chest, nor, unless he took them off of his own accord, his spiky gloves. Clearly there was something important—a clumsy, im-

portunate, entitled, colossal swagger—which she could not,
would not, must not mar. She needed this about him. She
needed as well his bumptious vigor, the susceptibility of his
youth. She needed his utter strangeness. She was not at all
sure where his intransigence left off and her needs began.

And sex was not the main thing here, after all. She knew
Henry needed some modernizing. But, she feared that as the
lover of a modern man she wasn't married to, she would have
to be "good in bed," and she had almost no notion of what
that meant. She knew from novels that some women dressed
in bizarre outfits and did stripteases for men to excite them.
Of course that wasn't in bed, exactly. Anyway, if she could
keep Henry in the Middle Ages, she wouldn't have to worry
about being good in bed. She wanted a little more romance
than he'd supplied that first time (she didn't want to be just
a receptacle), but not too much awareness. She didn't want
his expectations moving into the twentieth century.

First she circumcised him ("This won't hurt much more than
the teeth," she promised him with a wavering smile) because
that was what she was used to. Then after a nasty outbreak
of acne around his mouth made it difficult for her to look at
him she firmly aged him a touch. He began to speak in a
language she could never have spoken herself, but which she
understood perfectly, effortlessly. His words were vague like
music, like the sound an ocean makes, simple but arcane,
archaic but neither Shakespearean nor Chaucerian, spiritual
and earthy. He read poetry to her while she cooked.

They liked the same poems. He read Tennyson's "Morte
D'Arthur" over and over to her one night while she stirred
a white sauce which refused to thicken. Each time Bedivere
whipped Excalibur in the air, trying to let it go, she saw Henry
and his sword and the orange daisies on her bedspread. She
trembled, and her whisk sprinkled floury milk all over the
stove; when the mysterious arm rose from the water, "clothed
in white samite, mystic, wonderful," and caught the sword,
she wept again and again.

He was particularly fond of Marvell's "To His Coy Mistress."

While he read it, his beautiful metaphysical voice filled her up, and she stared at the red stain from the beet juice they had spilled that first time. She was hypnotized into an ethereal passion. From Marvell he flipped back a few pages in her anthology of the metaphysical poets and found the Donne poems her English teachers had skipped. She left a roast beef blackening in the oven the day he found this:

> *And yet no greater, but more eminent,*
>   *Love by the spring is growne;*
>   *As, in the firmament,*
> *Starres by the Sunne are not inlarg'd, but showne.*
> *Gentle love deeds, as blossomes on a bough,*
> *From loves awakened root do bud out now.*

She did not count the centuries by which Henry antedated Donne (they had world enough and time). She was only astonished at how long she had yearned for some gentle love deeds. They understood each other perfectly, effortlessly.

She went from day to day flushed and flustered, half aware of the material world. Her friends asked if she had changed her makeup. Her husband wanted to know if she was having hot flashes. Her skin felt tight; she was full as an egg. She saw beautiful people — beautiful men, rather — everywhere. At the coffee shop downstairs from the radio station she sat at the counter between two men so lovely she moved to a table so she could see them better. Henry wasn't with her. The one on the left had a sumptuous beard and burly hands. The other had sad downslanting eyes and a wide mouth like Rudolf Nureyev's. She forgot to drink her tea. She still didn't care much for tea anyway. She kept trying to drink it because Henry liked it. She felt sexy. She felt that, perhaps, if the beautiful men were to turn around, they might look at her too. She had a revelation. She had always assumed that sexy women attracted men. Now it occurred to her that it might be the other way round: that the ones who have plenty of sex look sexy. And she was, after a fashion, experiencing such plenty.

She may even have become, without knowing it, "good in bed." Very likely there wasn't as much to it as she had used to think. And sure enough, she fancied, as she stood at the cash register paying her bill, that bearded man was staring at her. She was afraid to look up; as she walked up the five flights of stairs back to the station (she had decided to try to lose a few pounds), she was sure she did look different, having reacted to Henry's lustful gaze like a plant to the sun.

She felt sexy even around her husband. She wore sweaters she'd kept since before the boys were born (they fit tightly now) and lipstick. When Henry was not around, she sat beside Kirk on the couch during the TV news and let her shoulder graze his. She laid her hand on his thigh; once she kissed him good night with her mouth wet and open, then (abandoning memory) shoved her face behind his ear and breathed: "What could I do to turn you on?" He neither moved nor spoke. She drew back to look at his face. He was frankly considering.

"Leave me alone maybe," he said at length, not unkindly. "You're scaring me."

After that, she left him alone, and he seemed to want to pick a fight with her. He complained that she wasn't paying attention to anything. When she served him and the boys a supper of peas, broccoli, coleslaw and warm milk, Kirk gagged and beat his fists on the table. He went in his underwear to the dryer to get his sweatpants and reported angrily to Maureen that he had found the dryer running hot but empty. His sweatpants were still wet in the washer. They went to watch their sons play basketball at the high school one evening, and he squirmed through a conversation Maureen began with the coach's wife about the beauty of the young boys' bodies, and how she preferred basketball to football because the uniforms showed them off so much better.

"You don't make sense anymore. The lights are on but nobody's home," Kirk said to her in the car on the way home.

She smiled and languidly apologized.

"The elevator doesn't go to the top floor."

She was driving. She had come recently to the conclusion

that she liked to drive. Henry found the certainty with which
she moved the stick shift arousing.

"You don't have all the little dots on your dice. Where did
you get that watch?"

"What watch?"

"What watch?" he yelled back at her. "This watch." He
snatched her right arm from the steering wheel and waved it
in the air between them. Maureen's hand flopped loosely from
the wrist. "This expensive-looking watch here with all the shiny
jewels on it."

She turned into their street, using one arm. He held onto
the other one. "I bought it for myself. I've always wanted a
nice watch." She glanced at him. His nose was moving up
and down as if it itched, but he didn't scratch it. He let her
arm go so she could downshift to enter the driveway. "You
can check the VISA bill," she added.

She called the boy-king Hal now. He still wore his gloves
and his high leather boots with the steel-armored toes, but
the noisy sword and scabbard had disappeared, his tunic was
cleaner, and his face was changing. It occurred to Maureen
that the scantly shrinking ears and lengthening jaw were sug-
gestive of a boy she had had a crush on in high school, but
she couldn't remember what that boy had looked like. She
wasn't too sure what anyone looked like anymore, except
Henry, and even he could be capriciously unstable and, at
times, still fuzzy around the edges.

He sat silently in the shadowy kitchen one evening while
Maureen and Iris Millikin stuffed invitations for the PTA auc-
tion into envelopes. Cicadas had begun that week to appear.
One had chased Maureen to the car that morning, flying upside
down. Iris and she worked in the dining room. Maureen
couldn't see Hal, but she could feel him there in the next
room, breathing, listening to her talk about her job and her
car and her teenagers, waiting for her. Iris asked about the
new watch.

"I hadn't realized it was so conspicuous," said Maureen.
"Several people have asked me about it."

"My God, Maureen, it's the flashiest watch I've ever seen. It's dripping with stones. Are they real?"

Maureen nodded, blushing. "My lover gave it to me." Iris looked slowly up from the invitation she was folding. Maureen giggled. She hadn't told anyone else. She didn't know Iris well enough for large confidences, but now she'd begun. Hal stirred in the next room; his steel toe clanged against a chair. Maureen hoped she hadn't disturbed him by telling.

Iris gaped. Maureen continued talking, deciding as she talked that talking was good: a verification.

"It's the best thing that's ever happened to me. We understand each other perfectly, effortlessly. We read poetry together. He talks to me while I cook. When he reads Tennyson the room shakes, he has such a voice. And I read aloud too, and when I'm with him my voice isn't a bit nasal."

"Shhhh!" urged Iris, tipping her head toward the living room. "Kirk is right in there."

"The TV is too loud. He can't hear anything."

Iris's face shed some shock and turned eager. "Is it anyone I know?"

"I don't think so. You may have heard of him, but I'm not going to say his name. Look." Maureen unclasped her watch and handed it to Iris.

"You mean he's famous?" Iris took the watch and reverently inspected it. "It's perfectly gorgeous. Do you wear it all the time? Hasn't Kirk seen it?"

"I told him I bought it for myself. Look at the inscription."

Lightly etched in florid italic behind the face was "Had we but world enough and time. . ."

"Oh my God," Iris groaned, as if with pain or longing. She returned the watch to Maureen. They were quiet while they finished the envelopes, except that every few minutes Iris looked at Maureen, shook her head and sighed.

Iris left by the back door. She had pulled her car into the driveway. Maureen went outside with her to help her load the boxes of envelopes into the trunk. Several cicadas clacked in the hawthorn tree by the garage. Lifting the top box off Iris's

stack, Maureen whispered, "His skin is fiery to the touch."
Iris let the remaining two boxes slide, and stuffed envelopes
splattered onto the driveway.

He never, after that first time, carried her up the stairs.
Rather, he waited for her to go up ahead of him. She knew,
though she didn't look back, that he liked to watch her
haunches shift and flex beneath her clothes, lifting her weight
deftly. She stopped wearing underwear, and she rolled up the
stairs on the balls of her feet, her torso listing easily forward.
She had never felt so lithe. She could see, though she didn't
look back, his face as he watched her, interested merely at
first, then lit by joy and a certain youthful astonishment. She
heard his naive, grateful breathing at the foot of the stairs.

Soon he would follow her. She would wait for him in bed
with a book open, her husband sleeping beside her. He would
enter the room naked. He was covered with down: hair light
and soft as corn silk, invisible in the daytime. But in the light
from the bedside lamp it shimmered around him. His face
and forearms glowed. "You look like an angel," she would
whisper, and she would move quietly and lift the comforter
to let him into bed beside her. "An archangel."

Late one night she sat in the kitchen with the lights off,
and there came the familiar thunking clamor up the basement
stairs. Her eyes popped open so suddenly she almost fell off
her stool; and she braced herself for a niggling barrage from
one of the boys: a shirt needed ironing, a book needed buying,
a failed summer-school test needed signing. She turned an
irritated face toward the head of the stairway, and Kirk
emerged. He had been working on the monthly bills downstairs at the family-room desk. He carried a creased piece of
paper, which he slammed onto the counter in front of her,
covering the beet stain. It was the VISA bill.

"I've had it." He swung his arm at the light switch, missed,
aimed again, swung furiously as if he were trying to kill a bat.
Fluorescence flickered, flashed, then illuminated the room.
Maureen blinked. Hal stood up from his chair by the table
and vanished.

Kirk's voice became quiet, and his face came close to Maureen's. His lips moved with a frightening elasticity. "You sit in the dark and talk nonsense." His mouth stretched toward his ears. Maureen flinched. "You, I used to know, I can't talk to you. You spend two thousand dollars on a watch when you already have a watch." He turned away from her. He sobbed once. His shirt was damp between the shoulder blades. "I wish someone else had bought it for you." He spoke normally now, as if after one sob he felt better. "I think you should see a doctor."

"Never," she said with equanimity. She guessed she would have something interesting to talk about to one now, but a doctor would surely kill Hal, expertly and without remorse.

She slid the VISA bill aside so she could see the red stain on the wood counter. It had soaked into the grain and gone brown. It could have been anything now: grape juice, mildew, a scorch from a hot saucepan, blood.

"I think you'd better get your brain in gear. Shape up. The next time you wreck the car the kids are likely to be with you. Really. Straighten up and fly right."

"Kirk, I wouldn't exactly call it a wreck."

"What would you call it?"

"A ding. Somebody sideswiped me in the grocery store lot. I wasn't even there. It wasn't my fault. I was parked just fine."

"I don't even know what you're talking about. So what else is new?" He flung his arms over his head hopelessly. "I'm talking about running into the light pole!"

"Oh, that." Maureen had forgotten. At work she had backed out of her parking place the week before. . . into a pole, crunching in the trunk of the car. Hal had been with her. He had laughed at the dismayed look on her face and at the way the damaged car looked—like a big blue duck, he said, with its turned-up tail.

Kirk got quiet again. "What's wrong with you?" he asked.

She saw the familiar mole on his forehead and a wet dab on his mustache—a tear? Something thick rose in her throat. "I want you to laugh when I bang in the car. I want you to understand me; and when you don't, I don't want to be told I'm crazy. I want to be told I'm mysterious."

Kirk pushed out his lower lip and blew a long breath upward, as if he were trying to dry the tear from his mustache. "Well, don't look at me," he said, leaving the room. "I'm telling you you're a pain in the ass."

She was sorry to have made Kirk angry; she didn't like to fight with him. But it gave her satisfaction to have expressed her simple desires in a straightforward manner. If they made him angry, she couldn't help it.

Meanwhile, her days with Hal went happily along. Some days Hal came to work with her. It was early summer, and together they took long walks through the neighborhood to see the trees sprouting new leaves. It had been a dryish spring — no storms to rattle the foliage — so the flowering shrubbery kept blooming through June. They had to push heavy lilac boughs from their faces as they walked the sidewalks. Hal kept pace beside her in his ambling, arm-swinging way. He walked unlike other men she knew, like someone who had never carried a briefcase. His own favorite was a pair of ornamental crab apples in a yard a few blocks from Maureen's house. Maureen did not know who lived there, but Hal admired the little pink trees so much that one evening they sat down under them and watched the dusk and listened to the neighborhood dogs start barking at each other until Maureen glanced at the house and saw one of the front room curtains jerk open and someone look out. They got up and moved lazily down the street, the length of their forearms touching.

At home, she heard his steel toes lightly clicking on the floors even when he was not visible. The sound reminded her of a time years before when one of her sons had decided to be a tap dancer. She had signed him up for lessons, bought him tap shoes; and for the next two months, until his interest waned, instead of walking he had inelegantly tapped everywhere, especially favoring the tiled bathroom floor. The clattering, the silvery marks throughout the house, and the danger of broken tiles had annoyed Kirk to no end; but Maureen was

sure she remembered enjoying those noisy days, even before
Hal's echoings highlighted their preciousness.

Hal usually came to the grocery store with her these days,
and her mind was more on him than on food. They were
playful and happy there. It was a hallowed place for them,
because they had met there. Weekly they bought pounds of
leeks. Maureen giggled and blushed whenever they came to
the cucumbers, and made the same joke each time: "One
still has to buy cucumbers, doesn't one?" And each time Hal
laughed. She danced to the jazz on the piped-in radio. She
dropped things: they seemed to turn slimy and slip through
her fingers. Often she came home with bruised apples and
melons preposterously squashed. Her boys insisted she should
switch grocery stores: the fruit was no good anymore at this
one. Once, during a discussion of warhorses and their saddles,
she dropped a stack of five chicken pot pies on the way from
the freezer to her cart; and the grocer helped her pick them
up and gave her five new ones, because the pastry might be
broken. Rather oversolicitously, Maureen thought, he helped
her unload at the register. "I think he thinks I'm palsied or
dim-witted," she confided later to Hal.

Maureen was as unprepared for Hal's death as she had been
for his arrival. The encyclopedia didn't say how it happened,
nor did Shakespeare, who left him gaily wooing in one play
and took up the next at his funeral. Kirk was out of town at
the time, at a convention of public-works executives. The last
cicada had attacked that day. It had veered at her drunkenly
from behind the back door as she was returning from dropping
the boys at baseball practice. She had ducked and closed her
eyes so she wouldn't see its fierce, red-eyed foolish face; and
when she made it panting into the house, she went straight
upstairs to get a sweater. She was cold, whether from a chill
in the air, fear of the cicada, or from a premonition of sorrow
she didn't know. She entered the bedroom and headed for
the dresser, but stopped short at the sight of a figure sitting
on her bed. She thought at first it was Hal, but only for a

second. It was a squat, menacing man, she saw, when he rose
noisily to stand, fully armored. Its arms splayed out far from
its sides because of the bulk of metal in its armpits; it could
not bring its legs very close together either, so it teetered as
it rose, then stood by Maureen's bed as if astride a short,
invisible horse. It was Hal's uncle, the Earl of Exeter. She
recognized him from the movie. He looked a little like an
actor she had seen once or twice on Masterpiece Theatre. She
had wondered, watching the movie, why, since this fellow
was apparently the only Briton who could afford a proper suit
of armor, he hadn't at least bought one for his nephew the
king, who went to battle in that flimsy padded tunic covered
with dirty lions. Immediately, before he even spoke, she felt
resentment toward her visitor. She decided she would take
up with him the questions of armor, stinginess and the value
of the king's body once they had introduced themselves. But
after a creaky bow and before she had a chance to open her
mouth, Exeter launched into a speech:

> *We mourn in black: why mourn we not in blood?*
> *Henry is dead, and never shall revive:*
> *Upon a wooden coffin we attend;*
> *And Death's dishonourable victory*
> *We with our stately presence glorify,*
> *Like captives bound to a triumphant car.*
> *What! shall we curse the planets of mishap*
> *That plotted thus our glory's overthrow?*
> *Or shall we think the subtle-witted French*
> *Conjurers and sorcerers, that, afraid of him*
> *By magic verses have contriv'd his end?*

Without a pause he clanged out of the bedroom and was
gone.

It took Maureen some while to digest his meaning. When
she understood that Hal was dead, she lay down on her bed
like an effigy, with her hands folded across her belly. She had
cramps. She knew the French had nothing to do with her

king's death: it was the planets of mishap. She knew she had
to construct a proper death. It would be good for her, something to occupy her mind. Illness was inappropriate — too un-
dramatic. He had to die in battle or be hit by a bus. She
settled upon battle. She rose, in pain, to do her little research,
then lay back down, grateful after all for the insubstantialities
of Exeter's and the encyclopedia's accounts. How nice that she
would be allowed to give Hal the sort of glorious passage to
Valhalla he would enjoy. She devised a wound, but not too
bloody a one, and nothing that would mark his ruddy young
face. She'd given birth to him without pain, and she wanted
to give him as little as possible in return when she killed him.
An arrow in the shoulder would be good, like cowboys used
to get in the movies, but more serious. As he expired in the
arms of a weeping foot soldier, he spoke of her, and gave
the soldier one of his muddy studded gloves to take to her.
Somehow it got lost later. Hordes of haggard warriors massed
round him, heads bowed, and hummed a requiem as he expired. Ravens the size of large cats tipped the branches of a
nearby oak. His horse stood over him until the last breath
(sweet pungent breath), then whinnied, reared, whirled, and
galloped away into the hills.

Maybe she had known since the parking lot, when she had
decided not to run him over with her car, that eventually she
would have to kill him. There was no avoiding the treacherous
ambiguities of their affair. (It had occurred to her, before he
had spoken, that Exeter had come to accuse her of incest and
haul her to the Tower, where she would melt into a retroactive
footnote.) She planned to choke back the feeling that she was
guilty of murder: some more or less scandalous end had been
inevitable.

After she had arranged the death, Maureen turned to her
grief. She cried every night for two weeks in the kitchen. Two
of her sons' white mice died the day after Hal did, electrocuted
by a naked wire behind the basement refrigerator where they
had fled when Maureen left the cage door ajar after feeding
them. The boys assumed, when she served them supper sob-

bing, that she was wracked with guilt because of her absent-
mindedness. Kirk stayed out of town for a week and a half and
when he returned he tried not to see her mourning. Perhaps he
accepted, by default, the mouse explanation from the boys.
He talked to her a little about his convention, about people
he had run into that she knew. "It's nice of you to talk to
me," she warbled, licking tears from her upper lip.

When she finally stopped crying, she still had her memories.
She remembered Hal's untameable hair. She re-created his
renderings of Keats, rifling through her messy library till she
found the lines from *Endymion*—

Why, I have been a butterfly, a lord
Of flowers, garlands, love-knots, silly posies,
Groves, meadows, melodies, and arbour roses

—and she remembered, without exactly locating it, ". . .
the spirit is beside thee whom thou seekest . . ." Keats had
been one of their joint favorites; *Endymion* took on new pro-
portions for her now—the story of a boy dreaming of loving
the moon—though she could not make the poetry sound like
Hal had. She remembered his lathery laughing mouth when
she had taught him how to brush his gleaming new teeth.
She remembered his acne, his habit of fiddling with his right
earlobe, and the way he liked to chomp his leeks raw and
unclean.

Her grief achieved now a certain calm, but these scattered
recollections were not quite satisfying; so she stayed home
from work one day and relived everything from beginning to
end—from cucumbers to Exeter, through beet juice to the
blood of the roast beef, which she saw now as allied omens
of startings and finishings. She stayed awake that night and
was done by the next afternoon. She moved fast, but never
got tired. It was recreation. The wild hair on his large head
was not as real as it could be. This murder turned out to be
the best thing she had made. Memory was memory, after all:
who could doubt it? Not even Kirk, nor Iris. She was now a

bona fide widow, as deserving of her sadness as any woman who had lost a lover or husband, because what she had now was as real as what any of them had. She was queen of England and France, and still alive to boot, unlike the poor widow Katharine, who hadn't even any brain scraps left to play among.

Yahoos

The following names are those of members of the U.S. House of Representatives who recently voted for the Stearns amendment, which in essence intends to abolish government aid to the arts. It would seem quite appropriate to offer this list (indeed it may be the funniest contribution in the issue) in a number devoted to humor . . . since jokers, fools, buffoons, yahoos have traditionally been figures featured in the various modes of comedy, usually low.

Wayne Allard (R-CO)
Bill Archer (R-TX)
Richard K. Armey (R-TX)
Bill Baker (R-CA)
Bob Barr (R-GA)
R. G. Bartlett (R-MD)
Joe Barton (R-TX)
H. H. Bateman
   (R-VA)
M. Bilirakis (R-FL)
J. A. Boehner (R-OH)
Henry Bonilla (R-TX)
Sonny Bono (R-CA)
Bill K. Brewster (D-OK)
Glen Browder (D-AL)
Ed Bryant (R-TN)
Jim Bunning (R-KY)
Dan Burton (R-IN)
Stephen E. Buyer (R-IN)
S. Callahan (R-AL)
Ken Calvert (R-CA)
Dave Camp (R-MI)
Charles Canady (R-FL)
Steven Chabot (R-OH)
S. Chambliss (R-GA)

Jim Chapman (D-TX)
Helen Chenoweth (R-ID)
Jon Christensen (R-NE)
Dick Chrysler (R-MI)
Bob Clement (D-TN)
Howard Coble (R-NC)
Tom Coburn (R-OK)
Michael Collins (R-GA)
Larry Combest (R-TX)
Wes Cooley (R-OR)
C. Cox (R-CA)
Robert Cramer
   (D-AL)
Philip Crane (R-IL)
Michael Crapo (R-ID)
Frank Cremeans (R-OH)
Barbara Cubin (R-WY)
Randy Cunningham
   (R-CA)
Nathan Deal (R-GA)
Tom DeLay (R-TX)
Lincoln Diaz-Balart
   (R-FL)
Jay Dickey (R-AK)
John Doolittle (R-CA)

Robert Dornan (R-CA)
David Dreier (R-CA)
John J. Duncan (R-TN)
Robert L. Ehrlich, Jr.
   (R-MD)
Bill Emerson (R-MO)
John Ensign (R-NV)
Terry Everett (R-AL)
Thomas W. Ewing (R-IL)
Jack M. Fields (R-TX)
Gary Franks (R-CT)
Dan Frisa (R-NY)
David Funderburk (R-NC)
Elton Gallegly (R-CA)
Greg Ganske (R-IA)
George Gekas (R-PA)
Peter Geren (D-TX)
Bob Goodlatte (R-VA)
Bart Gordon (D-TN)
Porter J. Goss (R-FL)
Lindsey Graham (R-SC)
Gil Gutknecht (IR-MN)
Ralph M. Hall (D-TX)
Mel Hancock (R-MO)
D. Hastert (R-IL)

Richard Hastings (R-WA)

James A. Hayes (D-LA)

J. Hayworth (R-AZ)

Joel Hefley (R-CO)

Frederick Heineman (R-NC)

W. Herger (R-CA)

Van Hilleary (R-TN)

D. Hobson (R-TN)

J. Hostettler (R-IN)

Duncan Hunter (R-CA)

Y. T. Hutchinson (R-AR)

Henry Hyde (R-IL)

Bob Inglis (R-SC)

Ernest Istook (R-OK)

Sam Johnson (R-TX)

John Kasich (R-OH)

Jay Kim (R-CA)

Peter King (R-NY)

Jack Kingston (R-GA)

Scott Klug (R-WI)

Steve Largent (R-OK)

Tom Latham (R-IA)

Greg Laughlin (D-TX)

Ron Lewis (R-KY)

Jim Lightfoot (R-IA)

John Linder (R-GA)

Frank Lucas (R-OK)

Donald Manzullo (R-IL)

Bill McCollum (R-FL)

Jim McCrery (R-LA)

John McHugh (R-NY)

David McIntosh (R-IN)

Howard McKeon (R-CA)

Jack Metcalf (R-WA)

John Mica (R-FL)

Dan Miller (R-FL)

Susan Molinari (R-NY)

G. Montgomery (D-MS)

Carlos Moorhead (R-CA)

John Myers (R-IN)

Sue Myrick (R-NC)

George Nethercutt (R-WA)

Mark Neumann (R-WI)

Bob Ney (R-OH)

Charles W. Norwood, Jr. (R-GA)

Jim Nussle (R-IA)

Solomon Ortiz (D-TX)

William Orton (D-UT)

Michael Oxley (R-OH)

Ron Packard (R-CA)

Mike Parker (D-MS)

Bill Paxon (R-NY)

Thomas Petri (R-WI)

Richard Pombo (R-CA)

John Porter (R-IL)

Rob Portman (R-OH)

Deborah Pryce (R-OH)

James Quillen (R-TN)

George Radanovich (R-CA)

Frank Riggs (R-CA)

Pat Roberts (R-KS)

Harold Rogers (R-KY)

Dana Rohrabacher (R-CA)

I. Ros-Lehtinen (R-FL)

Charlie Rose (D-NC)

Toby Roth (R-WI)

Edward Royce (R-CA)

Matt Salmon (R-AZ)

Marshall Sanford, Jr. (R-SC)

H. J. Saxton (R-NJ)

J. Scarborough (R-FL)

Dan Schaefer (R-CO)

Andrea H. Seastrand (R-CA)

F. James Sensenbrenner, Jr. (R-WI)

John Shadegg (R-AZ)

Christopher Shays (R-CT)

E. G. Shuster (R-PA)

Ike Skelton (D-MO)

Nick Smith (R-MI)

Christopher H. Smith (R-NJ)

Lamar S. Smith (R-TX)

Linda Smith (R-WA)

Gerald B. H. Solomon (R-NY)

Mark Souder (R-IN)

Floyd D. Spence (R-SC)

Cliff Stearns (R-FL)

Charles W. Stenholm (D-TX)

Steve Stockman (R-TX)

Bob Stump (R-AZ)

James Talent (R-MO)

John Tanner (D-TN)

Randy Tate (R-WA)

W. J. Tauzin (D-LA)

Charles H. Taylor (R-NC)

Mac Thornberry (R-TX)

Todd Tiahrt (R-KS)

James A. Traficant, Jr. (D-OH)

Barbara F. Vucanovich (R-NV)

Robert S. Walker (R-PA)

Zach Wamp (R-TN)

J. C. Watts, Jr. (R-OK)

David J. Weldon (R-FL)

Jerry Weller (R-IL)

Roger F. Wicker (R-MS)

C. W. Young (R-FL)

Don Young (R-AK)

Dick Zimmer (R-NJ)

DJ

A manuscript page from a recent script by Woody Allen.

Woody Allen

The Art of Humor I

*As New Yorkers know, Woody Allen is one of its more
ubiquitous citizens — at courtside in Madison Square Garden
watching the Knicks, at Michael's Pub on Monday evenings*

playing the clarinet, on occasion at Elaine's Restaurant at his usual table. Yet he could hardly be considered outgoing: shy on acquaintance, he once expressed an intense desire to return to the womb — "anybody's." In fact, his career is one of prodigious effort in a number of disciplines — literature, the theater and motion pictures. "I'm a compulsive worker," he once said. "What I really like to do best is whatever I'm not doing at the moment."

Allen's career in comedy began as a teenager when he submitted jokes to an advertising firm. In 1953, after what he called a "brief abortive year in college," he left school to become a gag-writer for Garry Moore and Sid Caesar. In the early 1960s, his stand-up routines in the comedy clubs of Greenwich Village gained him considerable recognition, and eventually several television appearances. In 1965, shortly after he produced three successful comedy records, Allen made his debut as an actor and screenwriter in What's New, Pussycat? *His 1969 film,* Take the Money and Run, *was the first project that he not only wrote and starred in, but directed as well. Though many of his early films (*Bananas, Sleeper, Love and Death*) were critically acclaimed, it wasn't until 1977 and the release of* Annie Hall, *which won four Academy Awards, that Allen was recognized as an extraordinary force in the American cinema. Fifteen of his motion pictures have appeared since, which works out at almost a movie a year. He has also written several Broadway plays, the most successful of them,* Don't Drink the Water *and* Play It Again, Sam, *also were made into films.*

Allen has written three collections of short pieces, many of which first appeared in The New Yorker: Getting Even, Without Feathers, *and* Side Effects.

The major portion of this interview, much of it conducted by Michiko Kakutani over dinner at Elaine's Restaurant, was completed in 1985. Since then, the editors — by correspondence and conversations with Mr. Allen over the phone — have brought it up to date.

— A.B.

INTERVIEWER

Do you think the humorist tends to look at the world in a slightly different way?

WOODY ALLEN

Yes. I think if you have a comic perspective, almost anything that happens you tend to put through a comic filter. It's a way of coping in the short term, but has no long term effect and requires constant, endless renewal. Hence people talk of comics who are "always on." It's like constantly drugging your sensibility so you can get by with less pain.

INTERVIEWER

That's very unique, don't you think?

ALLEN

It's one way of dealing with life. People think it's very hard to be funny but it's an interesting thing. If you can do it, it's not hard at all. It would be like if I said to somebody who can draw very well, "My God, I could take a pencil and paper all day long and never be able to draw that horse. I can't do it, and you've done it so perfectly." And the other person feels, "This is nothing. I've been doing this since I was four years old." That's how you feel about comedy: if you can do it, you know, it's really nothing. It's not that the end product is nothing, but the process is simple. Of course, there are just some people that are authentically funny, and some people that are not. It's a freak of nature.

INTERVIEWER

Who were the writers who made you first want to write?

ALLEN

I remember the first person I ever laughed at while reading was Max Shulman. I was fifteen. I have a couple of old books of his. The one that I found the funniest was *The Zebra Derby* . . . funny in a broad sort of way, though you have to appreciate the context within which it's written, since it's about veterans

returning here after World War II, returning to the land of
promise. Then I discovered Robert Benchley and S. J. Perelman, two other very funny writers who were truly great masters. I met Perelman at Elaine's restaurant one night. I came
in with Marshall Brickman, and a waiter came over and gave
me a card. On the back it said something like, "Would love
you to come over and join me for a celery tonic." I figured,
"Oh it's some out-of-town tourist," and I threw the card away.
About an hour and a half later, someone said, "You know,
it's from S.J. Perelman," so I retrieved the card from the floor.
It said "S.J. Perelman," and I raced around to where he was
sitting around the corner and we joined him. I'd met him
before and to me he was always warm and friendly. I've read
he could be difficult, but I never saw that side of him.

INTERVIEWER

When did you start writing?

ALLEN

Before I could read. I'd always wanted to write. Before
that—I made up tales. I was always creating stories for class.
For the most part, I was never as much a fan of comic writers
as serious writers. But I found myself able to write in a comic
mode, at first directly imitative of Shulman or sometimes of
Perelman. In my brief abortive year in college I'd hand in my
papers, all of them written in a bad (or good) derivation of
Shulman. I had no sense of myself at all.

INTERVIEWER

How did you discover your own voice? Did it happen gradually?

ALLEN

No, it was quite accidental. I had given up writing prose
completely and gone into television writing. I wanted to write
for the theater, and at the same time I was doing a cabaret
act as a comedian. One day, *Playboy* magazine asked me to
write something for them, because I was an emerging come-

dian, and I wrote this piece on chess. At that time, I was almost married — but not quite yet — to Louise Lasser; she read it and said, "Gee, I think this is good. You should really send this over to *The New Yorker*." To me, as to everyone else of my generation, *The New Yorker* was hallowed ground. Anyhow, on a lark I did. I was shocked when I got this phone call back saying that if I'd make a few changes, they'd print it. So I went over there and made the few changes, and they ran it. It was a big boost to my confidence. So I figured, "Well, I think I'll write something else for them." The second or third thing I sent to *The New Yorker* was very Perelmanesque in style. They printed it, but comments were that it was dangerously derivative, and I agreed. So both *The New Yorker* and I looked out for that in subsequent pieces that I sent over there. I did finally get further and further away from him. Perelman, of course, was as complex as could be — a very rich kind of humor. As I went on I tried to simplify.

INTERVIEWER

Was this a parallel development to what you were trying to do in your films?

ALLEN

I don't think of them as parallel. My experience has been that writing for the different mediums are very separate undertakings. Writing for the stage is completely different from writing for film, and both are completely different from writing prose. The most demanding is writing prose, I think, because when you're finished, it's the end product. You can't change it. In a play, it's far from the end product. The script serves as a vehicle for the actors and director to develop characters. With films, I just scribble a couple of notes for a scene. You don't have to do any writing at all, you just have your notes for the scene, which are written with the actors and the camera in mind. The actual script is a necessity for casting and budgeting, but the end product often doesn't bear much resemblance to the script — at least in my case.

So you would have much more control over something like
a novel.

That's one of its appeals—that you have the control over
it. Another great appeal is that when you're finished you can
tear it up and throw it away. Whereas, when you make a
movie, you can't do that. You have to put it out there even
if you don't like it. I might add, the hours are better if you're
a prose writer. It's much more fun to wake up in the morning,
just drift into the next room and be alone and write than it
is to wake up in the morning and have to go shoot a film.
Movies are a big demand. It's a physical job. You've got to
be someplace, on schedule, on time. And you are dependent
on people. I know Norman Mailer said that if he had started
his career today he might be in film rather than a novelist. I
think films are a younger man's enterprise. For the most part
it's strenuous. Beyond a certain point, I don't think I want
that exertion; I mean I don't want to feel that my whole life
I'm going to have to wake up at six in the morning, be out
of the house at seven so I can be out on some freezing street
or some dull meadow shooting. That's not all that thrilling.
It's fun to putter around the house, stay home. Tennessee
Williams said the annoying thing about plays is that you have
to produce them—you can't just write them and throw them
in the drawer. That's because when you finish writing a script,
you've transcended it and you want to move on. With a book,
you can. So the impulse seems always to be a novelist. It's a
very desirable thing. One thinks about Colette sitting in her
Parisian apartment, looking out the window and writing. It's
a very seductive life. Actually, I wrote a first draft of a novel
in Paris when I was doing *Love and Death*. I have it at home,
all handwritten, lying in my drawer on graph paper—I've had
it that way for years. I've sort of been saving it for when I'm
energyless and not able to film anymore. I don't want to do
it while I still have enough vigor to get out there early in the
morning and film. It's a good thing to look forward to a novel.

I know one day they'll either pull the plug on me for filming and say, "We don't want you to do this anymore," or I'll get tired of doing it. I hope the novel's all right. I mean, it's no great shakes, but it's a novel, a story that could only be told that way. I've thought at times of taking the idea and making it into a play or a film, but oddly it doesn't work that way. If it works at all, it's a novel. It happens in the prose.

INTERVIEWER
How did this novel come about? Had you thought about doing it for a long time?

ALLEN
Not really. I started on page one. It's an old habit from writing for the stage. I can't conceive of writing the third act before the first, or a fragment of the second act out of order. The events that occur later—the interaction between characters, the development of the plot—are so dependent on the action that takes place in the beginning. I can't conceive of doing it out of sequence. I love the classic narrative form in a play. I love it in the novel. I don't enjoy novels that aren't basically clear stories. To sit down with Balzac or Tolstoy is, in addition to all else, great entertainment. With a play, when the curtain goes up and people are in garbage cans, I know I may admire the idea cerebrally, but it won't mean as much to me. I've seen Beckett, along with many lesser avant-gardists, and many contemporary plays, and I can say yes, that's clever and deep but I don't really care. But when I watch Chekhov or O'Neill—where it's men and women in human, classic crises—that I like. I know that it's very unfashionable to say at this time, but things based, for example, on "language"—the clever rhythms of speech—I really don't care for. I want to hear people speaking plainly if at times poetically. When you see *Death of a Salesman* or *A Streetcar Named Desire* you're interested in the people and you want to see what happens next. When I had an idea for the play I wrote for Lincoln Center—*The Floating Lightbulb*— I was determined that I was going to write about regular people in a simple situation.

I deliberately tried to avoid anything more elaborate than that.
In film, oddly enough, I don't feel as much that way. I'm more
amenable in film to distortions of time and abstractions.

A lot of writers find it very hard to get started on the next
project, to find an idea they really want to work on . . .

Probably they are casting aside ideas that are as good as the
ideas I choose to work on. I'll think of an idea walking down
the street, and I'll mark it down immediately. And I always
want to make it into something. I've never had a block. I'm
talking within the limits of my abilities. But in my own small
way, I've had an embarrassment of riches. I'll have five ideas
and I'm dying to do them all. It takes weeks or months where
I agonize and obsess over which to do next. I wish sometimes
someone would choose for me. If someone said, "Do idea
number three next," that would be fine. But I have never had
any sense of running dry. People always ask me, "Do you ever
think you'll wake up one morning and not be funny?" That
thought would never occur to me—it's an odd thought, and
not realistic. Because funny and me are not separate. We're
one. The best time to me is when I'm through with a project
and deciding about a new one. That's because it's at a period
when reality has not yet set in. The idea in your mind's eye
is so wonderful, and you fantasize it in the perfect flash of a
second—just beautifully conceived. But then when you have
to execute it, it doesn't come out as you'd fantasized. Produc-
tion is where the problems begin, where reality starts to set
in. As I was saying before, the closest I ever come to realizing
the concept is in prose. Most of the things that I've written
and published, I've felt that I executed my original idea pretty
much to my satisfaction. But I've never, ever felt that, not
even close, about anything I've written for film or the stage.
I always felt I had such a dazzling idea—where did I go wrong?
You go wrong from the first day. Everything's a compromise.
For instance, you're not going to get Marlon Brando to do

your script, you're going to get someone lesser. The room you see in your mind's eye is not the room you're filming in. It's always a question of high aims, grandiose dreams, great bravado and confidence, and great courage at the typewriter; and then, when I'm in the midst of finishing a picture and everything's gone horribly wrong and I've reedited it and reshot it and tried to fix it, then it's merely a struggle for survival. You're happy only to be alive. Gone are all the exalted goals and aims, all the uncompromising notions of a perfect work of art, and you're just fighting so people won't storm up the aisles with tar and feathers. With many of my films—almost all—if I'd been able to get on screen what I conceived, they would have been much better pictures. Fortunately, the public doesn't know about how great the picture played in my head was, so I get away with it.

INTERVIEWER

How do you actually work? What are your tools?

ALLEN

I've written on legal pads, hotel stationery, anything I can get my hands on. I have no finickiness about anything like that. I write in hotel rooms, in my house, with other people around, on matchbooks. I have no problems with it—to the meager limits that I can do it. There have been stories where I've just sat down at the typewriter and typed straight through beginning to end. There are some *New Yorker* pieces I've written out in forty minutes time. And there are other things I've just struggled and agonized over for weeks and weeks. It's very haphazard. Take two movies: one movie that was not critically successful was *A Midsummer Night's Sex Comedy*. I wrote that thing in no time. It just came out in six days— everything in perfect shape. I did it, and it was not well received. Whereas *Annie Hall* was just endless—totally changing things. There was as much material on the cutting-room floor as there was in the picture—I went back five times to reshoot. And it was well received. On the other hand, the exact opposite has happened to me where I've done things that just flowed easily and were very well received. And things I agonized over were not. I've found no correlation at all. But, if you can do it, it's not really very hard . . . nor is it as tremendous an achievement as one who can't do it thinks. For instance, when I was sixteen years old I got my first job. It was as a comedy writer for an advertising agency in New York. I would come into this advertising agency every single day after school and I would write jokes for them. They would attribute these jokes to their clients and put them in the newspaper columns. I would get on the subway, the train quite crowded, and strap-hanging, I'd take out a pencil, and by the time I'd gotten out, I'd have written forty or fifty jokes . . . fifty jokes a day for years. People would say to me, "I don't believe it—fifty jokes a day, and writing them on the *train*." Believe me, it was no big deal. Whereas I'll look at someone who can compose a piece of music—I don't know how they ever begin or end or what! But because I could always write, it was nothing. I could always do it—within my limitations. So it was never hard. I think if I'd had a better education, a better upbringing, and perhaps had a different kind of personality, I might have been an important writer. It's possible, because I think I have some talent, but never had the interest in it. I grew up without an interest in anything scholarly. I could write, but I had no interest in reading. I only played and watched sports, read comic books; I never read a real novel until I was college age. Just had no interest in it at all. Perhaps if I'd had a different upbringing, I might have gone off in a different direction. Or if the interests of my parents, my friends, and the environment in which I was raised had been more directed towards things I was later responsive to, maybe things would have been different. Maybe I would have been a serious novelist. Or maybe not. But it's too late, and now I'm just happy I don't have arthritis.

INTERVIEWER

Can you remember one of the jokes you wrote hanging on a subway strap?

ALLEN

This was typical of the junk I turned out: "Kid next to me
in school was the son of a gambler—he'd never take his test
marks back—he'd let 'em ride on the next test." Now you see
why it wasn't hard to do fifty a day during rush hour.

INTERVIEWER

Agreed. But you mentioned this novel . . .

ALLEN

I'm not sure I have the background and understanding to
write a novel. The book that I have been working on, or planning, is amusing but serious, and I'll see what happens. I'm
so uneducated really—so autodidactic. That's a tricky thing,
because there are certain areas the autodidact knows about,
but there are also great gaps that are really shocking. It comes
from not having a structured education. People will send me
film scripts or essays or even a page of jokes, and they'll say, "Is
this anything—is this a short story? Is this a comedy sketch?"
They'll have no idea if it is or isn't. To a degree, I feel the
same way about the world of prose. When I brought something
into *The New Yorker*, I didn't know what I was standing there
with. Their reaction could have been, "Oh, this is nothing.
You've written a lot of words, but this isn't really anything,"
or, "Young man, this thing is really wonderful." I was happy
to accept their judgment of it. If they had said, when I first
took those pieces into *The New Yorker*, "We're sorry, but this
isn't really anything," I would have accepted that. I would
have said, "Oh really? Okay." I would have thrown the stuff
away and never batted an eyelash. The one or two things
they've turned down over the years, they were always so tentative and polite about; they always said, "Look, we may publish
something else a little too close to this" or something tactful
like that. And I always felt, hey—just tear it up, I don't care.
In that sense, I never found writing delicate or sacred. I think
that's what would happen if I finished the novel. If the people
I brought it to said, "We don't think this is anything," it
would never occur to me to say, "You fools." I just don't know

enough. I'm not speaking with the authority of someone like James Joyce who'd read everything and knew more than his critics did. There's only one or two areas where I feel that kind of security, where I feel my judgment is as good and maybe even better than most people's judgment. Comedy is one. I feel confident when I'm dealing with things that are funny, whatever the medium. And I know a lot about New Orleans jazz music even though I'm a poor musician. Poor but dedicated.

INTERVIEWER

Why did you start out writing comedy?

ALLEN

I always enjoyed comedians when I was young. But when I started to read more seriously, I enjoyed more serious writers. I became less interested in comedy then, although I found I could write it. These days I'm not terribly interested in comedy. If I were to list my fifteen favorite films, there would probably be no comedies in there. True, there are some comic films that I think are wonderful. I certainly think that *City Lights* is great, a number of the Buster Keatons, several Marx Brothers movies. But those are a different kind of comedy — the comedy of comedians in film stands more as a record of the comedians' work. The films may be weak or silly but the comics were geniuses. I like Keaton's films better than Keaton and enjoy Chaplin and The Marx Brothers usually more than the films. But I'm an easy audience. I laugh easily.

INTERVIEWER

How about *Bringing Up Baby*?

ALLEN

No, I never liked that. I never found that funny.

INTERVIEWER

Really?

ALLEN

No, I liked *Born Yesterday*, even though it's a play made into a film. Both *The Shop Around the Corner* and *Trouble in Paradise* are terrific. A wonderful talking comedy is *The White Sheik* by Fellini.

INTERVIEWER

What is it that keeps a lighthearted or comic film from being on your list of ten?

ALLEN

Nothing other than personal taste. Someone else might list ten comedies. It's simply that I enjoy more serious films. When I have the option to see films, I'll go and see *Citizen Kane*, *The Bicycle Thief*, *The Grand Illusion*, *The Seventh Seal* and those kind of pictures.

INTERVIEWER

When you go to see the great classics over again, do you go to see how they're made, or do you go for the impact that they have on you emotionally?

ALLEN

Usually, I go for enjoyment. Other people who work on my films see all the technical things happening, and I can't see them. I still can't notice the microphone shadow, or the cut that wasn't good or something. I'm too engrossed in the film itself.

INTERVIEWER

Who have had the greatest influence on your film work?

ALLEN

The biggest influences on me, I guess, have been Bergman and the Marx Brothers. I also have no compunction stealing from Strindberg, Chekhov, Perelman, Moss Hart, Jimmy Cannon, Fellini and Bob Hope's writers.

INTERVIEWER

Were you funny as a kid?

ALLEN

Yes, I was an amusing youngster. Incidentally, people always relate that to being raised Jewish. It's a myth. Many great funnymen were not Jewish: W.C. Fields, Jonathan Winters, Bob Hope, Buster Keaton . . . I never saw any connection between ethnicity or religion or race and humor.

INTERVIEWER

Were you asked to perform at school functions?

ALLEN

I didn't perform a lot, but I was amusing in class, among friends and teachers.

INTERVIEWER

So it wasn't the sort of humor that would upset the authorities?

ALLEN

Sometimes it was, yes. My mother was called to school frequently because I was yelling out things in class, quips in class, and because I would hand in compositions that they thought were in poor taste, or too sexual. Many, many times she was called to school.

INTERVIEWER

Why do you think you started writing as a kid?

ALLEN

I think it was just the sheer pleasure of it. It's like playing with my band now. It's fun to make music, and it's fun to write. It's fun to make stuff up. I would say that if I'd lived in the era before motion pictures, I would have been a writer. I saw Alfred Kazin on television. He was extolling the novel at the expense of film. But I didn't agree. One is not comparable with the other. He had too much respect for the printed word. Good films are better than bad books, and when they're both great, they're great and worthwhile in different ways.

INTERVIEWER

Do you think the pleasures of writing are related to the sense of control art provides?

ALLEN

It's a wonderful thing to be able to create your own world whenever you want to. Writing is very pleasurable, very seductive and very therapeutic. Time passes very fast when I'm writing — really fast. I'm puzzling over something, and time just flies by. It's an exhilarating feeling. How bad can it be? It's sitting alone with fictional characters. You're escaping from the world in your own way and that's fine. Why not?

INTERVIEWER

If you like that solitary aspect of writing, would you miss the collaborative aspect of film, if you were to give it up?

ALLEN

One deceptive appeal of being out there with other people is that it gets you away from the job of writing. It's less lonely. But I like to stay home and write. I've always felt that if they told me tomorrow I couldn't make any more films, that they wouldn't give me any more money, I would be happy writing for the theater; and if they wouldn't produce my plays, I'd be happy just writing prose; and if they wouldn't publish me, I'd still be happy writing and leaving it for future generations. Because if there's anything of value there, it will live; and if there's not, better it shouldn't. That's one of the nice things about writing, or any art; if the thing's real, it just lives. All the attendant hoopla about it, the success over it or the critical rejection — none of that really matters. In the end, the thing will survive or not on its own merits. Not that immortality

via art is any big deal. Truffaut died, and we all felt awful
about it, and there were the appropriate eulogies, and his
wonderful films live on. But it's not much help to Truffaut.
So you think to yourself, "My work will live on." As I've said
many times, rather than live on in the hearts and minds of
my fellow man, I would rather live on in my apartment.

INTERVIEWER

Still, some artists put such an emphasis on their work, on
creating something that will last, that they put it before everything else. That line by Faulkner—"The 'Ode on a Grecian
Urn' is worth any number of old ladies."

ALLEN

I hate when art becomes a religion. I feel the opposite.
When you start putting a higher value on works of art than
people, you're forfeiting your humanity. There's a tendency
to feel the artist has special privileges, and that anything's
okay if it's in the service of art. I tried to get into that in
Interiors. I always feel the artist is much too revered: it's not
fair and it's cruel. It's a nice but fortuitous gift—like a nice
voice or being left-handed. That you can create is a kind of
nice accident. It happens to have high value in society, but
it's not as noble an attribute as courage. I find funny and silly
the pompous kind of self-important talk about the artist who
takes risks. Artistic risks are like show-business risks—laugh-
able. Like casting against type, wow, what danger! Risks are
where your life is on the line. The people who took risks against
the Nazis or some of the Russian poets who stood up against
the state—those people are courageous and brave, and that's
really an achievement. To be an artist is also an achievement,
but you have to keep it in perspective. I'm not trying to under-
sell art. I think it's valuable, but I think it's overly revered.
It is a valuable thing, but no more valuable than being a good
schoolteacher, or being a good doctor. The problem is that
being creative has glamour. People in the business end of film
always say, "I want to be a producer, but a creative producer."

Or a woman I went to school with, who said, "Oh yes, I married this guy. He's a plumber but he's very creative." It's very important for people to have that credential. Like if he wasn't creative, he was less.

INTERVIEWER

When you're writing, do you think about your audience? Updike, for instance, once said that he liked to think of a young kid in a small midwestern town finding one of his books on a shelf at a public library.

ALLEN

I've always felt that I try to aim as high as I can at the time, not to reach everybody, because I know that I can't do that, but always to try to stretch myself. I'd like to feel, when I've finished a film, that intelligent adults, whether they're scientists or philosophers, could go in and see it and not come out and feel that it was a total waste of time. That they wouldn't say, "Jesus, what did you get me into?" If I went in to see *Rambo*, I'd say, "Oh, God," and then after a few minutes I'd leave. Size of audience is irrelevant to me. The more the better, but not if I have to change my ideas to seduce them.

INTERVIEWER

Film's not the easiest art form in which to do that; it involves a lot of people, requires a lot of money.

ALLEN

There are certain places like Sweden, where you're partially state subsidized. But in the United States, everything's so damned expensive. It's not like painting or writing. With a film I have to get millions of dollars—to make even a cheap film. So attached to that is a sense that you can't get along without a big audience. Therefore it's a bit of a struggle, but I've been lucky: I've always had freedom. I've been blessed. I've had a dream life in film—from my first picture on. It's been absolute, total freedom down the line. Don't ask me why. If I decided tomorrow to do a black-and-white film on sixteenth-century religion, I could do it. Of course, if I went in and said, "I'm going to do a film about monads," they'd say, "Well, we'll give you this much money to work with." Whereas if I say, "I'm going to do a big, broad comedy," they'll give me more money.

INTERVIEWER

What sort of development do you see in your own work over the years?

ALLEN

I hope for growth, of course. If you look at my first films, they were very broad and sometimes funny. I've gotten more human with the stories and sacrificed a tremendous amount of humor, of laughter, for other values that I personally feel are worth making that sacrifice for. So, a film like *The Purple Rose of Cairo* or *Manhattan* will not have as many laughs. But I think they're more enjoyable. At least to me they are. I would love to continue that—and still try to make some serious things.

INTERVIEWER

Was it *Interiors* that if anybody laughed during its making you took that part out? Is that so?

ALLEN

Oh no, no, not true. Good story but totally untrue. No, there are never any colorful stories connected with my pictures. I mean, we go in there and work in a kind of grim, business-like atmosphere and do the films, whether they're comedies or dramas. Some people criticized *Interiors*, saying that it had no humor at all. I felt that this was a completely irrelevant criticism. Whatever was wrong with it, the problem is not that it lacks humor. There's not much humor in *Othello* or *Persona*. If I could write a couple of plays or films that had a serious tone, I would much prefer to do that than have the comedy hit of the year. Because that would give me personal pleasure — in the same sense that I prefer to play New Orleans jazz than to play Mozart. I adore Mozart, but I prefer to play New Orleans jazz. Just my preference.

INTERVIEWER

But, when you're writing a script and humor surfaces you grasp it with pleasure, no?

ALLEN

Yes, it's always a pleasure. Usually what happens is that there are a number of surprises in films, and usually the surprises are the negative ones. You think you have something funny in a joke or a scene, and it turns out not to be funny, and you're surprised.

INTERVIEWER

And you're stuck with it.

ALLEN

Or you throw it away. On the other hand, once in a great while you get a pleasant surprise, and something that you never thought was going to be amusing, the audience laughs at or howls at, and it's a wonderful thing.

INTERVIEWER

Can you give an example of that?

ALLEN

When I first made *Bananas* years ago, I was going over to the dictator's house — I was invited for dinner there in this Latin American country. I brought with me some cake, in a box, a string cake from one of the bakery shops. I didn't think much of it at all, but it consistently always got the biggest howls from the audience. What they were laughing over was the fact that my character was foolish enough to bring some pastries to a state dinner. To me it was incidental on the way

to the real funny stuff — to the audience it was the funniest
thing.

INTERVIEWER

It seems as though when an artist becomes established, other
people — critics, their followers — expect them to keep on doing
the same thing, instead of evolving in their own way.

ALLEN

That's why you must never take what's written about you
seriously. I've never written anything in my life or done any
project that wasn't what I wanted to do at the time. You really
have to forget about what they call "career moves." You just
do what you want to do for your own sense of your creative
life. If no one else wants to see it, that's fine. Otherwise, you're
in the business to please other people. When we did *Stardust
Memories*, all of us knew there would be a lot of flack. But
it wouldn't for a second stop me. I never thought, I better
not do this because people will be upset. It'd be sheer death
not to go through with a project you feel like going through
with at the time. Look at someone like Strindberg — another
person I've always loved — and you see the reaction he got on
certain things . . . just brutalized. When I made *Annie Hall*,
there were a lot of suggestions that I make *Annie Hall II*. It
would never occur to me in a million years to do that. I was
planning to do *Interiors* after that, and that's what I did. I
don't think you can survive any other way. To me, the trick
is never to try to appeal to a large number of people, but to
do the finest possible work I can conceive of, and I hope if
the work is indeed good, people will come to see it. The artists
I've loved, most did not have large publics. The important
thing is the doing of it. And what happens afterward — you
just hope you get lucky. Even in a popular art form like film,
in the U.S. most people haven't seen *The Bicycle Thief* or
The Grand Illusion or *Persona*. Most people go through their
whole lives without seeing any of them. Most of the younger
generation supporting the films that are around now in such

abundance don't care about Buñuel or Bergman. They're not aware of the highest achievements of the art form. Once in a great while something comes together by pure accident of time and place and chance. Charlie Chaplin came along at the right time. If he'd come along today, he'd have had major problems.

INTERVIEWER

Don't you think that as serious writers mature they simply continue to develop and expand the themes already established?

ALLEN

Each person has his own obsessions. In Bergman films you find the same things over and over, but they're usually presented with great freshness.

INTERVIEWER

What about your own work?

ALLEN

The same things come up time after time. They're the things that are on my mind, and one is always feeling for new ways to express them. It's hard to think of going out and saying, "Gee, I have to find something new to express." What sort of things recur? For me, certainly the seductiveness of fantasy and the cruelty of reality. As a creative person, I've never been interested in politics or any of the solvable things. What interested me were always the unsolvable problems: the finiteness of life, and the sense of meaninglessness and despair, and the inability to communicate. The difficulty in falling in love and maintaining it. Those things are much more interesting to me than . . . I don't know, the Voting Rights Act. In life, I do follow politics a certain amount—I do find it interesting as a citizen, but I'd never think of writing about it.

A word about this interview. It was hard for me because I don't like to aggrandize my work by discussing its influences or my themes or that kind of thing. That kind of talk is more applicable to works of greater stature. I say this with no false modesty — that I feel I have done no really significant work, whatsoever, in any medium. I feel that unequivocally. I feel that what I have done so far in my life is sort of the ballast that is waiting to be uplifted by two or three really fine works that may hopefully come. We've been sitting and talking about Faulkner, say, and Updike and Bergman — I mean, I obviously can't talk about myself in the same way at all. I feel that what I've done so far is the . . . the bed of lettuce the hamburger must rest on. I feel that if I could do, in the rest of my life, two or three really fine works — perhaps make a terrific film or write a fine play or something — then everything prior to that point would be interesting as developmental works. I feel that's the status of my works: they're a setting waiting for a jewel. But there's no jewel there at the moment. So I'm starting to feel my interview is pompous. I need some heavy gems in there somewhere. But I hope I've come to a point in my life where within the next ten or fifteen years I can do two or three things that lend credence to all the stuff I've done already. . . . Let's hope.

— Michiko Kakutani

Squeak, Memory

Melvin Jules Bukiet

It was 1973, the summer of Watergate, but my mind was not on politics, but literature. While the parade of unreliable narrators told their stories on daytime television to be followed by their nightly commentators, I read, mostly Russians, mostly classics: Tolstoy, Dostoyevsky, Chekhov. I didn't really enjoy Chekhov, those lonely doctors, shabby and sentimental. I preferred the grandiose passions of their fathers, and thought I understood them.

There was a girl—there were still twenty-year-old "girls" then. How long ago was it, oh, about as many springs as she was young that summer. You can always count on a thief for a fancy prose style. And you, the one with the degree, you already think you know where I'm going, you've already overleaped the transition from the blunt forms of Czarist fiction into the heady flamboyance of the twentieth century.

It was actually Andrei Biely who led me to Mr. Nabokov. Usually it's the other way around, but I was an autodidact without benefit of tutelage, and relied upon one volume to pull me to another. I haunted the used bookstores of Fourth Avenue, inhaling the must from Dauber and Pine's basement

as if it were motes in the rose window at Chartres. Even then
the grand street was a shade of its glorious past, but there
were remnants of the glory. I found a dog-eared Grove Press
edition of *St. Petersburg*. The title called to me and even more
so the quote on the back, declaring this book one of the four
great works of the century, along with *The Metamorphosis*,
Remembrance of Things Past and *Ulysses*, so I bought it for
a dollar, but what really thrilled me was not the unknown
masterpiece, but its unknown advocate who dared to place it
in the same pantheon as those other monuments—as if he
defined such realms. The arbiter's name was Nabokov.

I had heard of *Lolita*, but only after reading the author's
extravagant, arrogant blurb for the esoteric symbolist, Biely,
did I dredge his own lurid best-seller out from the disorganized
bins in front of the Pageant, several blocks and a half-dozen
other venerable antiquarians away from Dauber and Pine, and
fell in love—with the author as well as his heroine. Every word
fell into place, each syllable echoed, and I sought out his other
books. None were less thrilling. In *Ada*, he penned the best
parenthesis in literary history, describing a character's tragic
demise "(picnic, lightning)." After several wrong guesses, I
made it a point to learn how to pronounce his name, moving
from Nah-bah-kov, accent first on the first, then on the second,
and third on the last syllable, to Nuh-boak-off, accent dead
center.

I found a photograph taken of him sitting on a stone-
balustraded terrace in the Alps, a delicate *kirschwasser* at hand,
a butterfly net angled against his rattan chair. He was wearing
thick loden shorts with a button-down shirt. In this first image,
I saw no shoes, but had an image of immense, puckered knees.

First I saw him in my mind, and then in the flesh.

I was walking the streets of the city that summer, map in
hand, determined to cover every block on the magic island
before Labor Day. Don't ask why. It was the literal-minded
youth's manner of making the city his own. Sometimes this
led me to inspiration, more frequently to a mathematical rigor.
I learned the best pattern to cover the most blocks without
overlapping footsteps, the snake, river to river, east to west,

down a block, river to river, west to east. Later I strode in 100-block straight lines down the avenues. I took in brownstones, warehouses, office towers, imagining the lives led there, as I avoided dragging my march sore feet to soak in the bathtub in the kitchen of my girl's apartment on West Fourth, near where it intersects West Eleventh, where the grid gets tangled and you can't pursue a simple snakewind.

That day, July 15, as the proceedings were broadcast from Washington to every television in the nation, I was on Madison Avenue in the thirties when I was yanked from my plan to cover Turtle Bay by a familiar profile not twenty feet away. It was Mr. Nabokov himself (despite our subsequent intimacy, I will never be able to refer to him as Vladimir, emphasis on the first or second syllable, let alone the sweet diminutive Vlady). I recognized him as much by stature as profile. He was a heavy man — made substantial by vocabulary — and had thin hair swept back off a high, sweaty forehead. It was summer, and Nixon was sweating too. The novelist had smallish eyes and a prominent nose and presidential jowls that I could not see at first, since he was angled, keeping a watch on a checker cab — there were still checkers then — taking a too tight right turn in order to pick up a woman holding a small dog. Perhaps he was thinking of Chekhov, whom he admired.

Then he crossed the street. Maintaining a subtle distance, I followed, although it took a few moments for me to realize that I was following. "Hey," I said to myself, "this is a creepy thing to do. This is what G. Gordon Liddy did." Then I relaxed and enjoyed my transgression.

I assumed that he was heading for the Morgan Library, to examine the antique etchings in the mansion that may have reminded him of his family home confiscated by the Revolution sixty years earlier. But he passed directly by the stately porte cochere. We continued northward against the pedestrian traffic flowing southward from Grand Central Station. I was astonished that people did not recognize him, pester him, adore him. I turned to make certain I was not the lead sheep for a flock of acolytes and nearly lost him. He wove with an elegant, even mincing, gait through the commuters' rough oceanic flow. At Thirty-eighth Street, he paused to examine a hot-dog-and-pretzel salesman, inhaling the scent of the New World. But despite the apparent randomness of his path, I was sure he had a destination.

Perhaps he was in New York for a meeting of a genealogical society or to confer with a lawyer suing the Soviet regime for restitution of stolen property, an estate roughly the size of Connecticut, or to make a presentation at a symposium on the sexuality of verbs. Or perhaps he was en route to a lunch date with his publisher, some bushy-haired thug who planned to berate him for not repeating the succès de scandale of *Lolita*. The man clearly had a reason for being on this block in this unseasonable city.

There was a bookstore on the corner that specialized in travel writing, its window full of Baedekers and memoirs. Perhaps he required some esoteric volume on Micronesia for research into a new project, *Pnin in Tahiti*. By following I might anticipate his next novel. But he passed the store without so much as a glance.

He veered off the avenue at Thirty-ninth Street, where the buildings rose in height, and I hurried and nearly bumped into him. He was stationary in front of a different window, that of a shoe store with a slim brown awning—perhaps to catch me off guard. I think he sensed my presence all along, but was too generous, or too removed to take offense, and the sinister bend in his path was meant to allow me to pass ahead gracefully and leave him be. Instead, I pretended great interest in a sign designating local parking regulations, as if the low-slung sports car at the curb belonged to me. I noticed that the meter had expired, so I fished into my trousers and found a dime and gave it another half hour, and leaned against the hood I felt I had rented for half a circle on the tiny municipal timepiece of sorts.

But the master's absorption in the wares of the shoe store seemed genuine, and then he entered. I was close enough to feel a draft from within. Since then I've learned that shoe stores always turn the air-conditioning way up, so that sweaty socks do not create unpleasant odors to offend other customers.

A salesman not much older than myself but with a tired manner appeared, to join him on the inside of the front window. Words were exchanged.

The fellow took a pair of wing tips from the window, but Mr. Nabokov shook his head and gestured several inches to the side, moving his finger in an arc that bisected the window and my stomach like a surgeon's blade. I could have told the clerk which shoes such a man preferred, an oxblood cordovan, with cylindrical laces like spaghetti rather than the more common flat linguini style. They were comfortable, elegant, Italian.

Suddenly I was keenly aware of my own footgear, a pair of Converse All-Stars that had seen better days. How long ago, oh, you know that one. A lace had broken and I had made an awkward knot between grommets that kept it from tying snugly. There was a tear in the side and, worst, a worn spot in the sole. I was standing in a slight depression in the asphalt in which a pool had gathered and the water was seeping in, and wetting my socks. It was the third day I had worn those socks and they were stiff. The puddle was a cooling lubricant to my chafing toes.

Mr. Nabokov held the sample and flexed it to make certain it had the suppleness he required to cushion his great bulk. It was a left shoe, as were all the samples. I wondered if Mr. Nabokov knew that the right foot is usually larger than the left, the reason why stores always use left shoes for samples, to fool people into thinking their own feet are minimally more tasteful than they really are. Of course, he knew everything; he would factor that into his decision and did not require my advice. Appreciating the texture, he nodded, and lowered himself ponderously into a row of chairs linked together like those in a movie theater as if he had hemorrhoids.

The clerk then knelt at his feet—I would have exchanged positions with him in a flash—and placed the novelist's rather small hoof into a contraption that measured it. The thing resembled a small silver tray with sliding extrusions, ridged to simulate toes, that came from the top to the black marking that read 7 1/2, while another bar slid in from the side to determine width. The result was unusual; his feet were wide, perhaps splayed from Alpine hikes in search of rare butterflies. By then I knew his hobbies, habits and obsessions. Now I knew his shoe size.

Then the clerk disappeared into the back room to fetch the requested shoes while Mr. Nabokov peered about the store, at the other styles of left shoes on display together with wooden stretchers and other accoutrements of the trade. The store also sold umbrellas, but it wasn't raining; it was humid.

The clerk returned, and knelt again to insert Mr. Nabokov's foot into the merchandise. Thus shod, he paced back and forth in front of a mirror set upon the carpeted floor. He looked out the window at me, and I patted the car proprietarily while a man in a suit rushed toward me down the block.

The man looked at the meter, perplexed, and then at me. Distracted, I missed the next phase of the transaction, but when I looked back Mr. Nabokov was at the counter, reaching into his vest pocket to extract a wallet whose Florentine leather was as luscious as the shoe, and then came the moment I was not waiting for. Apparently spontaneously, he plucked a pair of shoelaces from the spindly, multiarmed rack on the counter beside an enormous brown cash register. I might have guessed he would purchase an extra pair of laces; the man was fastidiously prepared for any contingency a traveler might face. I was caught with a hole in my sneakers, wading in a puddle, prepared only to make rubbery squishing noises for the rest of the afternoon. There was only one problem. The laces were yellow.

I was so shocked at this whimsy I forgot the fellow whose car I had usurped, and hardly heard as he cleared his throat and said, "Excuse me."

Bright, beaming sunshine yellow.

I heard the ring and authoritative chunking open of the cash register.

"Please get off my car."

Lemon yellow.

"I'm going to call the police."

Crayola yellow.

•

Fortunately, Mr. Nabokov left the store. He was cradling a rectangular box presumably containing his old shoes, since he was sporting his new ones, enjoying every step, dancing a one man quadrille between sidewalk squares, composing a line in his furrowed forehead, something about a chessboard.

"Take your fucking car," I sneered, and gratuitously kicked the fender of the steel perch I had been evicted from, as we moved further north, past the railroad terminal, toward the hotel.

It wasn't the Algonquin, which I would have expected from my callow early readings, but an anonymous hostelry on the same block, also named for an Indian tribe—in those days there were still "Indians."

Pretending that water was not cascading back and forth in the cavity below my instep like a tide, I sloshed past the liveried doorman as if I belonged, or maybe my parents belonged, and I, the impoverished prodigal, was visiting them for a good meal and a handout designated to pay the rent but destined to be squandered in used bookstores. My first thought once past the sentry was that the state of the air-conditioning he guarded was far from the shoe store's. The lobby was nearly as sultry as the street. It had a few sickly palms in pots.

Mr. Nabokov made a side trip to the thick mahogany receptionist's desk to check for messages, but there were none in whichever empty pigeonhole the clerk cast his bored glance upon. If there had been, I was ready to note the room number, but there wasn't. I was already plotting how I might call in from the lobby phone booth in order to see which slot he placed a faint blue "While you were out . . . " slip into, but then Mr. Nabokov moved toward the elevator.

It was an old-fashioned glass enclosure topped by a semicircular position indicator with a working arrow without a tip, and it was protected by an art nouveau gate operated by an elderly man, who was either a midget or looked like one, sitting on a stool behind the large brass lever that controlled the elevator. He wore a rumpled brown uniform and matching cap clamped low over his brow. The fellow saw me and paused, to avoid a second trip, but I quickly feigned interest in the sundries stand, examining a *Time* magazine with John Dean on the cover. Nonetheless the operator's wait was well-timed for purposes of saving his own labor because a well-dressed woman entered the elevator a second before his left arm, elongated by decades of single-limbed exercise, stretched to pull the gate closed. Then I rushed for the stairs that spiraled around the vehicle as it rose. At each floor, I glanced at the position indicator atop each closed entry door. At each floor, the arrow was still ascending. I was out of breath, but determined. I was dizzy, circling, rising and circling only several feet below the elevator and could hear its chains clanking. It stopped on six, and I halted several feet below, directly behind the cab, gasping for breath, looking down at all the flights I had climbed and the wet sneaker prints evaporating in my wake. The woman got off.

Once stopped, it was hard to recapture my breath, but I followed again as the elevator recommenced, and the woman stared at me as I brushed past her in my eagerness to match the elevator's pace. We passed seven and eight and then, thank God, it stopped again on nine and Mr. Nabokov alit. I peered from behind, while the operator continued upwards alone in response to an urgently blinking light that summoned him to twelve, the penthouse.

Mr. Nabokov, who did not lodge in the penthouse, walked down the hall, its carpet thinner than the shoe store's plush, and stopped in front of the third door on the right. If I was correct in my estimation of direction, room 918 would not have had a street view, but one to the rear, from the hotel into an air shaft between it and another ninth floor in a building fronting on the next block. He shifted the box with his old shoes from one arm to the other and removed the key from his trousers pocket. I heard it click, and saw the door swing open, revealing a glimpse of an unmade bed and a plaid suitcase. Then it closed.

I was steeling myself to knock, to introduce myself, and perhaps kneel. I walked to the door, and stopped. Brass numbers were glued onto the ersatz wood-grain surface glued to the steel that the hotel's original portals had been replaced with in order to comply with city fire regulations, one askew. A yellow shoelace was strung around the knob.

•

There was a bar off the lobby of the hotel, but it was more of an extension of the lobby than a room of its own. It was a dark alcove, suitable for assignations and mediocre salesmen. I ordered a Scotch; it was the most continental drink I could think of, and I tried to look as if the bartender did not need to request identification from me, as if I was used to drinking by myself in midtown hotel bars on Tuesdays in July. The television in the corner showed Senator Ervin, full of righteous indignation.

Did Mr. Nabokov purchase the shoe merely to justify purchasing the laces? That yellow strand was obviously a symbol, but of what, and to whom? Or was it some aristocratic Russian custom, gone with the monarchy in all but his own personal etiquette? I ransacked my recollection of his books in search of a clue.

Of one thing I was certain, it was not an affectation. Neither was he here for a publisher, nor did he say to the members of the genealogical association, "I'll be in the Hotel Mohawk, on Forty-fourth Street, in the room on the ninth floor with a yellow shoelace draped over the knob." Was this a message left for a salacious schoolgirl by her Humbert?

Three Scotches stiffer, I decided to return to the ninth floor and confront the mystery. I thought He would do no less. This time I took the elevator, despite the smirk of the operator.

As soon as he let me off onto the stained carpet lit by dim fixtures, I knew that something had changed between the thickly impastoed walls during my sojourn in the bar. In front of Room 918, there was a pair of shoes. The great man had left them for shining, but they were his brand-new cordovans, which did not require shining. They fairly glowed with their own pale fire. Nonetheless, my first inclination was to expedite the great man's request, to take them down to the bar and caress them with the cocktail napkins embossed with a cartoon of a martini glass and an olive on a pike. Then I thought of peeing in the shoes.

It was a moment of high giddiness, the liquor speaking, I told myself. But what would he think? Perhaps that the color of the congealed urine was like butter? Or that the texture of the ruined leather now resembled the flakiness of a butterfly's wings.

Or would he fail to think in images, and merely fume with outrage at the vulgarity — or delight in the vulgarity — of American culture? Or would he remember a day back at the homestead when, four years old say, and already quadralingual, he peed in his family's butler's boots, and chuckle at the reminiscence of how the man had to wear them anyway, squishing around for afternoon tea as if he was a child in water-sodden sneakers much to the young Vlady's (I mean Mr. Nabokov's) barely restrained hilarity.

Then I noticed the really remarkable thing; the shoes were there, but the yellow lace was not.

•

It was back to the bar, shattered by the strangeness. I scribbled frantically on the napkins I would have used to shine the shoes if I had made that decision. I made diagrams and charts of the series of events. First shoes; that made sense. Then laces. Then the lace on the door. Then the lace off the door and the shoes in front of the door. I made arrows back and forth, like the arrows atop the elevator. Perhaps he was a spy — there was still a U.S.S.R. then — and this was an elaborate code meant to convey information.

I tried to recall if the lace had been looped around the knob in a particular knot, the shape of a double helix connoting biological research or coiled in representation of a hydroelectric plant or tied into crisscrossed ovals for uranium. I flailed myself for my lack of perception and analytical capacity. I considered returning upstairs, but was terrified that I might find no shoes, and laces again, and began to question my own sanity.

"Another?" the bartender said.

I thought I had had enough.

"This one's on the house," he said.

I didn't know that this was standard procedure. It's called a buyback, and occurs after the third round, if the customer has tipped well. I hadn't intended to tip well, but had miscalculated in my confusion. Ignorant of my generosity, I thought he recognized me, admired me. So I accepted his gift, as graciously as a Nobel Prize. I started to make an acceptance speech, but he was called to the other end of the bar by the woman whom I had last seen on the sixth-floor landing. She must have changed out of her uncomfortable heels and taken the elevator down while I was pondering the situation on nine. I think she winked at me. I gulped the drink and fled, leaving no tip.

Much as I wanted to exit onto the street and return to my grid, I was compelled upstairs one last time. I knew my behavior was suspicious, but I was beyond caring. I think the elevator operator would have called the house detective if he gave a damn. I couldn't tell if it was me or him who smelled of Scotch. The cage came to a shuddering stop at nine.

"Watch your step," the man said.

I did. The difference in levels was so miniscule I could barely discern it, and I wondered if he was sarcastic. I might have ripped that dumb monkey's cap from his head, or thrown him down the shaft.

The cage lingered while I inspected the safety certificate framed beside a standpipe with a hose like an endlessly elongated shoelace for a giant's seven-league boot. It was expired. I was about to turn to check on the elevator certificate too, me, Mr. Probity, when the vehicle was summoned, probably by the woman downstairs, disappointed in the bar's booze or the company.

As warily as if I had been invited to a beheading, I tiptoed down the hall, studiously keeping my eye on the doors on

the odd-numbered side until I was about even with his door
to my blind side.

I didn't know what to expect when I turned: a lace without
shoes, a pair of shoes without laces, an open door with a pot-
bellied genius demanding to know why I was dogging him,
a jar of live butterflies, Vera, or an autographed copy of *Lolita*
inscribed, "To Kevin, With Lust." In any case, I knew, knew
in my belly, that I would not be faced with a blank door.

It was the least dramatic of these alternatives, the shoes,
alone, again, as if the lace had been my mistake, a mirage.
For a second I wondered if I was not mad, but simply wrong,
if the man I had followed was not Mr. Nabokov at all, but
just a salesman, in town for a convention and a little shopping
and maybe some hanky-panky, and if the shoes were not new,
but overdue for a shining. It was a service of the hotel that
anyone would use, like the shampoo in the complimentary
miniature tubes. But the shoes *were* new and they were beautiful.

Before I knew what I was doing, I had slipped off my sneakers and tried on the left shoe, fully aware that my left foot
was a tiny bit smaller than my right. I didn't pace the corridor
to make certain of the fit. I didn't ask the clerk or the genius
for another size. I slipped on the right. And then, dear reader,
I fled. I honestly can't say whether it was because I didn't have
a box to place them in, or in shabby recompense, but I left
my wet sneakers in front of the door without the shoelace.

I didn't dare face the elevator operator and took the stairs
three at a time, slipping on my new shoes' barely scuffed soles,
but on six, as I rounded the corner toward five, I could have
sworn that I saw another shoelace, lime green, Crayola green,
hanging from a knob several doors down the corridor.

The palmed lobby was different in my new shoes. And the
city was different in my new shoes. I tossed my idiotic map
of the grid into a garbage can on the corner of Sixth Avenue,
and headed downtown. Already my feet ached a little, for
the fit was imperfect. My feet were larger and narrower than
His.

The real problem came later when I arrived in the West Village. I walked up four steep and creaking flights to my girlfriend's apartment without leaving a single wet footprint, and I wasn't happy when I turned my key in the lock. Vanessa didn't read and she didn't steal, not even shoplift.

Nixon resigned later that summer.

Como Conversazione
26 - 29th May 1995

A Conversation on Literature and Comedy in our time.

Ut honesto otio quiesceret

Hawthornden Institute

Participants

Roy Blount	John Gross	Mordecai Richler
Malcolm Bradbury	Drue Heinz	Calvin Trillin
Tibor Fischer	John Mortimer	Auberon Waugh
Grey Gowrie	George Plimpton	John Wells

"Moult no feather, I have of late,
but wherefore know not, lost all my mirth"

—*Hamlet*, Act II, Scene 2

Como Conversazione

A Conversation on Literature and Comedy in Our Time

Roy Blount, Jr. and I were the first arrivals at the Casa Ecco on Lake Como where the "conversazione" on the topic "Whither mirth?" was scheduled. Calvin Trillin, his wife Alice (who begged off being a panelist), and a British contingent of wits and humorists (Lord Gowrie, Auberon Waugh, Malcolm Bradbury, John Wells, John Mortimer, Tibor Fischer, John Gross, and Mordecai Richler, a Canadian writer working and living in London) turned up later in the day. The event was sponsored by The Paris Review, *and also by the Hawthornden Institute, which offers one of the more prestigious literary prizes in England as well as providing retreats for writers both at the Casa Ecco and at a castle in Scotland.*

Blount and I were met by Drue Heinz, who runs the villa and is the driving force behind both the Review (she is its publisher) and the Institute. She showed us around Casa Ecco—a quaint mock fortress complete with serrated battlements and painted a non-military pink; it stands on groomed lawns that slope down toward the lake. Back of the casa is the Guest House where the American contingent is to stay—

a large, roomy residence, the hills rising up steeply behind. The others are in various "workhouses." A large statue of a Great Dane at rest stands in front of the main-house terrace, one paw draped over the other. The villa is named after a dog, Ecco, long gone but which has also given its name to the distinguished publishing house, the Ecco Press which Drue Heinz founded.

At lunch we were joined by Brian Urquhart, aide to a number of U.N. Secretary Generals, who has been touring Germany and is on his way to Israel. What an extraordinary career—a wartime soldier who survived two parachute jumps when his parachutes failed to open properly, and a diplomat who talked his way out of execution in the turmoil of Zaire in the late 1960s. Hearing about our conference on matters comic, Brian entertained us at lunch with a story he felt reflected the rather odd comic sensibilities of the Brazilians—a number of whom had been with him in Germany. The story involved Santos Dumont, the great pilot, who may have flown before the Wright brothers. He was on his way home from Europe via ship. The authorities in Brazil felt he should be greeted in carnival style, so they sent a seaplane out to drop flowers and petals on the ocean liner to welcome him. The seaplane went out of control and crashed into the ship, killing the pilot and quite a few passengers. The Brazilians, according to Brian, roared with laughter as they told him this, rocking back and forth on their heels, tears in their eyes. Brian commented, "Odd, what?" and at the table we broke into laughter. Roy then chimed in with what he felt was an appropriate story about "Kissing" Jim Folsom, a former governor of Alabama—that he and a large entourage were watching a naval display in Mobile which included a flyby by an aerial acrobatic team. One of the planes tipped the wing of another; one or two piled into the bay. After an interval Folsom returned to his entourage and announced: "Kiss my ass if that ain't a show." Again, considerable laughter on our part, even a wry smile from Brian Urquhart . . . what is wrong with us? It rather refutes George Meredith's theory that comedy and laughter

belong to the intellect. Perhaps the conference will shed some
light on this sort of reaction . . .
The principals met the next morning around an oval table
in a room in the Guest House. Excerpts from the first session
follow—the main topic "Political Correctness." The first re-
marks were made by Grey Gowrie who with Malcolm Bradbury
were the two cochairs of the conference.

Grey Gowrie: The idea behind this first session, which I'm
kicking off, is to look at humor from a great height and under
the eye of eternity. You might—from a Britocentric view—
argue that political correctness has been around for a long
time for us. One has only to think of Malvolio in *Twelfth
Night*, or a mere hundred years ago when rat catchers became
"rodent officers." But we are certainly reimporting a new and
virulent strain of political correctness which I look upon as a
form of moral relativity—all sorts of strains but which I think
need watching and are in need of debunking and ridicule.

My theme is really that satire and humor keep the enemies
from the gates. The ancient Britons are said to have painted
their bottoms blue—a sort of collective mooning to cast doubt
and despair among their rivals. Perhaps it simply broke the
rivals up by rendering them helpless with laughter. Of course,
humor is there to entertain, and to relieve the route-march
to oblivion. A steady litany of complaint is what gets the poor
bloody infantry through its wars.

The older I get, the more convinced I become that W.H.
Auden is a fortress with two towers—the greatest English poet
born in this century and the greatest defender of the faith in
civility of post-medieval western liberalism. Auden's vision
was comic, not tragic—comic in the sense of Shakespeare's
plays—in which humor, satire, and the blowing of deflationary
raspberries were weapons against religious, political, and
moral enthusiasm. Auden's church, both literally and meta-
phorically, was high not low. As he put it in a famous sonnet,
"Churches beside the brothels testify / that faith can pardon
natural behavior."

Robert Hughes once told me that he thought the best prose writing at the present time was not in fiction or learning, but in polemics, or literary journalism, if you like. A low form perhaps in the canon, but the jackals do at least see to it that the ground is not reeking with corpses.

. . . A word about last night. Brian Urquhart is a remarkable man — the individual who, more than any other, held the fragile but needed structure of the United Nations together for forty-five years following World War II. There were two circumstances in Brian's life which give us a metaphor or context for our discussion. There was a film made about the Arnhem campaign in the war, *A Bridge Too Far*. In it General Urquhart (no relation) was played, I think, by Sean Connery. Dirk Bogarde, a very fine actor and writer played the young British intelligence officer who warned the generals that this particular adventure would end in disaster, as it did. His name was also Urquhart — Brian Urquhart. But Hollywood couldn't manage that — the concept of two people being called Urquhart. So the true hero had to have his name changed to Jones, or whatever. The second circumstance is that Brian, more than perhaps any of us here, understands the absolute necessity of wit. Condemned to death with just five hours' notice in the Congo in the late 1960s, he talked and joked his way out of execution. And perhaps that's the underlying theme of this morning's session.

As Gowrie was making his remarks I was reminded of a curious anecdote Brian told a small circle of us last night which rather illustrates his somewhat pessimistic view of mankind — that it has its continual problems with communication. He said he was visiting the Central Park Zoo some years back — at a time when one of its main attractions was the hippopotamus, Rosie the Hippo. Rosie sat most of the day in a small indoor tank, far too small for her vast bulk. Brian was standing looking at Rosie when a father passed by with his son, a little boy about four, perhaps five. The father pointed at Rosie and said in a loud clear voice as if to press the information forever in the small boy's brain, "Rhino!" He kept jabbing his finger in

Rosie's direction. "Rhino, rhino," he repeated, and then spelt it out: "R-H-I-N-O. Got it?"

Malcolm Bradbury: I started writing in the 1950s in Britain. My hero was Auberon's father Evelyn Waugh, who seemed to me the greatest twentieth-century humorist. His humor was one that had a great deal to do both with an idea of protecting a certain kind of civilization—a civilization that in fact seemed to cease somewhere around Henry VIII—and at the same time with an absolute fascination with the opposite . . . which was barbarism and strangeness and savagery . . . surely another part of the stuff of the comic. Comedy is interested in order, but it's interested in anarchy as well. So the meshing and mashing of those two things was what was interesting about Evelyn. One of the books he wrote was about a visit to the United States, to Hollywood, and not just to the Hollywood cemeteries. *The Loved One* is a novel which constitutes America as savagery, with American death practices as a classic example of that savagery. The hero comes back to his ancient and uncomfortable British shore and then writes out of savagery. When I started writing I actually wished to reverse that myth. So I went to America in 1956. I loved America. I wanted to write the story of a young man going from anarchy, which was Britain, to civilization, which was America. Who were the American writers who constituted, as it were, the opposite to Evelyn Waugh? The *New Yorker* writers to some degree: Peter DeVries, Mary McCarthy, and James Thurber— a clear American tradition of civilized humor. I stayed in the States, and began indeed to write for *The New Yorker*, and in the end, I became so much a *New Yorker* sort of writer that you couldn't have told whether I was British or not! Other British writers became regular contributors—Anthony Bailey would be an example. Now, of course, there's the new Tina Brown generation.

In the fifties, humor was generally seen as something rather civilized, literary and benign. Then in the sixties, as a result of the publication of books like Beckett's novels and plays, *Lolita* and *Catch-22*, we started to think of humor as a quite different sort of discourse: anarchic, bitter, enraged, and alienated. It was about culture as disorder, knowledge of the absurd. It's not about the making of culture; it's about the breaking of culture. And so we start to reach for terms like "the comedy of absurdity," "black humor," "gallows humor," and "sour humor." To go along with this was the great boom in satire, television programs like *That Was the Week That Was* in Britain and all sorts of satirical rage expressed in the United States — Mort Sahl and Lenny Bruce, things like "performance art." So in the sixties you had a period when comedy actually seemed to reverse on itself and become something else. We seem to be the inheritors of both those traditions. Now there's a new age of analysis which seems to me terribly important, which has taken on all the arguments that have grown up about the nature of postmodern multicultural and multiethnic culture, and its politics, which have been challenged and analyzed and formulated by people like Robert Hughes, Allan Bloom and Harold Bloom. In this post-canonical age, we've entered an era when everyone has an agenda and is trying to compose their own rules on discourse; when there isn't a common agreement about what culture is, what stability is, what order is, and therefore about where the edges of order and anarchy lie. It seems to me that here the current debate begins.

John Mortimer: Our discussion must be on the assumption that humor and jokes are an absolute good. They puncture political correctness and they're always on the side of the angels. Humor is a wonderful benefit to mankind. When I defended in people's court, the defense always had to go for laughs. Once you get the jury laughing you can get an acquittal. The prosecution always goes for deep solemnity, and of course the judges wish to impose an extraordinarily solemn atmosphere on the proceedings. The great thing was to get the jury laughing. Perhaps the most successful instance of this was when I was defending a work by Linda Lovelace. Not a great literary distinction. But there was an item in this book about a wickerwork chair suspended on an elastic band from the ceiling. The point of it was that you wound it up like a model airplane and the lady seated in the wickerwork chair was above a gentleman; so she twiddled round at high speed. This was being taken enormously seriously by the prosecution and by the judge. An incredibly serious psychiatrist came into the witness box to describe the effect that reading this passage would have on a fourteen-year-old schoolgirl. As I rose to cross-examine him, I saw that the little judge had gone very pink in the face and was giggling helplessly, trying to conceal his giggles behind his notebook. So I was able to say to this psychiatrist, "Do you honestly think that the effect on a four-teen-year-old schoolgirl would be any different from the effect that it's clearly having on a seventy-year-old judge?" A moment of triumph! And of course we were acquitted. If you can get them laughing, you can probably get them off.

The test of obscenity in English law is that a book should tend to deprave or corrupt. It's been awfully hard to find anyone who's actually been depraved or corrupted by a book, though, in fact, at one of the Oz magazine trials a very famous Oxford book fellow gave evidence to the effect that he'd been completely depraved, utterly corrupted by reading a book. But he was seventy-five years of age at the time, so it didn't really seem to matter. What I said about the Oz trial was that you're never corrupted when you're laughing, which is a point for the defense. Recently I read a review of Richard Neville's latest book which criticized what I had said as a terrible thing to say because you can easily be corrupted when you're laughing—Nazi officers laughing at the Jews in the deathcamps, or soldiers laughing at the Crucifixion. Now, does he have a point? We've assumed that laughter should mock political correctness, which I think is a dead hand on our freedom of thought. Certainly I believe that everybody should be able to make jokes, and that unless you can have jokes made against you, you're not really worth troubling about.

Roy Blount, Jr.:   I think that at some point somebody needs to say that political correctness is less a dead hand than a dead horse. I mean I think the joke was *on* political correctness as soon as it was named—it was more an object of mirth than a repression of mirth. I've never quite understood why it seems so ominous to people, at least outside academia.

Calvin Trillin: I think the blight is the bad humor having to do with political correctness—the lame jokes. I mean as we sit here somebody somewhere is making up some euphemism for a cleaning lady or a double amputee, thinking he's the cleverest person alive. These days political correctness is a sort of easement for whatever you really want to say . . . the same old Blimps sitting in their country-club bars, who have been saying the same thing to the same kind of people for thirty years, now can say, "Well, this may not be politically correct, but these black people have to pull themselves up by their bootstraps." Or, "It may not be politically correct to notice this about that lady over there, but what a pair of hooters on her!" They have a little easement by saying it that way. But I think when it gets right down to it, who at this table has ever not written anything because of political correctness? Is there anybody here who has actually suffered from this?

Mordecai Richler: In Canada, we have a writer's union which is very politically correct. As a Canadian, born and bred, who happens to be Jewish, I now find I'm a member of a non-visible minority and a writer of pallor.

Auberon Waugh: I write four or five columns a week. Every time I write I have an invisible lawyer on one shoulder and on the other somebody advising me that, "No, people won't think that's funny, that's not funny in the present state of circumstances." So the answer is yes; everything one writes is conditioned by what you can get away with.

I think it's much more interesting, Calvin, than you think it is, because we're not talking about the effect it has on a bunch of fools, racists, and twerps who have always been like that. I'm talking about the American intelligentsia. It's very largely an American phenomenon, although in England we're borrowing it a bit. It's an American phenomenon because you're all dead scared. It's the uneasiness of the rich. You're aware of being the richest society in the world, and lots of things can go wrong. Underneath this rich society you've got the underclass—the blacks, the Hispanics, poor whites. The question you must ask yourselves is why do you put so much importance on not offending these minorities? I agree one shouldn't offend them—it's a boorish and beastly thing to do. But why is it to be of such prime consideration in America? I have a highly intelligent, beautiful, charming, humorous deputy editor, an American. One sees the moment a blanket comes over her mind. We were subbing a review by a former Conservative minister, who was writing about pouring money into South America. He made a slightly tasteless remark, asking if it was wise for these bankers to pour money into Mexico which regards its president as an Aztec king and where in places they genuinely worship Pepsi-Cola bottles. My deputy editor said, "No, that's not true. That's not right. They don't regard their president as an Aztec king." I said, "Well, steady on. The Conservative minister thinks they do, you know." She said, "But that's not right." She suggested that it was racist. I said, "Well, even if it's a bit racist, it's *his* responsibility . . . We don't want to censor him, do we?" She said, "It's not censorship. It's responsibility." A total blanket had come over her mind. That's because she'd been trained. Though she's a highly intelligent, humorous and sensible girl . . . er *(whoops!)* woman, she has an inability to see all that as anything but totally wrong.

Calvin Trillin: I think I would put that down to the editor's not getting that business about Pepsi bottles. I must say I don't get it myself. It sounds like a cargo cult joke, and I don't see what it has to do with Mexico. But the notion that somebody's walking around behind writers in America saying, "You can't say that, that'll offend the Mexicans," is nonsense. None of us have ever had this sort of problem. I think what you've brought up is an argument whether there should be editors. That'll take a whole new symposium.

Grey Gowrie: I doubt if those remarks Auberon referred to
could get published in the two most influential papers in the
United States, *The New York Times* and *The Washington
Post*.

Calvin Trillin: Oh, but they would *jump* on those remarks,
though it's true that in America, newspapers are the most
conservative, small 'c', periodicals. I can write stuff in *The
New Yorker* that you can't write in *The Washington Post* and
that would be blue-penciled in the *Times*. I did a piece on
a camp with kids with cancer and blood diseases. One kid
had a baseball hat that said, "Cancer Sucks," which I thought
was kind of a nice touch. But you can't say that in the *Times*.
The *Times* is an awful lot stricter than the outlets that most
of us write for.

John Mortimer: I mean are we any more threatened by political correctness than a nineteenth-century novelist was by sexual
respectability?

Mordecai Richler: A far more serious problem than political
correctness is we can no longer assume that we're writing for
a cultured audience. In my last book I made a passing reference
to Jacob and Esau, and my editor at Knopf wrote in, "ID
please."

Calvin Trillin: Did you identify Esau as "an hairy man?"

Grey Gowrie: Can we get back to writing and writers? Civilization requires writers to take their role seriously, and certainly
for readers to try to be serious about them — but not in a way
that can be humorless and malign. Let me give you a couple
of examples of a form of feminine censorship in both Britain
and America. The American one affects a dear friend of mine
and a fine writer, Ted Hughes. His relationship with his celebrated first wife, Sylvia Plath, made him a figure of hate for
the feminist movement in America. Yet from a literary point

of view he was both an impeccable husband and a husbander of talent. Her own poetry leaped forward after they split up. The other instance was two years ago when I was the chairman of the Booker Prize, not the biggest, but probably the longest-running, most celebrated literary prize for fiction in the Commonwealth and English-speaking countries. I had asked why *London Fields*, Martin Amis's novel, did not win. He has a formidable use of English, and it was a very remarkable book that I thought would last. If I understand him rightly, Martin Goff, the administrator, said, "Well, the judges all judged that it should be the winner." But it seems that one of the judges, a fine feminist writer called Maggie Gee, delivered a forty-minute speech saying that what Mr. Amis stood for made him absolutely unacceptable. This was weakly cheered and everybody collapsed; somebody else was given the prize. It made me think, proudly, of an aspect in America which as a young man I enormously respected. Ezra Pound was awarded the Bollingen Prize in 1949. That was a very marked contrast . . . that they had awarded the prize to a guy who was probably lucky to have escaped execution for his opinions and broadcasts. Intolerance is a threat to letters. It may have receded. It may be something that we play up too much. But topic tribalism, topic intolerance is much bigger than the political-correctness issue and is, I think, a threat to letters. The best way to fight it is to laugh at it.

John Wells: I mean to pick up, Grey, your line about what you call "deflationary raspberries." I don't want to get too *anal* about this, but I think a joke is a fart in a way. There's a sort of release of hot air, something kind of instinctive.

Malcolm Bradbury: True, a lot of humor is a fart. But a lot of humor has a context, a social context.

John Mortimer: Also, it's social action, that particular raspberry, because in fact a fart in solitude is not funny.

George Plimpton: It's not necessarily funny in company, though. Certainly not to the fart-er . . .

Grey Gowrie: A childish fart is not funny.

John Wells: It's amusing, not really funny.

Grey Gowrie: A fart is not especially amusing to the ladies.

John Wells: I withdraw the fart. I really withdraw the fart.

Calvin Trillin: The fart business is in the record. Sorry.

Drue Heinz: Perhaps we should get back to something else.

Calvin Trillin: I'd like to say that there was a time in America when very few things could be said. I remember somebody coming to *The New Yorker* after seeing a screening of *Dr. Strangelove*. It opened with the credits showing above a bomber being refueled in the air—a long funnel attached between the two planes. The music was playing something like "You Always Hurt the One You Love." He said, "Oh God, I don't see how they can show that here." These days that's pretty tame stuff. The only complaints I've ever had were from the Irish, oddly enough. I once mentioned the word *paddy wagon* in a column, and an Irish reader said it was a slur on the Irish. I actually looked it up and it doesn't say that the Irish have anything to do with the origin of *paddy wagon*.

John Gross: That was probably a politically-correct dictionary!

Auberon Waugh: All this suggests you've got to trim your sails to the prevailing wind. I'm saying I'm trimming them harder now than I've ever done before.

John Gross: It's certainly true that artistic success is the big deflator of certain kinds of pomposity of opinion! Italian-American groups once endlessly complained about any films about the Mafia, until the success and brilliance achieved by both Francis Ford Coppola and Martin Scorsese in these fields really meant that the complaints dried up or became too eccentric to bother about.

Roy Blount, Jr.:   It seems to me that political correctness is a challenge. It's fun to try and get away with something that people don't think you ought to say. Or rather to get away with something *enlightening* that people *didn't* think you ought to say. That's the point of the whole thing.

Auberon Waugh: Yes, but there's a certain sort of heckling which kills any attempt at humor. If you say something which would be harmless to anybody else but you've got some feminist or an animal activist in there who suddenly stands up and shouts, "How dare you say that?" you know, it kind of kills everything.

Drue Heinz: I suggest when we come back we dispense with the word *political correctness.* Is that fair?

One of the pleasures of the occasional break was the opportunity to get to learn something about the others. We meandered across the lawns in the wan spring sun. Refreshments were set out on tables. Lord Gowrie, lean, aristocratic, the head of the British Arts Council, enjoyed an ongoing banter with John Mortimer about the animal-rights controversy in England. Apparently, Mortimer and his wife are pro-fox hunting, and Gowrie, though he allowed being "virtually conceived in the saddle" had turned against such blood sports, admitting, though, that he doesn't approve of states (as I hear him say) "meddling with cultural pursuits which have a great deal of soil and manure of history and time behind them." John Wells, who once taught German at Eton, is a marvelous mimic in a number of languages. He seems too young for the massive variety of things he's done—acting in a Tarzan movie, translating Beaumarchais for the National Theater, writing a history of the House of Lords. He is especially known for his Dear Bill *letters published in* Private Eye—*purported to be the private correspondence of Margaret Thatcher's husband Dennis to a golfing buddy—a meal ticket lost, alas, when Mrs Thatcher resigned.* John Gross, once a critic for The New York Times, *also turned out to be a considerable mimic—doubling me over in laughter at his imitation of the rapid-fire verbosity of my friend, Noel Annan, the former provost of King's College. Malcolm Bradbury towers above the others as we move about the lawns and look down between the cypress trees at the lake. He is a substantial figure in my eyes having produced through his literary program at East Anglia University that remarkable clutch of writers including Ian McEwan, Julian Barnes, and Martin Amis. Auberon Waugh sits next to me at the conference table, taking notes with a pen for his literary journal,* The Literary Review. *Out on the lawn we chat about ways to keep our respective journals afloat. His columns flare with sentiments, precisely and amusingly reflected, which are opposed to just about everything . . . feminism, modern art, the United States in particular though not exclusively. Drue showed me a column which starts as follows: "I begin to have the feeling that the time has come for another war. We have done the Germans and the Japanese, but Swedes are particularly annoying people. They have no body hair and never stop grumbling about all the acid rain and atmospheric pollution we send them . . ." Tibor Fischer, of Hungarian descent, whose book* Under the Frog *was a Booker Prize nomination, is by far the youngest of the European contingent. He is scheduled to lead off the afternoon session.*

Tibor Fischer: One of the things about the high circles of literature is that humor, although recognized for its value as entertainment, is often seen as something slightly second-class, that real literature should be about suffering, pain, misery, and darkness. If it's funny it might be pleasant, but it can't really tackle the big issues. I take exception to that.

Humor can be a very effective way of addressing big questions. While it's a less painful way of doing so, humor also has an advantage in that it can be a shorthand. Jokes tend to be short; comic writing can often cover a lot more ground than a straightforward novel. This is not a particularly new observation, but most situations of a painful nature can be seen either as tragedy or comedy. The line can be very fine. *Tartuffe*, Molière's play, is a very good example. With a few very subtle adjustments it could be made quite tragic, and similarly the comic element in the play is often slightly marred by the fact that rather unpleasant things are going on.

Roy Blount, Jr.:   John Gielgud was once asked for advice on how to play Lear. Gielgud said his only advice was to be sure you have a "light Cordelia." If Lear weighed 150 pounds, Cordelia 149 pounds, 15 oz—tragedy. Lear 150 pounds and Cordelia 150 pounds, 1 oz—comedy. It seems to me that tragedy is a lot harder to sustain than comedy. Being funny is a fallback, a consolation. Woody Allen once said, before he got into various family problems, that being funny was the second choice. The first choice is to be noble.

John Mortimer: I would totally disagree with that. Anyone could toss up a tragedy on a wet afternoon. Anyone can write a serious Booker-prize book. But to be funny? I think it's the hardest possible thing. Only the greatest writers can do it. Shakespeare is infinitely a better writer than Milton is because Milton couldn't do any jokes. In fact, *King Lear* is full of jokes. So is *Hamlet*. I think comedy expresses the truth about the human situation because our lives are totally funny. I mean here we are, poised for a little murmur between two eternities, taking ourselves hugely seriously, discussing comedy or politics as though we really matter. If you want to tell the truth, you do it in comedy and probably in comedy which is also sad, as in Chekhov. But it's very very difficult. The most difficult things to write are comedies and detective stories because both of them require huge skill, whereas being sad and serious doesn't require much skill at all.

John Wells: Sometimes if you speed up tragedy it can become very funny. If you play Feydeau very, very slowly with a man saying, "Who-is-that-man-in-the-cupboard?" and the woman replying, "That-is-my-husband," then it becomes very serious and could be played, indeed, as tragedy. Speeded up, "Whoisthemaninthecupboard," and the woman replying, "Thatismyhusband," it becomes very funny. Do you think, John, you could actually take a tragic plot and make it wildly funny?

John Mortimer: It's interesting that with Feydeau the whole situation starts when the husband's braces arrive through the post. Why had he taken off his braces in some strange house? That's exactly the same plot as Othello's handkerchief. So you can make a comedy or a tragedy out of either of these situations — comedy, as you say, being tragedy played at a hundred revolutions a minute. In the theater you find that the biggest laughs you get are not from some wonderful epigram you've thought up, but when somebody says "What?" or "Who?" or "Who's at the door?" In the correct place, they're huge laughs. Comic writing isn't actually being able to be funny; it's being able to construct that situation which will fulfill the audience's expectation. Can I say a word about Feydeau? All his characters are extraordinarily serious, respectable, middle-class people. You can't write a really funny play about Swedish teenagers embroiled in free love. But you can write funny plays about extraordinarily respectable doctors, serious lawyers, and politicians.

Auberon Waugh: John Wells asked how you set about comic writing. I haven't written novels for about twenty years and can only talk about journalism. It seems to me that as soon as journalism is labeled comic, it's dead. Those comic columns don't work; humor's got to come out of apparent seriousness, an alternative perception, which you use humor to illuminate. I think if you set out to be funny, it's death.

Mordecai Richler: I come from a country where for a novel to pass muster it should be intractable and worthy, like health foods. If you actually enjoy reading it, and God help you, laugh aloud, it's somehow suspect. It's not cultural. Also, a big problem is that it's increasingly difficult to keep up with newspapers. This is an argument Philip Roth made about twenty years ago, and he's absolutely right. Only a few months back, there was a story about a legal secretary in San Francisco who had one of her breasts fondled and sued successfully for five million dollars. It's difficult to do satire when you're reading this kind of thing every day.

Roy Blount, Jr.:   I'm glad somebody mentioned Roth, who I think was a kind of transitional figure out of black humor into genuinely funny stuff. The largest writers—Twain, Dickens—are all funny. But they didn't work at being funny. They were able to give in to some sort of inherent humor.

Auberon Waugh: We think quite rightly that *Portnoy's Complaint* is a great comic novel, but it's rather like the Finns reading Wodehouse. It was read by all those sophomores who didn't realize it was comic at all, and that's why it made the big time.

Roy Blount, Jr.:   I think that any good writing, especially comedy, is visceral. You can get satisfaction from Wodehouse without knowing anything about his milieu because his language is so pleasant—in some sense *physically* pleasant—to read.

John Mortimer: They're great imaginative creations. It's a wonderful dream world. What Wodehouse did was what Dickens did: he painted an entire world of his own, which is a superb act of imagination.

Grey Gowrie: Nabokov's *Lolita* is a great post-war masterpiece. It is a very tragic book that you can be perfectly solemn about because it is about the variety and the impossibility of love. You could give a very long-faced lecture about it, but the moment you illustrated your lecture with some passages from the book, you'd have people breaking up as Nabokov is a Geiger counter of the absurd. Wodehouse is not thought of as a solemn literary critic, but he made a brilliant autobiographical critical comment. Famous for reading the Bible and Shakespeare every year (not just taking them to his desert island, but reading them through), he thought, basically, literature had either to be involved in the big stuff or be light. Auberon wrote five brilliant comic novels. I appear as the villain in one of them. It's interesting to me why you gave up.

Auberon Waugh: You won't get a personal statement from me. I just don't find novels so much fun as journalism. People are drawn to writing novels because they wish to expose or discover themselves. Those deeply boring selfish desires have nothing to do with entertaining other people or projecting some humorous perception of the world.

John Mortimer: That's the key word, isn't it. *Entertaining*. Somehow that's become a dirty word. Whereas it's the prime function of any art. There's a wonderful passage in one of Matisse's letters when he says that people lead very hard lives, work hard, and then come home, and what they want to be given is pleasure.

Calvin Trillin: To be funny, I think, is the least teachable and improvable part of writing. It's certainly not correlated with intelligence or talent. A gland or a gene or something. It has to do with a way of looking at things. I read somewhere that Updike didn't see any reason for comic novels—that a novel, a good novel, was comic. Although I have to say, most of Updike's novels are not terribly funny.

Grey Gowrie: Wordsworth was a great, moving writer, but funny he isn't.

Mordecai Richler: Woody Allen once said, "You don't get to sit at the big table if you're a comic novelist." So if a novel is not punishing Americans . . . I think in England people bear their culture much more lightly, and take it for granted in a way that Americans don't.

Malcolm Bradbury: It's interesting that in the fifties there was a culture in favor of comedy—Kingsley Amis, Muriel Spark, Anthony Burgess. All the interesting writers were writing in a comic frame. They saw the world through comic eyes, which doesn't mean they saw it trivially or emptily. Far from it.

Grey Gowrie: *Naked Lunch* is a great American comic novel. It was phantasmagoric and violent, but I still read it through.

John Gross: Did I hear lunch? What *about* lunch? Yeah, a naked lunch!

[Lunch]

The topic in the afternoon session, when we once again collected around the conference table in the Guest House, was the variety of humor.

Malcolm Bradbury: Where does the genre that I practice, fiction, come from? It does seem to me that the key date is 1605 with the book written by that wounded survivor of the Battle of Lepanto, Cervantes. *Don Quixote* is about the end of an old kind of book and the making of something new. What Cervantes conceives are actually comedies played against the romantic world that existed before. The two books (the second volume in 1615) are the beginning of the modern novel. The British are very slow people, so it took them a hundred years to figure out the value of this extraordinary generic invention. But then they did. In about forty years in Britain, from the early eighteenth century, they produced six great novelists, of whom four were comic writers. The two who were not comic writers are Defoe and Richardson. The four who were, of course, are Fielding, Swift, Sterne, and Smollett. Those four, between them, have invented a variety of comedic forms which are still profound and important to this day. Taking them in a kind of order, Fielding produced one of the classic definitions of comedy in the preface to *Joseph Andrews*, where he spoke about the novel as a comic epic poem in prose. The age was drunk on Aristotle and he had to produce an Aristotelian definition of what it was that he was doing. What did he mean? The novel is comic because it's not tragic, it's epic because it's big and wanders, a prose poem because it's not written in poetry. Then he goes on to define some of the essential characteristics of what he is doing. He says that comedy is a wandering between the creation of character and the creation of caricature. So words like caricature, burlesque, pastiche, and parody begin to frame the vocabulary of what he was doing. Swift is writing, of course, satire — the satire of blatant rage. Rage against the human condition and against the political order of the day, and in the end a kind of rage against living and dying: the human condition is abased. Smollett, who translated *Don Quixote*, is writing picaresque comedy — mad adventures, wanderings around the world, going everywhere. Sterne, who is perhaps the most interesting of the lot, takes this new form which has just been invented, reverses it and says, "Okay, we've got something called the novel. So let's have something else called the anti-novel." So, in *Tristram Shandy*, instead of starting as most novels at that time did, with the birth of the hero, he starts with the conception of the hero, a botched conception, so Tristram is born by temporal interruption. The rest of the novel is about not being able to write it. Sterne actually invents perhaps the most profound comic device ever invented, which is that the ending of the novel is his own death. He just keeps writing it until he drops dead. What finishes *Tristram Shandy* is indeed what Roland Barthes would call "the death of the author." So by the 1760s we actually have the comic novel fully in business as a basic British genre. At the same time

the French are busily doing the Encyclopedia and learning to
be philosophers, and Diderot is off advising Catherine the
Great, exporting hard thinking, though his *Rameau's Nephew*
is one of the great comic novels. Voltaire was also advising
princes and writing *Candide*. So the French too have their
comic fictional tradition. Americans at this time were not even
writing novels. It was Charles Brockden-Brown, the gloomy
writer of the gothic, James Fenimore Cooper, who is not comic
at all, and Poe, who was miserable for the best of reasons,
who set the tone of American fiction, essentially a gothic and
dark tradition until it's re-flavored by Hawthorne and Melville.
Hawthorne, I think, writes the first great American comic
novel in *The Blithedale Romance*, the first campus novel,
about Brook Farm and its group of transcendentalists who
have decided to find utopia. The second great comic novel,
which is not usually read as comic, is *Moby-Dick*, by Hawthorne's friend Melville, where he too teases the condition of
American thought, and points out that the benign dreams of
transcendentalists actually are a fanciful version laid over the
darkness of the real world. When the Civil War is over and
American culture resumes its business, it then inherits both the
massive presence of Charles Dickens and the great American
humorist Mark Twain, who is the real hero of the comic in
American fiction. By the nineteenth century, the comic, the
tragic, the difficult, have met in a wonderful apparatus of
prose fictional writings called the novel. It's a tradition carried
on in writers like Kafka, who is comic for all his mortal pain,
and Beckett who is comic for all his absurdity. And in Evelyn
Waugh who is comic for all his isolated rage on the one hand,
and his extraordinary exposure to himself on the other in books
like *The Ordeal of Gilbert Pinfold*, an extraordinary novel
about the vulnerability of the writer. This comic intelligence
is filled with different types of writing postures—benign comedy, parody, burlesque, bitter rage, black comedy, the anti-
novel . . . all of these into the frame of what the writer today
might choose to borrow from, might choose to do. Then we
add to that the late twentieth-century crisis, perhaps expressed
in a writer like Beckett whose novels deal with a world that

appears to have become meaningless, a world that has taken in existentialism, a world that has grown nonsensical in many of the elements that have to do with the writing of novels — that is to say, the construction of character, the construction of a sensible universe. An awful lot of the writing of Beckett is a return to the anti-novel that Sterne created but with a quite different map of the world. Powerful writers were taking on this tradition in America — people like Joseph Heller and Thomas Pynchon. Other examples are found in Eastern Europe in the work of dissident writers like Milan Kundera and Peter Esterhazy.

What I moan about is that my students tend to take reality straight, not borrowing from this history. They're not interested in the generic characteristics of the comic, the games that can be played with it, nor in its philosophical tradition . . . its ways of thinking about life, its ways of seeing human pain, its ways of seeing contradiction, dealing with crisis, its ways of upturning the logics that have been constructed in historical order. I very much want to hear whether Tibor has things to say about this. One of the striking things to me being the powerful persistence of angry humor in Eastern Europe — the kind that has begun to die after a period of real energy in America in the 1960s when people like Heller and Vonnegut and Coover were pretty enraged about their country and were writing comedies that meant something. I mean you had to read those books, not just because they were funny, but because of what they were saying about the culture. You had to read Kundera for the same reason. Now comedy is either just jokes or it's not there at all. The casualties, the energies, seem to me to be missing. We lack access to the varieties of humor in a way that was not true a few decades ago.

Tibor Fischer: I'm not sure it's so much that we don't have access to all the varieties of humor. It's just that the joke assumed an enormous importance in Eastern Europe because it was the only sort of folklore form of resistance that people had. That's how people kept in touch with what was going on and had a bit of relief at the same time. The joke in comic writing can never have that sort of importance in a free and fairly content society. Certainly in Hungary, as soon as there was a free election, the jokes stopped. I mean almost overnight. You still get jokes, but they're much more like the standard jokes you get here. Political humor more or less ground to a halt overnight.

John Mortimer: That suggests that comedy is only possible in a very restrictive society. It obviously flourished in Eastern Europe because it was a way of protesting tyranny. It flourished in the nineteenth century because people were shocked. But if you live in a society like ours where you can say anything, nothing's funny anymore. I would like to ask you, Malcolm: would it help anyone to write funnily if, say, all those books you catalogue very happily were read through . . . would it make you a better, funnier writer than you were before?

Malcolm Bradbury: No, not necessarily. But the reason I catalogue them is, in part, to point out how many different destinations the comic impulse actually provides.

John Wells: That's an interesting question, whether or not reading all those funny novels would make you funny. I bet everyone around this table has had certain things read to them as a child which go very deep. Certainly in my case, Wodehouse, probably Stephen Leacock. But I don't think you can ever sit down and expect that influence to actually produce anything.

Calvin Trillin: I agree. I don't think you can sit down thinking, Oh well, I can do that, or I'll do one of those because that seems to be what people like. Even if it's a form that they find really almost demeaning, they find they can't do it. Because you're not following the idea; you're starting in the wrong place. You're working backward.

John Wells: Most of us think on paper, and not before.

Calvin Trillin: Humor, it seems to me, is almost always better in the specific than in the general. I can't think of an instance in which general things are funnier than specific. I think you have to know about something in order to write humorously. That is because so much of it is in the details. There used to be a writing course at Yale called "Daily Themes" in which you wrote a little vignette every day and turned it in for criticism. To have something to do in class, they invented some rules, and one of them was "Individualize by specific detail." Roy found it wonderfully convenient writing about the Jimmy Carter family, partly because he's from Decatur, Georgia. He knows the nuances, the little details; it's closer to home to him. I suspect that if he were writing about people in Dublin, it would be harder for him.

Roy Blount, Jr.:   I have argued that the Southern tradition is Afro-Celtic. At any rate, Southerners take the English language less for granted than most Anglo-Saxons do. We find it musical and strange, and like to play around with it, dragging chickens in with high-flown language and being tickled by the mix. Southern humor tends to involve eating. That's part of its orality. I wrote a small verse which goes like this: *"I like to eat an uncooked oyster. / Nothing's slicker, nothing's moister. / Nothing's easier on your gorge, / Or when the time comes, to discharge. / But not to let it too long rest / Within your mouth is always best. / For if your mind dwells on an oyster . . . / Nothing's slicker, nothing's moister. / I prefer my oyster fried. / Then I'm sure my oyster's died."* Southerners like to roll language around in their mouths, in a frolicsome way. They also like to take things literally: there's a joke about an old boy who's asked if he believes in infant baptism, and he says, "Believe in it? Hell, I've seen it done."

Malcolm Bradbury: I was really struck by something said this morning—the question of whether humor travels across the Atlantic. I had a weird experience when my second novel came out. I had sent the manuscript over to Knopf. After a while

I received the manuscript back, and it had been profoundly edited. I called up and asked, "Well, why has this book been edited?" I was told, "We decided you'd written a comic novel and we didn't want any humor so we've taken it all out." So I withdrew the book. Afterwards I met with Blanche Knopf and asked her, "Why take the humor out of my novel, there's nothing else in it." She said, "Oh well, the person who edited your book won the *Mademoiselle* short-story contest. The prize was to come to Knopf and edit a book, so she had to think of something."

[End of Session]

The schedule informed that in the evening after dinner we were to gather in the Guest House library for after-dinner drinks and where over the course of the conversazione *each of us was to read either from one's own work or a humorous passage that one especially coveted — "a cherished text" as Lord Gowrie put it in his opening remarks. I forgot to bring anything of my own — cherished or not. I looked through the books in the Guest House library — a magnificent collection — and noticed Ambrose Bierce's* Devil's Dictionary. *He always used a goose quill to write (as I read in the introduction) though hardly the most interesting thing about him. I copied down a few of his definitions ("Riddle (n) Who elects our rulers?; Non-Combatant (n) A dead Quaker; Propitiate (v) Calling a bulldog 'good boy' when he has a firm hold on you from behind"), thinking I would offer a collection as my contribution. John Mortimer and Auberon Waugh were scheduled for the first evening.*

John Mortimer: It's very much too late to make a speech. It's really way past my bedtime. Obviously, in a three-day seminar on the nature of comedy, jokes would be totally inappropriate, so I shan't do any of those. I haven't really rehearsed. You can rehearse far too much, and that's also a great error. The only rehearsal story I know is about a very puritanical

Welsh actor who had to play the part of King Duncan in *Macbeth*. I'm sure you remember that after coming on stage King Duncan is faced with a bleeding soldier who gives him news of the battle. King Duncan's first line is, "What bloody man is that?" This actor was extremely distressed at having to say this awful swearword in public, so he went to the producer and said, "How can I possibly come on the stage and say 'What bloody man is that?' The Broadcasting Standards Council will shut us down. William Rees-Mogg will write a letter in the *Times*. The whole thing will be . . . I cannot say 'What bloody man is that.'" So the producer said, "Well, go away and rehearse." So he went down to his cottage by the seaside and walked up and down the beach and said, "What bloody man *is* that? What bloody *man* is that? What bloody man is *that*?" Then, when it was time for the performance, he came straight out on stage and said, "Who is that bugger?" Which makes it plain why it's important not to rehearse.

Comedy, I think, comes from your experience in life, in my case from the law. One of the richest veins of comedy I struck was very, very early in my career when I became a divorce barrister. My father was one of the most famous divorce barristers of his day. In the nursery, instead of telling the story of Snow White and the Seven Dwarfs, we used to get "The Duchess and the Seven Co-respondents." I can think of no better source of comedy really than being a divorce barrister — particularly as the divorce law was in those days. In those days you couldn't get a divorce unless you could prove adultery or cruelty. I had a client who had enormous trouble finding anyone prepared to commit adultery with his wife. He was driven to such terrible lengths that he put on a false beard, mustache, and dark glasses and crept into his mobile home to sleep with his wife for the purpose of providing evidence. He was sent to prison for perverting the course of justice, which I thought was extremely unfair since most men sleep with their wives without being sent to prison.

When I got into murder cases I found out rather surprising things. Murderers, compared with people in divorce cases, are extremely agreeable clients. People in divorce cases ring you up at two in the morning and say, "You know what he's just done now, he's gone away with the telescope, that's what he's done." But murderers have usually killed the one person in life who's really been bugging them, and a kind of peace has descended over them.

On the nature of comedy, I would like to say that murder is the sort of crime that perfectly ordinary people can slide into. None of us would probably want to rob a bank, but we might find we were tempted to do away with someone. I want to read you two newspaper items in order to prove how a perfectly respectable person can slide into committing a murder. This little cutting from the *Edinburgh Evening News* of 18 August 1978 may come into use to you in the study of comedy.

While they were waiting at a bus stop in Clerimston, Mr. and Mrs. Daniel Thirsty were threatened by Mr. Robert Clear. "He demanded that I give him my wife's purse," said Mr. Thirsty. "Telling him that the purse was in her basket, I bent down, put my hands up her skirt, detached her artificial leg and hit him over the head with it. It was not my intention to do any more than frighten him off but, unhappily for us all, he died."

The other cutting which may be of use to you shows that the murderers I defended were not particularly good at it — a comic turn indeed. I suppose that if they had been good at it they wouldn't have been in the position of having to be defended.

Dwarfing all known records for matrimonial homicide, Mr. Peter Scott of Southsea made seven attempts to kill his wife without her once noticing that anything was wrong. In 1980 he took out an insurance policy on his good lady which would bring him £250,000 in the event of her accidental death. Soon afterwards, he placed a lethal dose of mercury in her strawberry flan, but it all rolled out. Not wishing to waste this deadly substance

he next stuffed her mackerel with the entire contents of
the bottle. This time she ate it, but with no side effects
whatsoever. Warming to the task, he then took his better
half on holiday to Yugoslavia. Recommending the pan-
oramic views, he invited her to sit on the edge of a cliff.
She declined to do so, prompted by what she later described as some "sixth sense." The same occurred only
weeks later when he urged her to savor the view from
Beachy Head. When his spouse was in bed with chicken-
pox he started a fire outside her bedroom door, but some
interfering busybody put it out. Undeterred, he started
another fire and burnt down the entire flat. The wife of
his bosom escaped uninjured. Another time he asked her
to stand in the middle of the road so that he could drive
towards her and check if his brakes were working. At no
time did Mrs. Scott feel that the magic had gone out of
their marriage. Since it appeared nothing short of a small
nuclear bomb would have alerted this good woman to
her husband's intentions, he eventually gave up and con-
fessed everything to the police. After the case a detective
said Mrs. Scott had been "absolutely shattered" when told
of her husband's plot to kill her. "She had not twigged it
at all and was dumbstruck."

Well, there you are. This is life. What I've found as a writer
is that you have to keep taming it down, making it less improbable in order to fit into some sort of fictional context. Wouldn't
you agree?

Auberon Waugh read from his Will That Do?*, an account
of his father, Evelyn, and the end of rationing in post-war
England.*

On one occasion, just after the war, the first contingent
of bananas reached Britain. Neither I, my sister Teresa
nor my sister Margaret had ever eaten a banana throughout the war, when they were unprocurable, but we had
heard all about them as the most delicious taste in the
world. When this first consignment arrived, the socialist

government decided that every child in the country should be allowed one banana. An army of civil servants issued a library of special banana coupons, and the great day arrived when my mother came home with three bananas. All three were put on my father's plate, and before the anguished, he poured on cream, which was almost unprocurable, and sugar, which was heavily rationed, and ate all three. A child's sense of justice may be defective in many respects, and egocentric at the best of times, but it is no less intense for either. By any standards, he had done wrong. It would be absurd to say that I never forgave him, but he was permanently marked down in my estimation from that moment, in ways which no amount of sexual transgression would have achieved. From that moment, I never treated anything he had to say on faith or morals very seriously.

Afterwards, John Mortimer showed me a little sketch he'd written about Robert Graves which he would have read if his allotted time had not run out. He gave me a copy:

I asked what Robert Graves had done in the last war. Was he, perhaps, in some secret service? We all know from *Good-Bye To All That* of his experiences in the First World War.

"In the last war," he said, quite without boasting, "I won the Battle of Anzio. Shall I tell you how I did it?"

I said I'd be very glad to know.

"Well, I was bicycling round the island of Jersey," Graves said, "and I met an officer from my old regiment, the Welsh Guards. I asked him what he was doing, and he said he was off to fight the Eyeties at the Battle of Anzio. So I said if he'd give me time to ride round a little more I'd come back to him in, say, half an hour, and tell him my plan for defeating the Eyeties."

"And did you?"

"Oh yes. I rode round and thought it all out and then I came back. My officer was still there and I said to him, 'Look here, I've thought out a perfect plan. Let me tell you the secret of the Eyeties. They cannot stand the sound of a woman in labor. If he hears the sound of a woman in labor, your average Eyetie will run a mile. So all you have to do is to go down to Queen Charlotte's Hospital and record the sound of women in labor. Then play them on your gramophones on the beaches and every Eyetie soldier will run a mile.' Well, he did and they did, and that is exactly how he won the Battle of Anzio."

The evening reading is invariably followed by standing around and trading ribald stories and jokes. Almost everyone in the English contingent had a sheep-shagging story. Of the Americans I drew a blank on this one, and I can't recall if Bud Trillin chimed in, but Roy pulled it out for the U.S. side by recounting a number of Southern variations on that particular theme. One of Roy's phrases—in that long, drawled Southern accent of his—will echo in my head for a long time. It was: "Someone was asking me last night if I'd ever had oral sex with a chicken."

So I was sitting with Roy in the Guest House after the evening reading. Suddenly, an odd thumping sound from upstairs—I first thought from the Trillins' room overhead. He and his wife, Alice, were celebrating their thirtieth wedding anniversary, and I thought it might have been a bit of Kansas City exuberance. Not at all. When I heard another thump, I realized what I was hearing were fireworks going off over the lake—fireworks, my passion! "Hey!" I cried to Roy, "Fireworks." Carrying my miniscule beaker with whatever after-dinner drink was in it, I rushed out the door into the blackness of the night, tore across the gravel of the driveway onto the lawn, and as I swept left around the corner of the villa onto the terrace to get a better view, the tantalizing half of a Chinese firework still hanging in the sky, I tripped over a low chaise longue and fell flat, as if I had been picked up and thrown down like a rag doll. "I'm damaged," I said to Roy who had come up behind me. I truly was. The left side of my face had been disarranged. A pool of DNA lay on the flagstones.

I was patched up at a little hospital above Menaggio. The

*reaction of the humorists to my plight, my being Bela Lugosied
by the flagstones of the Villa Ecco, has been interesting. The
British contingent is enormously sympathetic: "Oh, I'm sorry,"
"Oh, dear," "Oh, what a shame," as if somehow they were
culpable. The colonials are much nastier. "Hey, is that your
idea of a pratfall?", "Trying to make us laugh?" etc. The next
morning I stayed in bed recuperating while the session went
on below. The topic was "The Nationality of Humor." I could
hear them laughing . . .*

Grey Gowrie: George is not dead, but asleep.

John Gross: Jokes, those mysterious things that are manufac-
tured who-knows-where, still, in my experience, demographi-
cally loom as large about national and ethnic types as ever.
Not all nationality jokes are nasty, but they are a huge element
of humor as a mass product. Some of this is absolutely inevitable. Without going as far as being really hostile, foreigners
are odd. There's a character, identified only as an old gentleman who makes a single appearance in Boswell's *Life of Johnson*, and his only recorded remark is: "For ought I can see,
foreigners are fools." I think that's basic and also much better
than saying foreigners are dogs and ought to be put down.
The sense that there is something fundamentally foolish and
odd about foreigners is very widespread and not to be simply
wished away at the stroke of a humanitarian pen.
     It seems to me that a lot of humor is really about types
rather than nationalities. Humor, particularly mass humor,
needs categories, and if we all belong to one race, then we
invent them. Sagittarians would all be stingy, Librans would
all be drunk, Tauruses would all be stupid, and so on. However, we know that those types also bear some relation to
reality, and that they also relate in many cases to the misfor-
tunes suffered by these groups. We know that it's a touchy
problem.
     A lot of national jokes are reprehensible, but I think that
a good deal of what is or might be legitimately funny about

national groups is not that they have such and such attributes—because most of the faults and failings one laughs at are kind of universal—but that they have them in such and such a way: a Frenchman is greedy in a French way, an Englishman is snobbish in an English way, and so on. They have no monopoly on their faults. It's the accents to their vices and follies, not the vices and follies as such. Then, of course, the best exponents of national or ethnic failings are members of the group themselves. We know that protected minorities are often allowed to make irritating jokes about themselves which nobody else can make in decent company. This is also true at high levels, where they become something other than just national jokes. For example, a play like *The Playboy of the Western World* is not just about being Irish as such; it's about human failings to which the Irish, in some situations, might be more prone than other groups. The whole feel of it has a specifically Irish tone. Yes, anyone can be boastful, treacherous, or violent, but when rural Irish are boastful, treacherous, or violent, they are in this kind of way. Synge gets it exquisitely right because he knows the thing from the inside: it stings for many Irish who object to it, though not the sensible ones. On the whole, jokes about cultures, beyond very primitive levels, are best done within the cultures themselves.

An awful lot of humor turns on allusions, nuances, great precision—it's anything but universal in this sense—and it's a little bit like the problem of humor of the past. The allusions get lost or fade away, and of course a footnote or an explanation is the most fatal thing to a joke. At all levels of humor, even the most popular humor, when it's verbal, it is very finely calibrated. We all know that a single word, or a single intonation, a single placing of a word, or a single verbal shading is all the difference between being horribly jocular and just spot on. We do learn to an amazingly complicated degree, without being conscious about it, what works and what doesn't, what word or turn of phrase is inspired and which one is labored.

In trying to define national characteristics in humor, it's mainly a question of style, local reference, and various predilections. I don't think any major culture specializes in one form of humor at the expense of others. In Russia, the only two classic novelists who are actually funny are Gogol and Chekhov. They couldn't be more different; Gogol writes a kind of serious sitcom that's grotesque and a bit like Dickens, but obviously in a very Russian way. Chekhov's is a comedy of human nature of an utterly different kind.

In thinking of humor that doesn't travel, either Brian Urquhart or Conor Cruise O'Brien—I can't remember which—described the late Dag Hammarskjold, secretary general of the United Nations, as walking down a corridor toward him with a humorless twinkle in his eye. A hell of a lot of European humor approaches me with a humorless twinkle in its eye. I suppose British humor is seen by Europeans the same way, although it appears that a good deal of English humor travels. Maybe we flatter ourselves.

Calvin Trillin: Good jokes about different nationalities actually tell you something about the nationality rather than the person who's the butt of the joke.

John Wells: How could you possibly make an illuminative joke about a group of fifteen million people?

Calvin Trillin: Well, you could do the culture. There are certainly Jewish jokes that illuminate the Jewish tradition of complaining, for instance. There's the joke about the grandmother who dotes on her only grandchild, a three-year-old boy, and begs her daughter to leave the child with her in Florida while the daughter goes on a short vacation. So the daughter leaves for two weeks, goes to Nassau, and lets the grandmother have the child. The grandmother's in heaven. One day the little boy is walking along the beach in Miami, and suddenly a huge tidal wave comes, grabs him and sweeps him away. Gone! The grandmother looks up and cries out, "God, this is my whole world, this is my life. I can't stand this. I'll do anything, I'll feed the poor, I'll go to synagogue every day. Please bring back my grandchild!" Suddenly there's a flash of lightning, and another wave comes and deposits the boy back on the beach. He lands on his feet. He's fine! The grandmother looks up and says, "Hey, where's his hat? He had a hat." Now, this is a Jewish joke about complaint.

John Mortimer: You can't apply good taste to comedy, can you? Part of the pleasure of laughing is knowing you're probably doing something you shouldn't be doing.

That night the after-dinner session in the Guest House library included readings by John Wells, who read a section of the first chapter of Fielding's Tom Jones, *Tibor Fischer from his novel* Under the Frog, *Calvin Trillin a spoof on newspaper correction columns, Malcolm Bradbury a passage from his collection of essays* Unsent Letters, *about how German thesis writers examine British comic novelists, and Grey Gowrie, who read a passage from Alistair Horne's book* For the Price of Glory. *Mordecai Richler and John Gross offered the following extracts. I felt better, so I was able to enjoy the readings.*

Mordecai Richler: A couple of pages of an ordeal we have all gone through. A book tour.

No sooner did I fly home, boorishly refusing to answer my family's questions about the tour, feeling that to have lived through it once was sufficient, than I was off again, this time to speak at the *Detroit News* Book and Author Luncheon as well as handle the usual batch of TV and radio interviews. Upon arrival in a seemingly abandoned city at 7:30 on a Sunday evening, I checked into the hotel Pontchartrain. The desk man, noting my Canadian address, cautioned me, "You're in Detroit now. You're not to go out for a walk. Right?"

At 6:45 the next morning, I turned up as scheduled at TV-2 News, and there I encountered another speaker at the lunch, Irving Stone. After lighting up a Schimmelpenninck, a Dutch cigarillo, I offered him my hand.

Stone, glowering, snapped, "You're not going to blow that stuff in my face on camera, are you?"

At lunch, Stone began by telling the audience of 1,200 ladies that they were wonderful, absolutely wonderful; obviously not a walker, he added how pleased he was to be in Detroit. "Why," he asked in a booming voice, "do people read my books? I don't deal in sex or violence." The ladies applauded.

"They read my books because I tell great human stories."

More applause.

"And what are the great human stories?" he asked, "Tom Jones, The Brothers Karamazov, War and Peace, Madame Bovary."

Stone, a fine performer, speaking without notes, told the ladies that he did not want them to read his books, no, he wanted the ladies to *live* them, just as he had not merely written his historical novels, but had actually *become* Van Gogh and Michelangelo.

Well now, I've never been to Stone's house in Beverly Hills, and so I don't know what magic he's done to his ceilings, but I'm willing to swear he wasn't missing an ear. Anyway, I was grateful for the sake of all the ladies present that he hadn't also written *The Carpetbaggers*.

I appeared with Stone again on a radio show later in the afternoon; there was a live audience.

"Today," our ebullient host declared, "we have with us the great American novelist Irving Stone; one of the world's ten best-dressed men, actor George Hamilton; and a writer from Canada."

Soon Stone was saying, "Why do people read my books? Because I don't deal in sex or violence. They read my books because I tell great human stories . . ."

"And exactly how many books have you written, Mr. Stone?"

"Twenty-five."

"Twenty-five. That's amazing. And how many years did each one take?"

"Four."

George Hamilton was wearing a gold bracelet and gold ring; the first two buttons of his shirt were undone. As Irving Stone lived his books, so George Hamilton said he lived the characters he played. Then, turning to me, he added how much he had disliked the film of *Duddy Kravitz*. You start out by liking the character, he said, finding him funny, and then you discover he's nasty. With John Wayne, he pointed out, you always knew where you stood.

Now it was my turn to shine. Our host, glancing at the studio clock, said, "Sorry we never got a chance to mention your book."

John Gross: These are all from my *Oxford Book of Comic Verse* and they're all very short. The first one, by Hilaire Belloc, is about Lord Heygate.

> Lord Heygate had a troubled face,
> His furniture was commonplace—
> The sort of peer who well might pass
> For someone of the middle class.
> I do not think you want to hear
> About this unimportant peer.

This is an epitaph by Stevie Smith entitled "On the Death of a German Philosopher."

> He wrote *The I and the It*
> He wrote *The It and the Me*
> He died at Marienbad
> And now we are all at sea.

This is a Phyllis McGinley poem called "Squeeze Play."

> Jackson Pollock had a quaint
> Way of saying to his sibyl,

'Shall I dribble?
Should I paint?'
And with never an instant's quibble,
Sybil always answered,
'Dribble.'

And now a poem by a lesser-known British poet — Stanley J.
Sharpless. It's called "Low Church."

It was after vespers one evening
When the vicar, inflamed by desire,
Beckoned a lad to the vestry,
Dismissing the rest of the choir.

He said, "I've got something to show you,"
The boy followed hard on his heels,
Behind the locked door there was silence,
Except for some half-muffled squeals.

The vicar got two years (suspended),
The judge spoke of 'moral decay',
The vicar is sadder and wiser,
But the choir-boy is happy and gay.

Now a very short one by the American poet A.R. Ammons:

"Their Sex Life"

One failure on
top of another.

Here's another very short one, this by X.J. Kennedy:

"To Someone Who Insisted I Look up Someone"

I rang them up while touring Timbuctoo,
Those bosom chums to whom you're known as '*Who?*'

And finally a poem which might seem appropriate on this occasion. It's by Wendy Cope and is based on a reviewer's comment in the *Spectator*: "She is witty and unpretentious, which is both her strength and her limitation. They (Roger McGough and Brian Patten) have something in common with her in that they all write to amuse." It's called "Serious Concerns."

I'm going to try and overcome my limitation—
Away with sloth!
Now should I work at being less witty? Or more pretentious?
Or both?
Write to amuse? What an appalling suggestion!
I write to make people anxious and miserable to worsen their indigestion.

[*At the final plenary session we were
asked to make summary remarks.*]

Malcolm Bradbury: What has been interesting about the whole event, I think, is that it proves what I suppose we all knew from the start, which is that comedy and humor always break open the frames in which you try to put them. Theory dissolves into laughter and that is the fundamental pleasure of the whole affair. It was said yesterday that there are very few books on comedy, and I think that's one of the reasons. There is actually one good book, *Comedy*, by a guy called T.G.A. Nelson. It's perhaps worth just jotting down the contents list. It starts with "Laughter" and then "Comedy and Related Forms." There's a very long section on marriage which he obviously regards as the first essential aspect of comedy. Then "Procreation," "Death" (an extensive chapter), "Rogue and Trickster," "Dupers and Duped," "The Fool," "The Language of Comedy," "Reality and Fantasy," "Reflective Comedy," "Absurd and Existential Comedy," "Festivity," "Laugh-

ter or Harmony," and then "Suggested Further Reading."
"Suggested Further Reading" isn't all that much. There's a
man who lives in Brighton called John Hart who did a list of
the two-hundred and fifty humorous novels in English entitled
The Crinkly and the Comic, for some reason. Crinkly, by the
way, refers to the amusement factor which falls short of frank
comicality. Some of the books are about as funny as Wagner's
Ring Cycle. This is about as far as good scholarship goes.
Most people in most cultures laugh. The sense of contradiction and absurdity that they find to laugh at is a crucial human
possession. A definition of the human itself. But humor also
needs culture to shape it, to take it forward. It needs the
institutions, it needs the magazines, the *New Yorkers*, the
Punches, or whatever, the *Private Eyes*. It needs the theaters
and the theatrical spaces. It needs the movies. It needs the
conflicts and it needs the audiences. As we were dispersing
last night, the television came on in the other room and it
suddenly became apparent that the hideous conflict in Bosnia
had degraded into absurd comedy with chained-up Canadian
soldiers attached to lampposts by the Bosnian Serbs as hostages
in an act which can only be a kind of sick parody of war. As
I looked at that it struck me that even in the heart of war the
humorous instinct to degrade does not entirely disappear.

Humor may be under duress and human nature may be
going through some sort of change . . . and the only answer
to that as far as I can see is more humor . . . Long may it
flourish.

Grey Gowrie: I'm sure we agree with a great deal of what
Malcolm said. Comedy and humor are not necessarily the same
thing, which undoes the picture in a lot of discussions of
literary comedy. Comedy can be a literary form, yes, dealing
with things which are absurd, grotesque and so forth, but it's
not necessarily meant to make one laugh, and often doesn't
make one laugh. A simple joke obviously makes one laugh
more than many great works of literature which one could
fairly call comedy. More specifically is that Bosnian example —
comedy in some sense because it's grotesque, a kind of bizarre

carnival these people are making out of their situation. It's a source of comic reference. But in itself, I must say I don't think there's anything humorous about it. These people's lives are threatened and the symbolism of that threat is to try and prevent any peacemaking in the area. There are a lot of things which are comic in the sense of grotesque, bizarre, a distortion of reality, a deliberate caricature of things, but it's not the same thing as humor if humor is above all to entertain and to liberate . . . its main purpose, if you will.

Auberon Waugh: In America, to a certain extent, the word *serious* is the word of highest praise. Anyone who's "serious" is worth paying attention to. Anything else is frivolous and to be despised. I don't think we need worry too much about that. But where one does find these pressures against humor more particularly, I'm sorry to say, is from the feminist movement. That is the great area of opposition to humor in any form. They put on these absolutely frozen faces. That is the only point I wish to make at this plenary session.

Roy Blount, Jr.:   How many female humorists does it take to change a lightbulb?

John Gross: That's not funny.

Roy Blount, Jr.:   That's the answer!

John Mortimer: From the literary point of view I would be quite content to be left with the two great masters of this century, Wodehouse and Waugh, and Feydeau to tell me how to construct funny plots, and Chekhov to tell me how sad comedy is. With those I would feel that I had enough. Now if you're writing comedy, I don't think you should worry about whether you're going to change the world, or even think a great deal about the audience. What you're doing is translating the world that you see into some form of entertainment, hoping that you'll make people laugh by surprise and recognition.

When you write, if you can make yourself laugh, then there's a decent chance that you'll make everybody else laugh too. If you bore yourself and drop into a light doze, that's going to be the reaction you're going to have on everybody else. The audience will have to worry about whether we're making them better or worse for what we're doing with them. We're subject to no literary rules, no rules of taste since bad taste is a vital element of humor. The interesting thing is to push the audience towards the limits of its taste and just leave it there trembling. Certainly no political rules, certainly no feminist rules. We must go on trying to entertain ourselves and then hope that we'll entertain somebody else.

John Wells: I wanted really to praise Gowrie for expressing the greatest truth in the fewest possible words when he used the expression in his opening remarks, "The blowing of deflationary raspberries." Because it brings me back to my theme of the fart. If the human voice goes on uninterrupted by laughter, there is a very intensive unease that oneself is being very boring, or someone else is being very boring. When someone laughs, all that tension is released, just as one feels a certain physical malaise before flatulence. The moment everyone laughs, we're all immediately united, we all forgive each other, and you've got your grump out of the way about how much you're bored by yourself or by the person who's talking. Thus the right image in all this and our job is to blow off at every possible moment.

This generated cries around the table of "Hold on, now," "Just a moment," "Hey, wait!" etc., etc.

Roy Blount, Jr.:   The most edifying thing I've learned here is that ancient Britons painted their backsides blue to disconcert their enemies, which I think is a highly civilized form of warfare. I apologize for always having assumed that it was to attract sexual partners.

The other day I may have suggested that being funny was

a sort of a pathology, as if the ability to be professionally humorous derived from a form of dyslexia. I didn't mean to deny that there is artistry involved. Part of it involves finding the right distance — almost like finding enough leeway or elbow room to throw a punch in boxing. With enough distance, almost anything can be made funny. Bombing peacekeepers chained to posts might be funny in five hundred years — we joke about all sorts of horrific practices in earlier periods. Sometimes you haven't got enough distance, and that's part of the challenge.

Mordecai Richler: The pressures against humor that we cited here, such as militant feminism, are also a rich source of humor. Where would we be without the absurdities? The only point I'd like to make is that any humorist who thinks he's going to change anything is already in serious trouble. All we're trying to do is make reality somewhat more acceptable. In the West the only risk we run is winning a medal if you write a very good satire. But in the East it's a different story altogether, and those people had to be a very brave to do what they did.

Calvin Trillin: I can only actually make myself laugh about two or three times a year while I'm writing, but if they put me in solitary confinement I would not be totally without resources. I would have a couple of chuckles during the year. Humor was thriving in Eastern Europe under an extremely oppressive regime, and it seems to me it's thriving in America under a regime that if anything is too easy on people . . . that is you can say nearly anything and the worst punishment would be to be called "outrageous," which is probably good for your next book advance. It's all in the doing. It's either funny or it isn't. If it's not funny, it's much more likely to be offensive to people than if it is funny. In the end, if the lady in the second row laughs, it's funny.

I've done several stories on stand-up comedians, and they turned out to be among the most neurotic people I've ever met. This is not the only reason, but if no one laughs, you can't say, "Well, you're wrong. What I said was really quite funny. The audience in my previous gig, much better educated and more sophisticated than you, laughed their heads off." The difference is that if I did a piece for *The New Yorker* on a murder somewhere and someone said, "I have a cousin who lives in that town and he says you're wrong about this and that," I would probably say, "Well, your cousin has his big toe stuck in his ear; he is absolutely wrong for the following reasons . . ." You can't do that sort of thing with humor. Humor, I'm afraid, is indefensible — of all the forms of writing the least explainable, the least analyzable.

Tibor Fischer: In his *Poetics*, Aristotle doesn't say a great deal about comedy. When he's musing on the origins of comedy, he just says, well, it probably originated in village revelry or dirty songs. The scholars and literary folk at the time weren't particularly interested in and didn't make any record of it, unlike, for instance, the development of tragedy.

George Plimpton: Well, considering the state of my face, perhaps I should speak to the healing aspects of humor. If it had not been for Auberon's banana story about his father, John Gross's imitation of Lord Annan, the extraordinary number of sheep-shagging jokes, I probably would have died.

But Trillin's mention of stand-up comics being neurotic reminds me that I once tried a stint as a stand-up comic my-self — performing on the stage of Caesar's Palace in Las Vegas as part of a television documentary on humor. I had a number of splendid coaches — Buddy Hackett, Bob Hope, Steve Allen, among them, and also Woody Allen, who didn't think I'd have a very good time out there. I had a routine written for me by a pair of writers for a very successful television show called "Laugh-In." It was full of John Wayne and Howard Hughes jokes. I went to the writers and complained. I said to them, "I don't think you've captured my style." They said, "If we could capture your style, we'd put it in a cage and club

it to death." So anyway I went out and performed. Jonathan
Winters, one of my coaches, had suggested for my entrance
that I peek out between the curtains and call out to the audience in a simpering voice: "Hi!" I resisted.

The analogy that came to mind being out there on the stage
was that it was like fishing at night. You throw this joke far
out into this black lake and you hope for a strike. It's exhilarating, of course, when there is one, and it's magical that somehow you've performed a kind of service in making people
laugh. Sometimes, of course, you hurl the John Wayne joke,
or whatever, far out into the darkness, and nothing happens.
You keep on reeling in and nothing *touches* it. Despair. A
numbness . . . what they call out there "flop sweat."

I remember that John Mortimer in his interview for *The
Paris Review* some years ago mentioned that a writer-friend
of his had gotten onto the tube at Piccadilly and noticed a
young woman seated opposite reading one of his novels. He
looked to see where she was in the book and realized that
fifteen or twenty pages further on there was a big laugh. So
he stayed on the train through Green Park, which was his
destination, all the way to Cockfosters at the end of the line
. . . waiting for a laugh . . . which never came!

All of which suggests what a brave and intrepid breed has
turned up for this conference. I like to think that Tibor is on
the mark when he suggests that humor serves a very useful
purpose, it's most useful to transmogrify unpleasant aspects
of life into something agreeable. Would anyone like to hear
an old John Wayne joke . . . ?

—edited by G.A.P.

The End: An Introduction

John Barth

. . . As I was saying, ladies and gentlemen, before that little unpleasantness: I have just been assured, by those in position to know, that this evening's eminent "mystery guest" has arrived, and should be with us any time now.

Did I say "arrived"? In the literary sense and on the literary scene, our distinguished visitor "arrived," of course, with her first collection of poems, or at latest with her prizewinning second. On the international political scene, as the whole world knows, she arrived with a vengeance — excuse the poor joke, not intended — upon the publication of that more recent, truly epical poetic satire of hers whose very title it is dangerous to mention favorably in some quarters, though thank heaven not here. At least I *hope* not here; that unbecoming ruckus just now makes me wonder. And as of just a short time ago, I'm delighted to announce, she has arrived in our city. Even as I stretch out these introductory remarks — introducing my introduction, I suppose we might say, while we await together the main event — the most controversial poet of our dying century (*politically* controversial, it's important to remember, not artistically controversial, for better or worse) is in mid-whisk from the airport to our campus, to honor us by inaugurating this new lecture series. In that final sense, she should arrive here in the flesh — the all too mortal, all too vulnerable flesh — within the quarter hour.

In that meantime, I thank again the overwhelming majority of you for your patience with this unavoidable delay. It is owing, let me repeat, neither to any dilatoriness whatever on our visitor's part nor to transoceanic air-traffic problems, but solely to the extraordinary security measures that, alas, necessarily attend and not infrequently impede the woman's every movement. Who could have imagined that, at this hour of the world, a mere book, a mere *poem*, could provoke so dreadful a stir?

Well. As some of you may know, I myself am a writer, not of verse but of fiction: one whose "controversiality," such as it is, is fortunately of the aesthetic rather than the political variety. And I must acknowledge that although it is my professional line of work to imagine myself into other people's situations, I cannot for the life of me imagine what it must be like for such a free, proud, articulate, sensitive, gregarious, impassioned, and altogether high-spirited spirit as our impending visitor's to endure and even to go on making art under her constricted circumstances — not to mention courageously putting herself in harm's way by accepting from time to time such invitations as ours (whose absence of advance publicity I'm sure you appreciate, although your numbers suggest that word somehow got out despite our precautions). I shake my head; I am awed, truly humbled. It was my good fortune to first meet and enjoy the company of our eminent/imminent guest some years ago, before the present storm of political controversy broke upon her, back when she and I were happily just representative scribblers from two different countries sharing a lecture platform in a third — and I heartily do not envy her present celebrity! At the same time, for her sake if not for my own, I much wish that some Arabian-Nights genie could put me and every one of us who treasure artistic freedom

and deplore murderous zealotry into our guest's skin, each of
us for just a single day, and she in ours, to give us the chas-
tening, attention-focusing taste of terrorism and to give her,
who must surely crave it, a bit of respite therefrom: a souvenir
of the artist's more usual condition of being blissfully ignored
by the world at large.

But I was speaking of meantimes, was I not—indeed, both
of meantimes and of mean times, and of introductions to
introductions. For some decades, as it happens, I have belonged to that peculiarly American species, the writer in the
university. Indeed, it has been my pleasure and privilege for
many years now to be a full-time teacher at this institution
as well as a full-time writer of fiction. As, again, some few
of you may have heard, at the end of the current semester I'll
be retiring from that agreeable association (my replacement
has yet to be named, but I don't mind confiding to you that
we're taking advantage of this new lecture series to look over
a roster of likely candidates—not including tonight's visitor,
alas—to any one of whom I would confidently entrust the
baton of my professorship). There is an appropriate irony,
therefore, in its having devolved upon me, as perhaps my
final public action as a member of our faculty, to introduce
not only tonight's extraordinary guest speaker but also this
newly endowed "Last Lecture" series that her visit will so auspi-
ciously inaugurate.

Valediction, benediction: I see therein no contradiction—
and while I'm in the nervously-improvised-doggerel-verse
mode, let me pray that to my valedictory *introduction* there
may be no further *interruption*. . . .

So. Well. Until our guest materializes, kindly indulge me
now an impromptu brief digression on the subject of . . .
introductions.

The purpose of introductions, I have somewhere read, is
normally threefold: first, to give late-arriving members of the
audience time to be seated, as I notice a few in process of
doing even now; second, to test and if necessary adjust the

public-address system for the principal speaker; and at the
same time (third) to give her or him a few moments to size
up the house and perhaps make appropriate program modifi-
cations. Introductions, therefore, should go on for longer than
one sentence — but not much longer. And may Apollo spare us
the introducer who either in the length of his / her introduction
presumes upon the speaker's allotted time, or in its manner
attempts to upstage the introducee!

But tonight, it goes without saying, is another story. We
need not ask of it the traditional Passover question — "How
is this night different from all other nights?" — although that
is the question that I urge apprentice storytellers in my "workshop" to put to the main action of their stories. Why is it that
Irma decides to terminate Fred *today*, rather than two weeks
ago or next semester? What was it about *this* satirical verse-epic
of our visitor's that provoked so astonishing and lamentable
a reaction, which her scarcely less provocative earlier works
did not? You get the idea. I trust you'll appreciate, however,
that in all my years of introducing our visiting writers to their
audiences, this is my maiden experience of being not so much
an introducer as a warm-up act for "him who shall come after
me," as John the Baptist put it (in this instance, *her* who shall
etc.). The bona fide introduction that I had prepared — short,
short, I assure you, and not badly turned, if I do say so myself —
I am thus obliged to expand ad libitum like one of those
talking heads on public television fund-raisers, either until
there's mutiny in the ranks (but let it be more orderly, in that
event, than that uncivilized earlier disruption) or else until
our eagerly awaited guest . . .

One moment, please.

She is? Allah be praised for that! (No disrespect to that
deity intended.)

My friends: I'm perfectly delighted to announce that the
limousine of our so patiently awaited leadoff lecturer-du-soir,
together with its attendant security convoy, *has reached the
campus*, and that therefore it should be a matter of mere
minutes — another ten or fifteen tops, I estimate and profoundly hope — before I happily yield this podium to the Go-

dot for whom we've all been waiting. May that news update appease you while I now go straight to the matter of this series:

The anonymous benefactress who endowed "Last Lectures" (she was, like our guest, a she; that much I can tell you. Perhaps the muse?) throughout her long and prosperous lifetime was a perennial student, by her own description, and an inveterate "cultural attender," ever present on occasions like these. In her advanced age, she came to realize and even to derive some critical zest from the circumstance that, for all she knew, any given lecture or similar cultural occasion that she happened to be attending could feasibly be her last. It was her whimsical but quite serious inspiration, therefore, to endow handsomely a series of public lectures at this institution, with the stipulation that each speaker would be asked to imagine that this will be his or her valedictory presentation, her "last lecture" — as, for all any of us knows, any given utterance of ours might well turn out to be. Thus would we hear our visitors' "bottom-line" sentiments, their summings up; and thus by the way would the situation of the guest approximate that of the hostess — who, I'm sorry to report, went to her reward shortly after rewarding us with her philanthropy, and so cannot attend, at least in the flesh, this first Last Lecture, nor any of those to follow it (the interest on our muse's endowment being generous, we expect this series to extend ad infinitum).

Do I dare point out — indeed, I do so dare, for I knew this lady and her mordant wit well enough, once upon a time, to believe that she would enjoy the irony if she were with us — that tonight's circumstances have matched donor and donee even more aptly than intended, inasmuch as both are now . . . forgive me . . . *late?*

Well.

What?

Aha. Gentlemen and ladies, ladies and gentlemen: *She is in the building!*

Excuse me? Okay; sorry there: our distinguished visitor and her security entourage are *approaching* the building, it seems, although for several reasons I would prefer to say that she is "in the building"—for aren't we all, come to that, in the process of building and of being built every moment of our active lives: a-building and a-building until the end, whereafter our building, we may hope, will survive its builder?

Hum.

The end, I've said, and now say again: *the end*. And having so said, with those words *I* end, not my introduction—for our guest's custody, as it were, has yet to be officially transferred from the state and municipal security people to our own, I'm told, or to some combination of the two, or the three: a transfer now in progress elsewhere in this building even as I end, not my introduction of our visitor, whom I've yet to *begin* to introduce, but my introduction to that introduction. No fitter way to do that, I hope you'll agree, than with a few words about . . . endings.

Endings, endings: where to begin? I myself am not among the number of those Last Lecturers whose distinguished names you've seen on our posters and other advertisements (all except that of this surprise inaugurator, for good and obvious reasons). I don't mind declaring, however, that I could readily deliver a last lecture myself on the subject of endings. Further, that had I been invited so to do, I could not have done better than to begin with the opening exclamation of our Mystery Guest's world-challenging verse-epic, which exclamation I shall take the liberty of Englishing thus: "An end to endings! Let us rebegin!"

As we wind up our century and our millennium—this is Yours Truly speaking now, not our impending visitor, and you have my word of honor that the moment she enters this auditorium I shall break off my spiel in mid-sentence, if need be, as Scheherazade so often breaks off her nightly narratives, and go straight to the very brief business of introducing her— as we end our century and millennium, I was saying, it is no surprise that the "terminary malady" afflicts us. Of the End of Art we have been hearing ever since this century's beginning, when modernism arrived on the stage of Western Civ. Picasso, Pound, Stravinsky—all felt themselves to be as much terminators as pioneers, and where they themselves did not, their critics often so regarded them: groundbreakers, yes, but perhaps grave diggers as well, for the artistic tradition that preceded and produced them. By mid-century we were hearing not only of the Death of the Novel—that magnificent old genre that was born a-dying, like all of us; that has gone on vigorously dying ever since, and that bids to do so for some while yet—but likewise of the Death of Print Culture and the End of Modernism, supplanted by the electronic visual media and by so-called Postmodernism. And not long ago, believe it or not, there was an international symposium on "The End of *Post*modernism"—just when we thought we might be beginning to understand what that term describes! In other jurisdictions, we have Professor Whatsisname on the End of History, and Professor So-and-So on the End of Physics (indeed, the End of Nature), and Professor Everybody-and-Her-Brother on the End of the Old World Order with the collapse of the Soviet Union and of international communism.

In short and in sum, endings, endings everywhere; apocalypses large and small. Good-bye to the tropical rain forests; good-bye to the whales; good-bye to the mountain gorillas and the giant pandas and the rhinoceri; good-bye even to the humble frogs, one is beginning to hear, as our deteriorating ozone layer exposes their eggs to harmful radiation. Good-bye to the oldest continuous culture on the planet: the Marsh Arabs of southern Iraq, in process of extermination by Saddam Hussein even as I speak. Good-bye to once-so-cosmopolitan Beirut and once-so-hospitable Sarajevo, as we who never had the chance to know them knew those excellent cities. The end of this, the end of that; little wonder we grow weary of "endism," as I have heard it called.

And yet, my patient-beyond-patient friends, things do end. Even this introductory introduction will end, take my word for it—and I wish I could add "the better the sooner," as one might sigh at the end of splendid meals, splendid sessions of love, splendid lives, even splendid long novels: those life-

absorbing, life-enriching, almost life-displacing alternative
worlds that we lovers of literature find ourselves wishing might
never end, yet savor the more for knowing that they must.
Yea, verily, I declare, things end; our late muse / benefactress's
enviable life, our own productive lifetimes, and soon enough
our biographical lives as well — happily or haplessly, all end.
As I like to tell my students . . .

Excuse me?

Very well, and hallelujah: *She is proceeding at this very
moment with her security escort through the several check-
points between our improvised safe-reception area belowstairs
and our final staging area, just . . . offstage*, excuse that feeble
wordplay — and will you gentlemen in the rear of the hall
kindly return to your seats pronto and spare us all the indignity
of once again marshaling our marshals, so to speak — who, as
that earlier demonstration demonstrated, are standing by. I
thank you in advance. I thank you. Now, please . . .

As I was saying: I advise my student apprentices to read
biographies of the great writers they admire, in order to be
encouraged by and take comfort in the trials and discourage-
ments that attended *their* apprenticeship — but I recommend
they skip the final chapters of those biographies. For a writer,
after all, the alternative "last-chapter" scenarios are almost
equally distressing, quite apart from the critical reception of
one's works during one's mortal span: either the end comes
before one has had one's entire say (we recall John Keats's
fears that he might cease to be before his pen had gleaned
his teeming brain) — What an unspeakable pity, so to speak! —
or else one goes on being and being *after* one's pen has gleaned
et cetera: not so much a pity as simply pathetic. Therefore,
say I to my coachees: skip the endings.

The biographical endings, I mean: the endings of the great
authors' life-stories. To the endings of those authors' great
stories, on the other hand, I urge and enjoin apprentice writers
to pay the most scrupulous and repeated attention, for at least
two reasons, of which it won't at all surprise or distress me if
I have time to share with you only the first before this endless

introduction happily ends — its happiest imaginable ending
being that it never gets there, if you follow my meaning.
Reason One is that it's in a story's Ending that its author
pays (or fails to pay) his narrative/dramatic bills. Through
Beginning and Middle the writer's credit is good, so long as
we're entertained enough to keep turning the pages. But when
the story's action has built to its climax and started down the
steep and slippery slope of denouement, every line counts,
every word, and ever more so as we approach the final words.
All the pistols hung on the wall in act one, as Chekhov fa-
mously puts it, must be fired in act three. Images, motives,
minor characters — every card played must be duly picked up,
the dramaturgical creditors paid off, or else we properly feel
shortchanged on our investment of time and sympathy, the
willing suspension of our disbelief.

There are, to be sure, ways of paying one's bills by brilliantly
defaulting on them: apparent non-endings that are in fact
the best of endings, anyhow the most appropriate. We might
instance the alternative and therefore inconclusive endings of
Dickens's *David Copperfield* and John Fowles's *French Lieu-
tenant's Woman*; the roller-towel ending/rebeginning of
James Joyce's *Finnegans Wake*; the recombinatory "replay"
ending of Julio Cortázar's *Hopscotch*, to name only a few
examples; likewise the more immediately contemporary phenomenon of "hypertext" fiction: those open-endedly labyrin-
thine computer-novels that may be entered, transited, and
exited at any of many possible points and waypoints. Such
non-endings, I repeat, if managed brilliantly (and a mighty
if that is), can be the most apt imaginable, and ipso facto the
most satisfying.

And the reason for *that*, my friends (Reason Two of two,
which I, for one, never imagined or wished that I would find
myself giving voice to here tonight), is this: that every aspect
of a masterfully crafted story, from its narrative viewpoint
through its cast of characters, its choice of scene, its choreogra-
phy, tone of voice, and narrative procedure, its sequences of
images and of actions, things said and things left unsaid,
details noticed and details ignored — everything about it, in

short, from its title to its ending, may be (nay, *will* be) a sign of
its sense, until sign and sense become, if not indistinguishable,
anyhow inextricable.

Of this ground-truth, no apter demonstration can be cited,
I trust you will agree, than our first Last Lecturer's —

Will you *please*, you people there in the back! . . . What?
What?

Oh my. I say, there!

As . . . Dear me! What now? . . .

As I . . . As I was

NOTES ON CONTRIBUTORS

FICTION

John Barth is the author of nine novels. A new collection of short stories, *On with the Story*, will be published by Little, Brown next year.

T. Coraghessan Boyle's latest novel, *The Tortilla Curtain*, has just been published by Viking Penguin. He is a past winner of the John Train Humor Prize.

Melvin Jules Bukiet's collection of stories, *While the Messiah Tarries*, was published recently by Harcourt Brace & Company. He teaches writing at Sarah Lawrence College and is the fiction editor of *Tikkun*.

Marcia Guthridge's first published story, "Bones," won the 1993 *Paris Review* Discovery Prize. She lives in Chicago, Illinois.

POETRY

Lucille Clifton is the author of over thirty books. A new collection of poetry will be published in 1996.

Tom Disch's most recent books include a novel, *The Priest: A Gothic Romance*, and a collection of essays on poetry, *The Castle of Indolence*.

John Drexel spent 1994 in England on an Amy Lowell travelling scholarship.

Victoria Else lives in New York City.

Gary Fincke is the author of *Inventing Angels*.

Albert Goldbarth's most recent collection of poems, *Heaven and Earth*, received the National Book Critics Circle Award.

Beth Gylys is pursuing a Ph.D. in creative writing and literature at the University of Cincinnati.

Brooks Haxton's most recent collection of poetry is *Sonnet Night*.
David Lehman's most recent book is *The Big Question*, a collection of essays. His poetry collection, *Valentine Place*, will appear in February.
Campbell McGrath is the author of two poetry collections, *Capitalism* and *American Noise*. He lives in Miami Beach.
Gary Mitchner is Professor of English at Sinclair Community College in Dayton, Ohio.
Robert Phillips is the author of five books of poetry, including the most recent, *Breakdown Lane*.
Lloyd Schwartz is the author of two poetry collections, *Goodnight, Gracie* and *These People*.
John Updike's *Rabbit at Rest* was awarded this spring the Howells Medal by the American Academy of Arts and Letters for the most distinguished novel of American fiction in the past five years.

INTERVIEWS

Michiko Kakutani (Woody Allen interview) is the Senior Book Critic at the *New York Times*.
George Plimpton (Harold Bloom, Garrison Keillor, Calvin Trillin interviews) is the editor of *The Paris Review*. His latest book, published last spring by W. W. Norton and Company, is *The X Factor*.

FEATURES

Walter Abish's most recent novel *Eclipse Fever* was published in 1993 by Knopf.
Henry Alford is the author of *Municipal Bondage*, a collection of humor.
Dave Barry is a humor columnist for *The Miami Herald*. His most recent book is *Dave Barry's Complete Guide to Guys*.
Roy Blount, Jr. is the editor of *Roy Blount's Book of Southern Humor* and author of eleven other books, including *Crackers* and *First Hubby*.
Malcolm Bradbury is the author of six novels. His most recent is *Mensonage*, published by Penguin in 1993.
Art Buchwald's autobiography, *Leaving Home*, was published by G. P. Putnam's Sons last January.
Christopher Buckley is the author of *The White House Mess* and *Thank You for Smoking*.
Stephen Dixon's novel, *Interstate*, and his collected stories were published recently by Henry Holt. His new novel, *Abortions* will be published next year.
Jeffrey Eugenides is the author of *The Virgin Suicides*.
Tibor Fischer is the author of the Booker Prize-nominated *Under the Frog*. His second novel, *The Thought Gang*, was excerpted in issue 134 of *The Paris Review*.

Veronica Geng is the author of the humor collections, *Partners* and *Love Trouble is My Business*. She was an editor of humor and fiction at *The New Yorker* from 1977 to 1993.

Grey Gowrie is Chairman of the Arts Council of Britain.

John Gross, the editor of *The Oxford Book of Comic Verse*, is the theater critic for the *Sunday Telegraph*.

Donald Hall was the poetry editor of *The Paris Review* from 1953 to 1961. His latest book is *Principal Products of Portugal*.

Drue Heinz is the publisher of *The Paris Review*.

John Irving has published eight novels, including *The World According to Garp*; a collection of stories, essays and memoirs entitled *Trying to Save Piggy Sneed* will be published by Arcade Publishing next year.

George Kalogerakis is a contributing editor at *Vogue* and a former editor and writer at *Spy*.

David Kamp is the assistant managing editor at *GQ*

Alfred Kazin is the author of *A Walker in the City*, *New York Jew*, and most recently, *Writing Was Everything*, published by Harvard University Press.

Sean Kelly has covered civil wars in the Congo, Biafra, Laos, Cambodia, and El Salvador, and now works for the Associated Press.

Rick Moody is the author of the novels *Garden State* and *The Ice Storm*, as well as a collection of stories, *The Ring of Brightest Angels Around Heaven*.

Willie Morris's latest books are *New York Days* and *My Dog Skip*. He is currently working on a novel that will take place in Oxford, England in the late 1950s.

John Mortimer's new memoir, *Murderers and Other Friends*, was published last year.

Mark O'Donnell is the author of *Elementary Education* and *Vertigo Park and Other Tales*. Next year Knopf will publish his novel, *Getting Over Homer*.

P. J. O'Rourke is the author of eight books. He is the foreign affairs desk chief at *Rolling Stone*.

Mordecai Richler is the author of nine novels, including *The Apprenticeship of Duddy Kravitz*.

Mary Lee Settle's latest novel is *Choice*.

Wilfrid Sheed is the author of *In Love with Daylight*. He is currently working on a book about great American songwriters.

Daniel Stern is a past winner of the John Train Humor Prize for "The Psychopathology of Everyday Life by Sigmund Freud: a story." He is the author of nine novels and two collections of short stories.

Michael Thomas writes a column for *The New York Observer*, "The Midas Watch." His seventh novel, *Baker's Dozen*, will be published next year by Farrar, Straus & Giroux.

Calvin Trillin's memoir of his father, *Message from my Father*, will be published by Farrar, Straus & Giroux next year.

Frederic Tuten is the author of *Tintin in the New World* and *Tallien: A Brief Romance; The Adventures of Mao on the Long March.* He is currently a member of the graduate faculty in creative writing at the City College of New York.

John Updike's poem "Epithalamium," is also featured in this issue.

Auberon Waugh is editor and publisher of the *Literary Review.*

John Wells is at present writing a history of the House of Lords.

Paul West's novel *Love's Mansion* won the 1993 Lannan Prize for fiction. His next book, due from Viking next year, is a novella about John Milton.

Barry Yourgrau's new book is *The Sadness of Sex* published by Dell\Delta; a film version, which he cowrote and in which he stars, is forthcoming.

ART

Saul Steinberg received the Gold Medal from the American Academy of Arts and Letters in 1974.

Raffaele lives and works in Fiesole, Italy. His work is represented by Paolo Baldacci Gallery in New York.

NB: Reprinted from *The Really Short Poems of A.R. Ammons,* © 1991 by A.R. Ammons, with permission of W.W. Norton & Company. Wendy Cope's poem is reprinted with permission of Faber & Faber, Ltd. X.J. Kennedy poem, © 1995. Stevie Smith's poem is reprinted with permission of New Directions, ©1972. "Low Church," © Stanley J. Sharpless 1985.

STATEMENT required by the act of August 24, 1912 as amended by the acts of March 3, 1933, and July 2, 1946. (Title 39, United States Code, Section 233) showing the ownership, management, and circulation of THE PARIS REVIEW published quarterly at Flushing, New York, 11358.

1. *Editor:* George Plimpton, *Managing Editor:* Daniel Kunitz, 541 East 72 Street, New York, N.Y. *Business Manager:* Lillian Von Nickern, 45-39 171st Place, Flushing, N.Y.

2. The owners are: George Plimpton, Harold H. Humes, Peter Matthiessen, Thomas H. Guinzburg. All c/o Plimpton, 541 E. 72 Street, NY, NY 10021.

3. The known bondholders, mortgages, and other security holders owning or holding 1 percent or more of total amounts of bonds, mortgages, or other securities are: None.

4. Paragraphs 2 and 3 include, in cases where the stock holder or security holder appears upon the books of the company as trustee or in any other fiduciary relation, the name of the person or corporation for whom such trustee is acting; also the statements in the two paragraphs show the affiant's full knowledge and belief as to the circumstances and conditions under which the stock holders and security holders who do not appear upon the books of the company as trustees, hold stocks and securities in a capacity other than that of a bona fide owner.

5. Extent and nature of circulation: Average number of copies each issue during preceding 12 months (actual number of copies of single issue published nearest to filing date):

Total/number copies (Average): 50042 (1250½) Paid and/or requested circulation (Sales through dealers and carriers, street vendors and counter sales): 23447 (5606¾) Mail Subscription: 3243 (3240½) Free distribution by mail, carrier, or other means, samples, complimentary, and other free copies: 609 (648¼). Total Distribution: 10092 (9750½) Copies not distributed (office use, left over, unaccounted, spoiled after printing): 1458 (596¾). Copies not distributed (return from news agents): 8653 (2163¼). Total: 50042 (12510½)

Marjorie Kalman, Notary Public, State of New York   —Daniel Kunitz
No. 4955336   Managing Editor
Qualified in New York County
Commission Expires August 28, 1997